A Loving Voice

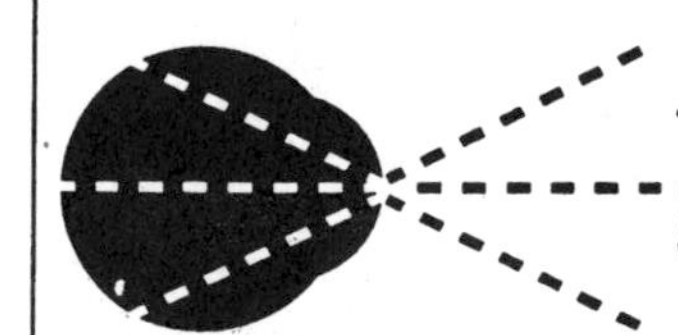

A Loving Voice

A Caregiver's Book of Read-Aloud Stories for the Elderly

Edited by
Carolyn Banks
and
Jane Rizzo

G.K. Hall & Co.
Thorndike, Maine

Published in Large Print by arrangement with
The Charles Press, Publishers.

G.K. Hall Large Print Book Series.

Printed on acid free paper in the United States of America.

Set in 16 pt. Plantin.

Library of Congress Cataloging-in-Publication Data

A Loving voice : a caregiver's book of read-aloud stories for the elderly / edited by Carolyn Banks and Janis Rizzo.
p. cm.—(G.K. Hall large print book series)
ISBN 0-8161-5620-4 (hard : alk. paper).—
ISBN 0-8161-5621-2 (pbk. : alk. paper)
1. American literature. 2. Aged—Books and reading.
3. Large type books. 4. Recitations. I. Banks, Carolyn.
II. Rizzo, Janis.
[PS507.L62 1993]
810.8—dc20 92-42562

Acknowledgments

"Grandmother's Amazing Chocolate Roses" © 1991 by Jean Langston Burgess. An original story published by permission of the author.

"The Greats" © 1988 by Carolyn Osborn. First published in *Antioch Review*. Reprinted by permission of the author.

"Battle of the Bees" © 1991 by Stacy Tuthill. An original story published by permission of the author.

"The Bear" © 1991 by C. S. Kittelmann. An original story published by permission of the author.

"Arkansas Summer" © 1991 by Betty Gray. An original story published by permission of the author.

"Oklahoma Blizzard" © 1987 by Dorothy Rose. First published in *Dustbowl Okie Exodus*. Reprinted by permission of the author.

"Afternoon Delight" © 1991 by Nancy Climer. An original story published by permission of the author.

"Friends, Lines, and Sinkers" © 1991 by Lucille Bellucci. An original story published by permission of the author.

This book is dedicated
to our mothers
Gilda Rizzo
and
Victoria Dogonka Kengerski

Acknowledgments

There were many who contributed time and advice to this project. We especially thank Diana Deaton, Executive Director of The Renaissance Senior Living Center, Austin, Texas and the residents of the Bastrop Nursing Center in Bastrop, Texas. Thanks, too, to Ray Bard, Robert Rafferty, Susan Wilder, Jon Reilman, and Amy Voigt. Finally, we are grateful to Dr. Lawrence Meltzer of The Charles Press, who believed in this project from the start.

Contents

Preface xxiii

Grandmother's Amazing Chocolate Roses
by Jean Langston Burgess 1

An inspiring story about a woman who saves her stricken grandson.

The Greats
by Carolyn Osborn 8

With quiet humor, a woman recalls her eccentric kin.

Battle of the Bees
by Stacy Tuthill 14

A comic story of one woman's exasperation when she moves into a bee-infested house in East Africa.

The Bear
by C. S. Kittelmann 28

A young boy makes his way across occupied Europe during World War II.

Arkansas Summer
by Betty Gray 35

A woman recalls the summer of 1937, when she and her giggly girlfriends contrived to meet a popular movie actor, Dick Powell.

Oklahoma Blizzard
by Dorothy Rose 42

A narrative poem about a family's activities during a fierce snowstorm.

Afternoon Delight
by Nancy Climer 45

A woman yearns for her husband to leave so she can indulge in some not-quite-sinful pleasures.

Friends, Lines, and Sinkers
by Lucille Bellucci 49

A humorous tale of one fisherman's revenge on his boastful friend.

Traces of the Past
by Leona Nogues 54

In diary form, a woman recalls her family's hardscrabble rural life.

The Virgin of Polish Hill
by Carolyn Banks 71

Set in a Polish neighborhood in Pittsburgh in the

1950s, this story recounts a miraculous appearance of the Blessed Virgin.

Up, Up and Away
by C. G. Segre 85

This humorous essay depicts the way one early riser starts his day.

Once is Enough
by Dorothy Rose 88

In this comic poem, a laconic man comments on becoming a widower.

A Need To Get Away
by J. Madison Davis 90

A young war veteran returns to Virginia to sort out his life.

A New Life
by Janis Rizzo 99

An aging woman learns that the young dog she loves is ill.

***Pies Sagradas:* Praying at the Feet of the Saint**
by Barbara Lau 108

This poem is about a pilgrimage to a Mexican shrine.

Cook's Choice
by Barry Bauska 110

Remember school lunch menus? Well, the man who wrote this funny story does too—with a vengeance.

West Texas Photograph
by Patricia Lewis Sackrey 119

A poignant description of an eight-year-old farm girl's life.

Outpatient
by Rosalind Warren 121

In this story, a hypnotist gets even with a doctor who has kept her waiting.

The Man Who Shot Bats
by Mary Connor Ralph 129

The story of one man's obsession with bats and his friends' response to it.

Grandpappy and the Indians and a Bear
by John H. Lambe 135

The old prospector in this story has a fortunate encounter with a grizzly bear.

The Quarry
by Christopher Woods 141

A mysterious story set in Mexico about the influence of a sculptor on her gardener.

Going Home
by Dotte Shaffer 147

In this love story, a widower is happily reunited with his wife.

No Butts About It
by Ruth D. Langston 162

One woman's amusing World War II recollection.

Old Women
by Barbara Lau 167

This poem celebrates aging women.

Everybody Has a Snake Story
by Kathleen Hoffman 168

A humorous and folksy account of real-life encounters between people and snakes.

The leap
by Louise Erdrich 176

A woman recalls, in crystalline language, the way her mother, a former trapeze artist, rescued her from a burning house.

The Pontiac Years
by Paul Estaver 187

A young boy links growing up with a series of Pontiacs his father owned.

Tale Spinner
by D. W. Wright 200

In this poem, a man remembers the seafarer's widow who lit his imagination.

Sweet Revenge
by Lisa Fisher 201

In this funny story, an exceptional young boy gets even with his father.

Dad's Wrench
by Bruce Wick 208

An exciting adventure story about a young man rescued by his remarkable dog.

Duststorm
by Dorothy Rose 224

A narrative poem about cleaning up after a duststorm.

Bookmark
by Penny Wilkes 227

Getting caught passing notes in school and puppy love are the subject of this funny little story.

Love for Things Unknown
by Phoebe Newman 232

An evocative look at the Rainbow Bar and its quirky clientele.

Training Wheels
by Lynne Conroy 236

A comic account of a mother teaching her daughter to drive.

Truth Like Enormous Flakes of Snow
by Barbara Lau 240

In this poem, a woman recounts the mysteries of her grandmother's life.

The Man Who Owned a Mountain
by Maureen Williams 241

An environmental parable about a man who inherits unspoiled Pennsylvania land and attempts to turn it into a ski resort.

The Black Sheep of the Family
by Thomas H. Davis III 250

A comic story about a young boy's embarrassing dinner with the local preacher.

Golfers in the Fog
by Richard Ploetz 259

A sixteen-year-old recalls his grandfather's

collapse and triumphant recovery on the golf course.

Sightseeing
by Thomas Claire 269

A poem about a blind woman whose husband provides a special sort of sight.

Alysa's Father
by Amy Schildhouse 273

An adolescent boy watches as his friend's father, whom he idolizes, is reduced to mere mortal status.

Blackberry Island
by Joanne Seltzer 280

A richly embroidered story about a girl's two-week stay in the Sault Ste. Marie.

Elly
by Stanley Field 288

A man celebrates his 23rd wedding anniversary recalling his marriage's early travails.

Dear Mary Lou
by Dorothy Rose 299

In this comic poem in the form of a letter home, a rural child marvels at city convenience.

Better Man
by Tricia Lande 302

A rough-and-tumble coming-of-age story.

Set Free
by Helen Peppe 317

A boy frees a chained dog with ironic results.

The Donation
by Marion Rosen 324

Two members of the church Ladies' Aid Society put one over on a couple of thieves.

Hot Chocolate for Two
by Dorothy Winslow Wright 333

A warm tale about a moving moment between a man and his nineteen-year-old granddaughter.

Crazy Hat
by Frederic Carpenter 339

Teenagers torment an old mountain man.

Jelly Rolls
by Jyl Lynn Felman 355

In this comic story, a woman who hates fat people gets her just desserts.

Boarding House Days
by H. Ray Pardue 369

A young man is caught up in some crazy goings-on in an old boarding house.

The Necessary Art of Salvaging
by Barbara Lau 381

In this poem, a woman loses her unborn child.

Missing Kin
by Shelby Hearon 382

Relatives mistakenly fear the worst when a 74-year-old woman doesn't answer her phone.

Notes on Contributors 388

Preface

I began to think about a book of read-aloud stories when I worked in an adult day care center a few years ago. Among the many elderly patrons of the center were some recovering from strokes and others in some stage of Alzheimer's disease. My job was to entertain them, to interest them in activities. No easy task.

Because reading has always been important to me, I thought it would be fun to read to them. I searched for suitable read-aloud material. Soon I found that there were read-aloud stories for children, but nothing specifically meant to be read aloud to adults. What I was looking for were short stories or poems that dealt with adult experiences but were clear and easy to follow, and written simply enough to be read aloud without stumbling over the vocabulary, getting bogged down in overlong descriptions, or twisted up in lots of hard-to-follow dialogue where the listener couldn't tell who was speaking.

I spent much of my free time searching for stories that met these requirements. On the infrequent occasions when I did discover a story or a poem that worked, I could see that the read-aloud experience was something that mattered to the people I was reading to. Even those I knew couldn't possibly be following the plot line would listen intently. I believe this is because most of us, when we were small, had someone read aloud to us—a parent, a teacher, a librarian—and we remember it fondly. Sometimes, too, I would find that a descriptive passage or a line of dialogue would evoke a memory in one of the listeners. They'd start talking, or they'd laugh. It was a wonderful shared experience.

I soon got enthusiastic feedback on this from some of the caregivers—usually the adults who'd dropped their elderly parents off at the day care center—who were pleasantly surprised to hear about some aspect of the stories later on at home. Frequently these concerned caregivers asked for copies of the stories I had read so that they could read them to their elderly loved ones again.

I began to realize that most caregivers are desperate for things they could do with the aging people in their care. They felt guilty consigning the old folks to the television set. Reading aloud was ideal. It was intimate. It was meaningful. And the stories were short so it didn't take long and tire either reader or listener. Again and again, I was told that it was a wonderful experience.

This was reinforced during the several years when my husband and I visited his mother in a nursing home. We found that after a few minutes of small talk we ran out of things to say. We didn't know what to do to make the most of these visits. In talks with others who were visiting residents in the home we found this was a common situation, one that made all of us feel uncomfortable.

These were relatives we loved and yet we all tended to look at the visits as a chore or obligation rather than a pleasant time. Here again, I turned to reading aloud—and it worked.

This unfilled need for a book of read-aloud stories led to conceiving the idea of *A Loving Voice*, an anthology that would not only be welcomed with open arms and hearts by those responsible for visiting or caring for the elderly, but also by family or friends visiting adults of all ages who could not read for themselves. It wouldn't matter if they were in hospitals, hospices, in nursing or retirement homes, or were shut-ins at home. If they liked stories but couldn't read for themselves, our book would fill the need.

I enlisted the aid of my friend Janis Rizzo, a freelance journalist and pharmacist. She, I knew, remembered well her struggle to communicate with her father after his capacities had diminished. We began work almost at once.

Although we had ideas of our own, we consulted experts in the eldercare field who could give us pointers on the sort of material we ought to select.

We learned several things. One was to include as broad a range of material as possible. Another was to make certain that the stories and poems were about people of various age—not just the elderly. We found out, too, that death was not a taboo subject. And we learned that laughter was an important response to court.

With these things in mind, Janis and I approached authors whose work we admired. We also asked writers' organizations to broadcast the word. In addition, we placed an ad in *Poets & Writers* magazine. The results were gratifying. Out of the several hundred submissions we received, we selected 52 stories and poems—one reading for each week of the year.

Variety was important. We wanted our book to have stories with all kinds of settings, all kinds of themes and we feel we have achieved this goal. We have snow stories and hot weather stories, stories about golf and fishing, stories about love and friendship, mystery stories, animal stories, stories about food, rural settings and urban, too. And we made certain that we included some rugged adventure pieces as well as romantic and even sentimental stories. We truly believe that everyone will find a favorite here.

At the same time, the pieces we've chosen are not insultingly simple. Even those who are able to read these selections on their own will find them engaging and entertaining. These are stories and poems with purpose, stories and poems with heart, stories and poems we are proud to present. Each, we hope, will help you find your own loving voice.

Carolyn Banks

Grandmother's Amazing Chocolate Roses

by

Jean Langston Burgess

Everybody had heard of my grandmother's way with roses. Her tiny yard was full of them, from early May through the whole summer: red ones, white ones, pinks and yellows in all shades. And lined up on the walls of her living room were the many ribbons she had won at our county fair for their unusual colors and fragrances.

She lived in a little house all by herself just down the road from our house. Mama's vegetable garden was in-between, with a gate on our side and a gate on Grandmother's side, and Daddy always left an extra wide space between the beans and tomatoes for a path. The gates had springs so they couldn't be accidentally left open to let in chickens or rabbits to ruin the vegetables.

We used those gates a lot in the summertime. The first thing my brother Ben and I always did right after breakfast was run over to Grandmother's to check on her. "As if I need checking up on," she'd say with a stretch of her neck. When she stretched her neck and raised one eyebrow you knew she was indignant, or so Mama said. It was a Patterson trait that went along with her determined nature.

Anyway, no matter how early we got over there, Grandmother was already busy at work in her yard, tending her roses. There she'd be in her long-sleeved shirt, khaki pants and her yellow straw hat with the red bandanna tied around it.

"Well, good morning, boys and girls," she'd always call out when she saw us coming, even though we were only one boy and one girl. "Come see!"

There was always something new for me to see. Ben, being a boy, thought he ought not to get too excited about such things as roses. He'd stuff his hands in his jeans pockets and look as bored as he could while Grandmother showed us the mass of white buds that had come overnight on the trellis over her back door, or the perfect salmon pink that stood so tall in the side yard against the old wagon wheel.

Ben would look and sniff, then shrug, asserting his ten years of male wisdom. "Just like women to get so wide-eyed over flowers and stuff." Then he'd arch his eyebrow, stretch his neck and plop down on the bottom doorstep to watch us in disdain.

Grandmother would snip and weed and spray and pat the ground with her outstretched hands.

"Lean over this way, Jo-Jo," she'd say to me, "so you can catch the fragrance of this one. No, don't touch it while it's wet. Just lean close and smell. Now what does it smell like?"

"Um-m, wonderful," I'd always say. "People are always asking me how you grow such beautiful, sweet-smelling roses, Grandmother." You see, I was already thirteen and, unlike my pesky little brother, could appreciate flowers and words like beautiful and fragrant.

Grandmother's blue eyes would crinkle and she'd say, "Oh, I've told you before. You have to take good care of flowers and love them, even talk to them, like you do for people you love, until they love you back. When they smile with their petals and let you lean in close to catch that special fragrance, you know they are loving you back. And if you listen with your heart, sometimes they'll speak to you."

Ben just snorted and rolled his eyes skyward. Grandmother would laugh and tousle his hair. "Well, then," she'd say, "let's take our break."

Then we'd go into Grandmother's kitchen and sit around her shiny, vinyl-topped table and have Kool-Aid and cookies. Sometimes they'd be homemade and still warm. Other times they'd be store-bought served out of her blue ceramic cookie jar. Mostly, though, they'd be some kind of chocolate, as that was Ben's favorite.

Our summer days flew by filled with pulling weeds and picking tomatoes, beans and squash with Mama in her garden, and riding the tractor with Daddy in the fields, and always, a part of every day with Grandmother in her rose garden.

Of course, we did other things, too, like swimming in the lake and going to the movies on the weekends. And I spent a few minutes, as many as I could get away with, everyday on the telephone with my best friend, Jennifer, who lived on the farm next to ours. We'd bicycle to each other's houses to listen to music together in the afternoons while Mama and Grandmother watched their soaps.

One morning, about midsummer, when Grandmother called out her usual, "Good morning" and "Come see," even Ben got a surprise.

"Okay you two, come on over here. Ben, you too," Grandmother insisted, her eyes bright. "Now what does it smell like?"

We both bent low over the rose, careful not to touch, closed our eyes, and breathed in deep.

"Hey!" Ben opened his eyes, incredulous, "that smells like chocolate."

And it did. The rose actually smelled like chocolate, and it even looked a little like it. It was of such a deep, deep red that it had a chocolate brown center where the bud had not fully opened.

"Grandmother, how did you do that?" I whispered, taking another whiff of the unbelievable rose.

"Yeah," Ben echoed, "how did you do that?"

Grandmother just laughed. "That's my secret. Besides, I've told you before, haven't I? Now let's go in for our break."

She winked at me as Ben ducked his head from her hand when he went in. Grandmother seemed very satisfied to have finally impressed Ben with one of her blooms.

It was late in the summer when Ben had his accident, and our good times came to an abrupt end. He was fishing with Jack and Tom Jarrett in the irrigation pond in our back field. They had all been warned not to swim there, but on a dare Ben dived in and hit his head. Probably he hit a submerged stump. When he didn't come right back up, Tom, the older of the two brothers, jumped in and pulled him out. But he had been in the water a long time. Jack ran to our house for Mama and she rushed Ben to the hospital. Even though Tom had done all he could for Ben in the meantime, he remained unconscious. All he did was belch up a lot of water.

The doctor said we would just have to wait and see. It was very possible, he said, very possible, that Ben would just wake up and be good as new. But he also said he just didn't know.

Mama wouldn't leave his bedside. Daddy and I came and went. The Jarrett brothers and their parents came also, their faces long with regret and sadness. Jennifer came, too, and our pastor, Mr. Roberts. Daddy shook all their hands but couldn't say much.

Grandmother came one time to sit beside Ben's bed and hold his hand. She spoke to him in soft words and put her hand gently on his head.

On the fifth day of Ben's unconsciousness, when the doctor's expression had become very, very serious, and we all were so frightened we could hardly think, much less pray our wordless prayers, Grandmother came back. She had brought with her a small yellow vase with three perfect red-brown roses in it. Their rich chocolate fragrance filled the room. Mama didn't say anything. She just squeezed Grandmother's shoulder, her teary eyes locked on Daddy's.

"Now Ben, you listen," I heard Grandmother whisper when she bent low over him to place the roses on the table right next to his bed.

The next morning I was sitting next to Grandmother on her bottom doorstep when her telephone rang. Daddy had told me to stay with her and that he would call us if there was any change with Ben.

I remember the fear that I felt when that phone rang. I thought my heart had stopped. Grandmother did not hesitate, but hurried inside and answered on the second ring. I followed, feeling like I was wading through a thick dream, and went to the kitchen where Grandmother had the phone to her ear.

She was not saying anything, just standing there with a strange look on her face. Then her eyes filled with tears and she handed the phone to me.

"Here, Jo-Jo, somebody wants to speak to you," she said.

I barely squeaked out my, "Hello."

"Hey, Jo, it's me." It was Ben's voice, weak but unmistakable. I don't remember what I said, only Grandmother's arms around me, hugging me tight.

In a few days Ben was home and soon he was just as aggravating as he ever was. Then some weeks later, we were at Grandmother's one morning, all three of us in her garden. We had taken our break on the doorstep, and were all lost in our own thoughts, when Ben started talking out of the blue. "You know, Grandmother, while I was in the hospital, I was so sleepy," he began, looking shyly at her. He had not talked about it at all up to now. "Sometimes I would almost wake up, and I could hear you all talking, but I was so sleepy, I didn't want to wake up. I thought I was dreaming and that you were all getting further and further away. Until I heard your chocolate roses, Grandmother. It seemed like they just wouldn't let me sleep. All I could think about was how hungry I was." Ben looked down at the chocolate chip cookie he was munching on. "So I just woke up, I guess."

I looked at Grandmother and neither of us said anything. I don't think Ben even realized he had said "heard" instead of "smelled." And neither of us ever thought to bring it to his attention.

The Greats

by

Carolyn Osborn

In my mother's family Great Uncle Ambrose is known as "the one who painted the fence blue." He did it when he was drunk, and everyone else had gone to town one remote Saturday in the early 1930s. The fence was a typical Middle Tennessee white post-and-rail arrangement surrounding five acres of the farm's front lawn, a small pasture for children, Shetland ponies, dogs, trees, and swings. No one knew why Uncle Ambrose was drunk. He was a visitor from Charleston. Perhaps he brought some sorrow with him, or some sudden joy demanded celebration. But why did he choose to paint the fence?

My grandfather, I was told, said, "By God, Ambrose, I wish you'd taken on the barn. It needed painting." (He didn't have much leeway for comment since he got drunk and did strange things himself.)

No one could tell me if Great Uncle Ambrose finished the job. When I was six, ten years or so after the deed was done, I used to get stuck on a mean-tempered Shetland who preferred grazing a corner of the lawn to trotting children about. When I wasn't bawling for someone to come and lead the pony away—quite logically I feared he'd bite me as he'd bitten one of my cousins already—I was looking for splinters of blue underneath the white rails. Other coats of paint and weather had washed it all off. Though I inquired, no one could explain Great Uncle Alnbrose's choice of color, nor could they remember why there were buckets of blue paint at the farm.

Grandfather Moore was a neat farmer. His place looked like the pictures in my first grade reader, or rather some of the outbuildings did. There was a log smokehouse, a red barn for livestock, a gray weathered wood house where "the help" lived, and a gray tobacco barn. The house was rose-red brick, two-story, antebellum—too southern for *Dick and Jane*. All were kept in good order though Grandfather collected things. Any number of half-filled buckets of paint were stored in the livestock barn along with a dilapidated buggy, old mule collars, singletrees, other bits of harness, and machinery. Ambrose might have wandered in there in the midst of a drunken reverie and picked up the first bucket of paint available.

However the fence-painting happened, Moore family mythology, which concentrates on deeds and neglects motivations, prevents further inquiry. And Great Uncle Ambrose, himself, returned to Charleston where he died before I was old enough to ask the right questions.

Great Aunt Eula is "the one who went to California to buy movie houses." This was sometime before 1927 when *The Jazz Singer* signaled the beginning of "talkies." Whatever possessed her? She was a middle-aged woman, married to an indulgent man. My grandmother said, "Maybe she was tired of playing lady up there in Kentucky." (Her guess was reliable as any since she played lady emphatically herself.) Great Aunt Eula was also the only one of the Moores who knew anything about family history. Except for their own memories, none of them were in the least interested in genealogy. "Eula knows all that," they would say. After a short visit to Tennessee the family chronicler arrived in Los Angeles where she did indeed buy a movie house, for she wrote to my grandparents offering them free passes to all the shows if they would only come out.

My grandfather scorned the idea as "one of Eula's notions" though Grandmother Moore wanted to go, a desire that categorized her as a great a day-dreamer as Eula. California was a good place for her, but no one else was supposed to fall under her spell. Grandmother Moore did allow my mother to answer Eula's summons. "Come on out and I'll get you in the movies," she said. Mother went to L.A., was photographed intensively by a friend of Eula's, and came home after a month without even seeing a movie. Years later she said, "There was never time. We always had to rush off to meet someone or other who made a lot of promises." The statement was made without rancor. Apparently she'd had a good time and she'd never believed Aunt Eula's expectations could turn her into an actress.

"You know Eula. She had to have her way." So say present-day survivors. She was, according to them, headstrong and inclined to overreach herself in business matters. When she was quite old one of her nephews had to rescue her. He found her sitting on a sofa surrounded by the rest of her furniture in the yard of a house she was renting. She refused to use the word "evicted" to describe her problem. "Temporarily low on funds," she explained. She died in California, and as far as I can find out, no one in the family ever entered one of her movie houses if, indeed, she ever bought more than one.

I don't think they were particularly angry at her. Great Aunt Eula simply left their sphere. My grandfather owned land, real estate in town, mules, horses, hogs. A woman who wanted to buy movie houses was, in all senses of the term, "outlandish" even though she was his sister.

She was gone before I ever got to California, but I like to think of her sitting in a darkened movie house in Los Angeles watching Mary Pickford, Charlie Chaplin, Theda Bara, Rudolph Valentino, and all the rest. And I also like to believe she enjoyed seeing *The Mark of Zorro* and *The Three Musketeers* a whole lot more than she liked icing tea cakes and collecting dates for the Moore family tree especially since they disdained her efforts.

Great Aunt Eula and Great Uncle Ambrose vanished. Great Uncle Howard who ventured out of the mountains of East Tennessee is, peculiarly, still with us. He was visiting my grandfather and died "of a fever" while staying at the farm. As children my cousins and I used to try to guess which of the house's four bedrooms he died in and what fever he died of. Was it typhoid, poliomyelitis, meningitis? No one could tell us. "People died of fevers back then," said my grandmother exasperated by such scientific research. (Self-interest was involved. We were all terrified of polio and wanted to keep away from dormant germs.) Neither could anyone tell us exactly where Great Uncle Howard was buried. "Somewhere in the family plot," they all said. The family plot has a general tombstone proclaiming MOORE; however, again for reasons no one can explain, he has no private stone, so when anyone dies Uncle Howard is "the one who has to be found." Some cemetery worker must probe the ground with a rod until Uncle Howard's casket is located. Why wouldn't my grandfather buy his brother a tombstone? Did he dislike him? Was he hiding him from the law? Or was the tombstone merely one of those details grandfather didn't get around to taking care of before his own early death?

I thought once to ask for contributions for Uncle Howard's stone, but I realized that the family preferred to let him stay as he is. Finding Great Uncle Howard is a welcome distraction when somebody else dies. And it is a ritual.

Though careless of ancestry, the Moores accept him as they do the other greats, their eccentric, willful, and finally, mysterious kin.

Battle of the Bees

by

Stacy Tuthill

When my husband Charles accepted a scientific research job in East Africa for a year to study the mating habits of hyenas, I expected to make some adjustments, but I wasn't prepared for what they would be. I also expected to conduct my life as orderly and as productively as I had back home in Illinois. I felt the first impact of change when the African Studies Institute near Lusaka, Zambia assigned us to an Old English house left over from days of colonialism. It was a tall two-story brick building with a steep roof and hadn't been lived in for years.

I was delighted at first but soon found the huge kitchen, workroom, and dining room so vast and unworkable I took a three-mile hike each time I served a simple meal. Electricity was off most of the time, but the tiny English "cooker" made mealtime a challenge even when it was on. Washing machines were things of the future; I did laundry by hand in concrete tubs in the back yard. Eventually we hired Abelo, a Chewa "houseboy" who was continually underfoot because I was not accustomed to dealing with servants.

The greatest cultural impact occurred with my sudden exposure to the variety of fauna which had taken possession of the house in the absence of human habitation. Tiny flesh-colored frogs with freckles and red feet plopped out of water faucets. Small lizards scurried about in vines on the outside walls and sometimes slithered into the house through an open door. Ants and roaches claimed the kitchen. Bush babies, small rodents with wide eyes and innocent faces, invaded the pantry, often leaping from silverware drawers when I opened them. Flying termites drifted in piles on the steps where African children popped them raw into their mouths, eating them like peanuts. Then those strange marching insects with big pinchers came out after the first rains—the kind children were fond of placing together in glass jars to watch a good fight.

And spiders! I remember the first night in our new house. I was sitting at the dining room table with a spoonful of custard poised in front of my mouth when at eye-level on the wall across the room, I saw a sprawled apparition of the arachnid genre—a huge flat spider. Leigh, our ten-year-old daughter, and I must have seen it at the same time; we both screamed. When Charles recovered from surprise, he scolded, "Don't be silly. Those spiders are harmless and quite useful. They eat malaria mosquitoes."

"Will the spiders get malaria, Daddy?" Leigh asked.

I wasn't impressed. During the remainder of the meal, every bite I swallowed seemed to have legs. Later, I rather enjoyed the antics of those lovely spiders hanging on the ceiling like dark stars.

The most shocking discovery was a hive of wild African bees that had taken residence in the chimney. On cool nights they were quiet, but during midday heat, they filtered down through the fireplace and buzzed to exhaustion in the living room. Bush babies, squeezing slender bodies through holes in screens, braved the presence of humans for a free meal. When I swept the bees, still buzzing and convulsing into the dustpan, Leigh begged me to leave them. "I like to watch bush babies eat bees," she giggled. "They hop about so funny when they get stung."

Later, when Leigh got stung, the bees weren't so funny. The poison from a single sting made a swelling the size of a fist. That same day, Abelo coaxed me outside into the garden to look at bees, and, pointing to the chimney, made a comment which became a common expression around our house. "Madam," he said. "The bees find that a good place." They did, indeed, find that a good place, and I decided it was time to do something about it. The battle began.

Abelo tried various ways to get rid of the bees. He popped their heads with his fingernails and swept them into dustpans. He built a roaring fire in the fireplace, but the bees abandoned the hive only while the heat was on. He tried to smoke them out by burning damp grass in the fireplace.

The bees left momentarily, hovered around the chimney, and returned when the smoke died down. Leigh, who is easy-going like her father, ignored the persistent buzzing around her head and feet and at the window screens while doing her homework in the living room. Meanwhile, Charles was away most of the time living somewhere in the bush or in a remote area of a game park gathering statistics on hyenas. When he emerged from the bush long enough one weekend to replenish his supplies of canned food and clean underwear, I tried to convince him of the danger, but he didn't seem to comprehend the aggressive nature of wild African bees.

"Aw, honey," he said, laughing at his own pun. "It can't be that bad." Then he joked about how lucky we were to have bees in our belfry rather than bats. Leigh joined in the fun by pointing to the places Santa Claus might get stung when he came down the chimney on Christmas Eve.

On Monday I called the African Studies Institute which, in turn, called the Lusaka Fire Department. Late that afternoon a fire truck came roaring up the driveway to assess the situation. The firemen looked impressive in navy blue uniforms and official red hats. Leigh had just come home from school and was delighted with all the excitement. Six firemen came again after dark to exterminate the bees while they were "sleeping." Two firemen climbed upon the roof to spray carbon tetrachloride *down* the chimney, and two went inside to spray *up* the chimney while two firemen watched and made jokes about bees. Then they zoomed away in the dark after assuring me I would have no more troubles. But my troubles were just beginning.

A few days later, Abelo called me again into the garden and pointed to the chimney. "Madam," he said, "the bees are not finished."

A strange new development prevented me from concentrating on bees. Live maggots, feasting off the rotting bee hive in the chimney, had begun to drop from the ceiling. They fell from a plugged opening used in colonial days to connect a wood-burning stove. For three days maggots rained down, making small clicking sounds on impact. There was nothing to do but assign maggot sweepers; Leigh and I took turns when Abelo was busy. If the maggots were left to their own devices, some built-in guide directed them to migrate across the kitchen, through the dining room, down the hall, and out the crack under the front door. Since nobody was willing to lose sleep to keep maggot watch, live maggots crunched under our feet when we came downstairs each morning.

As mysteriously as the maggots came, they disappeared. Then dirty honey began oozing in rivulets down the wall from the plugged opening. Some dripped on the stove and some made its way through rafters and dripped from the ceiling. I placed buckets under the drips while Abelo wiped walls, but we played a losing game. Ants, flies, and roaches came to sip at the poisoned honey even as Abelo cleaned it up. After collecting a quart of the sweet, sooty gook, I filed another complaint with the Institute, but someone else's plugged toilets took precedence over our dripping honey.

Charles came home over the weekend and, to my horror, *laughed* when he saw the condition of the kitchen.

"Wait till I tell you about the maggots!" I said.

He laughed again. "I was looking forward to some good home-cooked food," he said, "but fried maggots in honey was not what I had in mind."

I was furious. If I had not been so glad to see him, I would have suggested he cook his own maggots. I have never understood why he laughs at things I find so frustrating, but maybe that's one of the reasons I like him.

On Monday I called the Lusaka Fire Department. The firemen refused to believe the bees had returned. "Come and see for yourselves," I insisted. "In the meantime, we're in great danger here. We could be mortally stung."

Shortly after dark, the fire truck roared up the driveway again with six big firemen. They rushed in carrying galvanized tubs and more spray. They unplugged the stove flue and removed rotting honeycomb and bees. Working with long poles, they poked honey and honeycomb down the chimney and into the fireplace where a tall, broad-shouldered fireman shoveled it into a tub. He seemed to enjoy himself as he examined the contents of each shovel. Presently he shouted, "Look at the king bee!" He pointed to the large queen still intact and encased in a sticky jell.

“That’s the queen bee,” I said.

“Oh, no!” he insisted. “That is the king bee and he has all these wives.” I knew it was useless to try to convince him. While he carried out two tubs of rotting debris, I wondered how many wives *he* had tucked away in mud huts in the village.

A week later, Abelo was in the garden pointing to the chimney. “Madam,” he called. “The bees still find that a good place.” I nodded. I had seen them. Drawn by the odor of honey, a new hive of wild African bees had taken up residence. I was too embarrassed to call the fire department again. I thought if I ignored the bees, they might go away. I resigned myself to living as harmoniously with them as possible, hoping no calamity would occur before the end of the year. My state of mind was not eased when I read in the *Lusaka News* that a village man had died when attacked by wild bees.

Then, one evening just before dark, the bees descended upon us with a vengeance. Leigh, doing homework at a table in the living room, called with panic in her voice. “Hey, Mom! Come and look! There are so many bees!” I hurried in to find roaring, excited bees pouring out of the fireplace. I grabbed Leigh by the arm and dragged her from the room. “My books!” she protested. “I don’t want them to get stung. The bees might make them into honeycomb.”

“Forget the homework!” I screamed. “You’ll be killed. Get out!”

I slammed the door behind us but bees bombed

under the crack beneath the door. I packed towels around the door facing and ran to the telephone. The housing office was closed. I was too disoriented to think of calling the Lusaka Fire Department, but I'm sure they wouldn't have believed me; they thought they had solved my problem. I lay awake during the night listening to a roar like the droning of a jet engine. Sometime past midnight I eased my head through the door and marveled at the wonders of nature. Angry, hysterical bees buzzed at chairs, tables, and the mantle piece, covering the furniture and light fixtures in a solid mass.

Next morning I waded cautiously into the living room to retrieve Leigh's homework and, with a thumb and forefinger, shook her books and papers free of inert bees. Leigh, following behind me, called out in a tone that would have made her father proud. "Look, Mom! Wall-to-wall bees!" She was right. The bees had buzzed themselves lifeless; most were lying dead or exhausted on the tables and floor. A few, still active, straggled drunkenly out of the chimney, and I knew our troubles were not over.

After getting Leigh off to school, I called the Institute's housing office. Mr. Patel, the director, informed me I would have to come in to file a complaint and the matter would be taken care of as soon as possible. From past experience, I knew "as soon as possible" might be a matter of days or weeks.

"You don't understand," I pleaded. "Wild bees

have swarmed in my living room. We're in danger."

"You must be mistaken," Mr. Patel said with a thick British and East Indian accent. "Wild bees swarm outside."

"Please," I begged. "Send somebody at once to make a report. This is an emergency My living room is wall-to-wall with bees."

"You might call the Fire Department," Mr. Patel said. "We don't have the equipment or personnel to handle emergencies."

I called the Lusaka Fire Department again and talked to Mr. Zulu, the fire chief, who recognized my name. He laughed when I told him about the swarm. "Bees swarm outside," he said.

"These bees are inside," I said. "I have wall-to-wall bees in my living room."

He laughed again. "The bees wants to start a new village."

"Yes, I know," I sighed. "But can't you do something?"

"Maybe tomorrow they will go away," he answered.

"I can't wait," I said. "My daughter's life is in danger."

Behind me I listened, with one ear, to the accelerated rumbling of bees, and pressed the other ear to the receiver while Mr. Zulu lectured me on their habits and habitats. When he finished, he agreed to send a truck out after dark. When the fire truck arrived at dusk, the main swarm had clustered on a bougainvillaea bush outside the patio door, hanging lush and ripe like poison pear-shaped fruit. The firemen sprayed the swarm and told me they were paid to put out fires, not kill bees, and the Institute would have to "do something." I relayed the message to Mr. Patel.

"What would you suggest we do?" he asked. I couldn't decide from his tone of voice whether he wanted suggestions or was being sarcastic.

"Now that bees are out of the chimney," I said, "this would be a good time to tie a screen across the top. The odor of honey will attract another swarm if we don't."

There was a long pause on the other end of the line. "I can send someone out," he said. "Tomorrow morning."

The next morning an old Mercedes truck rattled up the driveway. A crew of twelve men climbed off a flatbed in back and the truck sped away. I stood at the window watching. Workers had arrived empty-handed—no screening, no ladder, no tools. The men drifted toward the back of the house, looked up at the steep roof, and shook their heads. Then they squatted by the washtubs, chattering in their native tongue. For most of an hour they looked up at the chimney, shook their heads, clicked their tongues, and emitted low rumbling sounds. I'm certain if Charles had been home, he would have laughed, but I was furious. Soon the truck returned, sat vibrating in the driveway while the twelve men climbed aboard, revved its engine and roared away. Nothing had been done.

I'm not a patient woman; I like to see things done right. If an entire crew of men couldn't do one small job, then I would have to do it myself. By Friday afternoon I had collected a ladder, a piece of strong wire, a length of screening, and a pair of pliers. I was ready to go to work. Looking up I realized the house was taller and the roof steeper than I had thought. My stomach felt queasy, but I was determined. I tied the pliers around my waist with the strip of wire and knotted a length of heavy twine to the light screening, tying the other end to my wrist. I removed my sneakers and placed them beside the tubs, remembering from my childhood years as a tomboy that bare feet have better grip. But I had misjudged the height of the roof; the ladder didn't reach the eaves. I dragged the ladder sideways until it touched the copper drain pipe. I shook the pipe vigorously, testing it for strength. It seemed steady enough. When I reached the top of the ladder, I threw my weight upon it and my heart almost stopped. I heard it crack, but I swung onto it and got a precarious grip on the edge of the roof. The shingles were old; I hoped they wouldn't break.

I hadn't realized how out of shape I was. My arms ached as I drew my body upward. I tried to forget the weight of the pliers around my waist and the tug of the twine at my wrist I heard the seams of my jeans rip when I threw my left leg over the shingled eaves, rolled onto the roof, and got a firm grip with my toes. At last I was balanced. I moved sideways, crablike, toward the gutter at the gable and inched my way up the steep incline, testing each move with fingers and toes. When I reached the top, I swung my leg over the ridge, straddled the peak, and fished the screen up with the twine tied to my wrist. Drawing myself toward the chimney, I leaned upon it.

It took only minutes to shape screening over the top. Drawing wire around the edges of the second row of brick, I pulled tight to prevent any loose edges where bees might find their way inside. Even as I worked, two yellow bees dove against the screen and took off. I tied the wire and twisted it with pliers, satisfied the plan was going to work. The screen sagged a little, but the job was done, and I had been able to do something a crew of twelve men had not. Smiling, I let the pliers slide down the steep roof, listening to the washboard effect as it rumbled down the shingles and struck with a metallic clink on the concrete below. Then I looked around at the magnificent view from the roof.

Along the front driveway bougainvillaea, which had not been trimmed for years, cascaded over the fence in unruly masses of color—fuchsia, lavender, burgundy, rusty orange. Hardy climbing roses decorated a peeling white trellis with splashes of green and bright red, and a poinsettia tree in full bloom stood in the corner beside them. To the left, beyond a cluster of jacaranda trees, the small houses of the workers for the Institute stood in neat rows, and to the right was an orchard of fruit trees—orange, lemon, guava, mango. In the back garden a pair of frangipani trees framed a thatched shelter, their fleshy, succulent branches reaching out like stubby fingers. And farther beyond was Kaunda Square where thousands of workers had migrated from villages and built modest homes. Viewing the world from above, I felt detached, serene, the kind of high a mountain climber might feel when reaching a distant peak.

I turned at the sound of a roaring engine. A big hook-and-ladder truck from the Lusaka Fire Department came zooming down the dirt road in a cloud of orange dust. It swung in a wide curve and turned into the driveway of the Institute. I looked around, puzzled, searching for flames or smoke, and saw Abelo outside our front door, arms flailing, pointing to the fire truck.

"Don't jump, Madam," he called. "We will save you. I called them for help."

My moment of triumph was reduced to humiliation. The big firemen in blue uniforms had come to my rescue for what I hoped would be the last time. While workers from the Institute drifted out of buildings to watch, men cranked the tall ladder to the pointed eaves of the house. Straddling the ridge of the roof, I worked my way to the edge and looked down. A fireman was on his way up. I wanted to tell him I could come down alone, but decided against it. I let him sling me over his shoulder and carry me down where other firemen stood shaking their heads and clucking their tongues. Mr. Zulu shook my hand and congratulated the men on getting me down safely.

Abelo stood to one side, proud and smiling, convinced he had saved me from disaster.

I was grateful Charles wasn't home; I know he would have laughed, and I would never have heard the last of it.

The Bear

by

C. S. Kittelmann

When my father was little there was a big war. A war is like a fight between adults, only worse. In a fight, adults yell and scream. In a war, they kill each other.

My father lived in Berlin. Berlin is in Germany. He lived with my grandmother and grandfather.

At first, the war was good. That's what my grandmother says. There was enough to eat, and shoes were cheaper. Then the bombing started, and there were fires everywhere, and there was nothing to eat except frozen potatoes.

But my grandfather could make everything all right. He was big and strong and had a wide chest. He would hold my grandmother on his lap, while she held onto daddy, and wrapping his arms around them both, he'd whisper, "Everything will be all right." And for a while, it was.

He didn't have to fight in the war because he was an accountant for the government. He calculated exactly how many socks and bullets Germany needed to invade France. Then he went home to take care of his family. At home, he locked the door and drew the curtains. On weekends he built my father a cowboy fortress, just like in the wild west, out of paper and cardboard.

One doesn't have to get shot to die in a war. One can die in a war from being sick. My grandfather died at home. Over the dinner table. My grandmother had pickled a herring. A herring, in a war, is a treat. Grandfather loved herring, with plenty of onions, and peppercorns. My grandfather said, "The herring is delicious, Marie." And then he died. It was his heart. His heart was sick. It hurt too much and then he died.

After he died, my grandmother and my daddy were alone. And the bombs and fires got worse. And there was nothing to eat. So my grandmother took the streetcar to Pankow, outside of Berlin, to get oats from her parents who lived in Pankow. They were farmers and kept animals. The animals ate oats.

When she walked back to the streetcar, carrying bundles of oats under her arms, she could see in the distance that bombs were falling over Berlin. The city was ablaze. The streetcar wasn't running. She began to walk and then she ran. She ran, and ran, and ran, carrying the oats, for two hours, through the rain of bombs, letting go of the oats at last, to get home, because daddy was alone at home, and he was ten years old, and might not think of hiding in the basement.

My grandmother had many sisters who helped her take care of daddy after my grandfather died. One, named Lotte, had died early in the war from consumption. She went blue and then white because she didn't get red meat to eat. But Trude, Erna and Ollie were alive and living in Berlin.

The sisters never fought. Sometimes they argued about silly things. None of them had children, except for my grandmother, because they were too poor and then came the war. When they got pregnant, they would jump off the kitchen table, over and over and over and over and over again, until they were pregnant no more. My father was stubborn, and strong, and couldn't be shaken out.

My grandmother wasn't the only one who lost her husband in those years. Trude's husband was sent to Africa to fight and was found missing. Ollie's husband got cancer in his mouth and couldn't eat anything, not even boiled oatmeal. He got skinny, and then skinnier, and then one day he was gone. Erna's husband was very sad and lay in bed most of the war.

Berlin was not a good place for a little boy. So my grandmother and her sisters had a big meeting to decide what to do about daddy. Grandmother, Ollie, and Trude met at Erna's because Erna was the oldest. They sat in the kitchen while daddy sat in the other room, the living/bedroom, with Erna's husband, who didn't say much.

The sisters talked softly, and sometimes not so softly, for a long time. They agreed in the end, to send daddy south to stay with distant relatives, far away from the bombs and the fires and the sick. To a place that was safe and where there was enough to eat. The relatives bred pigs and probably had food to spare. Then they pooled what little money they had for the train ticket.

At the station Ollie presented daddy with a sandwich of Limburger cheese and rye bread. She said she had been saving the cheese. It was very smelly and just right. He should eat it when he got hungry. Trude gave him a bar of bitter chocolate. It was bitter, but it was chocolate. Erna had found an orange who knows where.

And grandmother hugged him and cried and said everything would be all right. One day the war would be over and they would all be together again. And then she pulled from her bag a teddy bear, big enough to hug and hold. Daddy reached out and hugged the bear. Grandmother enveloped daddy and the bear in her arms, saying softly: "When you get sad and scared and lonely, give the bear a hug, and think of home, and the pain in your heart will go away."

Daddy stayed in the south for a few months, until the war ended. He was homesick and waited and waited and waited for my grandmother to come and get him. But the trains weren't running and there was no way for letters or people to get from one place to the other. Except by walking.

So my father walked home.

He left a note for the relatives that read: "Thank you for the pig knuckles. I am going home. Do not worry. I am a big boy now." He put boiled potatoes in his pockets and the bear under his arm and began walking.

He was eleven years old.

Five hundred miles through occupied Germany. He walked for four months.

Often he was scared and cold and hungry and then he hugged the bear until the bear's belly grew flat.

There were soldiers everywhere. Some spoke French, some English, some Russian. Daddy knew a little Greek and Latin, but they were of no use whatsoever.

Sometimes he went hungry for days. But again and again soldiers took pity and fed him man-sized portions of sweet beans that came in a can, and white bread that was all soft in the middle, and soup that was red and sour and stained his lips and tongue.

One night he stayed with a troop of American soldiers. Most of them were big and black. That's how you knew, from afar, that they were American, long before you saw the uniforms or heard them speak. It was a cold night.

One of the soldiers took off his coat and wrapped it around daddy's shoulders and kissed daddy's cheek, saying something soft in English, and then the soldier kissed the bear with a loud smacking kiss, placing the bear in the coat's pocket. The coat was enormous and trailed on the floor. It was warm from the soldier's body. The next morning the soldier motioned that daddy could keep it. The coat kept daddy and the bear warm until they reached Berlin.

It was easy to find Berlin. He just walked north

and asked questions. People pointed and he walked in that direction. But once in Berlin, it took him four days to find Togostrasse Number 54. Home.

Walking into Berlin he grew confused. Berlin had changed. Some sections had been razed, heaps of rubble, with children and grown-ups picking around in the rubble. Nobody lived there anymore.

It took him four days to find Togostrasse because he ran around so much, and wouldn't stop to think and find his bearings. Tired, he stopped running, and walking he found his way home.

As he turned into Togostrasse he began again to run, because he was almost there. And running he noticed that much had been leveled, including the apartment building at Number #54. But only half of it—the window in the living room was still in place. So he ran faster.

There were people on the street and they recognized him and said: "Marie's boy! That's Marie's boy! He's alive!" And a young girl who was bigger and faster ran ahead proclaiming: "Frau Kittelmann, Frau Kittelmann! Your boy is back!"

My grandmother came running out of Number 54 and ran toward my father, arms wide open. She hugged him until everything inside him hurt, and she was covered in his dirt because he hadn't washed in a long time. But she didn't mind. And neither did Erna and Ollie and Trude who also were there, full of breathing and smiles, all together, ready to squeeze daddy flat. All of them had lost husbands and homes, except for grandmother who still had a home, and Erna, who still had a husband.

Erna's husband also hugged daddy. Erna's husband wasn't so sad anymore. The war was over. He smiled, and stroked daddy's coat, saying, 'I'm glad to know you have been warm. And look at you! So lean and strong. Almost a man. And then he took the bear out of the coat's pocket. The bear's belly was flat and the seams around its chest had burst and split wide open, and its nose had been pushed in from too much hugging. The bear was covered in grime, just like dad.

Erna's husband, whose name was Erich, Uncle Erich, looked at the bear for a while, saying nothing but maybe wanting to. He put the bear in daddy's arms and smiled and said softly, "Everything will be all right."

And then he lifted daddy onto his shoulders and led the train of grandmother and her sisters back into Number 54, saying to the neighbors who had gathered around, "Marie's boy and his bear are back, and they will now take a bath."

Arkansas Summer

by

Betty Gray

Little Rock, Arkansas in 1937 was a typical sleepy Southern town. The summer heat was intense. Everyone who could, sat in the cool draft of an electric fan. Everyone, that is, except a certain group of young girls in that awesome stage between child and woman—that horribly restless time of life when adventure lies around every corner, if one only turns the right way.

Before we begin my adventure, you must understand that my beginning was a little unusual. I was born in a small frame metal-roofed house in Fordyce, Arkansas during a hailstorm on my parents' third wedding anniversary. After such a bodacious entry into Arkansas, I did not want to leave the state nor my large family there ever, ever! Then came the Great Depression. My father's business was closed. In order to survive, we were forced to move to Houston, Texas in 1930.

My body moved to Houston with my brother and mother and dad. My heart did not. The gloom I cast about me with my fierce loyalty to Arkansas extended into my life at school as well.

Each morning, as a prelude to class work, my third grade class at Houston's Woodrow Wilson Grammar School stood at attention and sang "Texas, Our Texas." That is, my classmates sang "Texas, Our Texas." I, too, stood with shoulders straight and head held high—and often with tears streaming down my cheeks. I, however, belted out "Arkansas, Arkansas, 'tis a name dear . . . !" The obvious solution to everyone was that I would return to Arkansas each summer to visit my grandparents. Houston breathed a sign of relief when I took my summer hiatus!

My grandfather was a minister in Arkansas. He was systematically transferred from a church in one town to another every few years. During my summer visits I became acquainted with five girls just my age from several different towns. Through the years we had become close friends and house-partied back and forth. Now it was Virginia's turn to share bed and board with the giggly group in Little Rock.

We strolled around the familiar streets beneath large oak and hickory trees, tastefully clothed in our best crepe dresses, brimmed straw hats and white mid-heel shoes. We sipped cherry phosphates and chocolate sodas at the soda fountain. We played croquet on manicured lawns—a hallmark of the well-to-do "older" prestige neighborhood.

We considered ourselves to be the most exciting and desirable young women in Little Rock, for we were the Secret Red Heart Girls Club. Could anyone possibly guess that we were the phantoms of the night who left red cardboard hearts on the doorsteps of the residences of handsome young men in the area? We were, indeed, "genteel young ladies" but out for excitement—and that commodity was hard to come by when you were fourteen, and a girl at that!

Half of my summer visit had passed and the usual activities had become a little wearing. We settled down in the cool parlor of Virginia's white frame house and turned on the radio. The strains of "Alexander's Ragtime Band," "Deep Purple," "Once in a While," and "Blue Moon" cast a spell over the group. Then came the news. "Little Rock is honored to have one of its famous sons back for a visit. Dick Powell will be here visiting his parents . . ." Wow! Dick Powell! Oh golly! The *real* Dick Powell!

The stars falling to earth could not have brought more glory to Little Rock. Our finest hour had arrived and we were ready! And just think—his parents lived only four blocks away.

Six giggly girls bounced down the steps and danced a Ruby Keeler tap all the way down the sidewalks of the four blocks. But when we arrived in front of the Powell house, sheer terror replaced our excitement. What were we going to do now? Someone would have to walk up that walk, up the steps, and turn the handle of the doorbell. Our hero must be summoned before his court of worshipers.

The other five girls were by far more grown-up looking than I. They seemed much more woman-of-the-worldish from their stores of knowledge revealed during the wee morning hours of our slumber parties. But I was determined to win Dick Powell for my very own. If I could not win him with beauty and sophistication, I would have to use nerve.

"I'll do it!" Had the words really come from me? The others practically pushed me up the steps of the wooden porch before they retreated to a safe distance back on the sidewalk. Dazedly I rang the bell. After what seemed an eternity, the door opened slowly and a gray-haired woman with a kind smile peered down at me. "Yes?"

I swallowed hard, took a deep breath and looked up into the eyes of the mother of my hero. I asked, "Is Dick Powell here?" Did this nice, but ordinary lady realize that she was the mother of the "Idol of Millions," the man who posed for the magazine ads for Calox Tooth Powder, the ads that I had tacked up on the door of my room?

"No," she said, "he hasn't come home yet. May I help you?" This was the mother of the man of my dreams—and here she was, casually talking to me as though she were just anybody's mother!

Now panic replaced my cockiness. What now? I tried to keep my voice as steady as possible. "I am writing an article for the neighborhood paper and we would like to have an interview with him," I improvised. Oh-oh . . . what if she calls the paper and they have never even heard of me!

She wasn't at all suspicious. "He should be here

soon," she told me. "Would you like to come in and wait?"

Would I! I threw a gloating glance back over my shoulder to the five wide-eyed, open-mouthed girls on the walk and followed the mother of my idol into the living room.

"Dad," she announced, "this young lady has come to see Son."

The slender, gray-haired gentleman rose from his chair, extended his hand and smiled down at me. How could they be so casual? Didn't they realize that they were the parents of the most wonderful man in the world?

A door closed in the back of the house. There were footsteps. *He* stood in the doorway of the room! His brown tweed double-breasted suit, white shirt and brown-striped tie gave him the appearance of a typical Arkansas businessman returning home after a day at the office. But this man was a star! The entire female population adored him in *Stage Struck* and *Varsity Show.* Ruby Keeler and all of the other beautiful women were his at the snap of a finger. Oh my! I had fully expected a production number complete with fifty lovely ladies and a 100-piece orchestra. But there he stood, smiling, and as natural as any ordinary man, his dark wavy hair brushed back from his forehead, his eyes sparkling.

His mother said, "This young lady is writing an article about you, Son."

As he turned toward me my knees began to tremble. I realized that he could feel my panic.

My moment had come and instead of being a sophisticated big-city reporter, I was on the verge of fainting—or even worse—giggling! Suddenly I was just a very young stringy-haired, awkward, frightened girl.

"Well, just have a seat and I'll try to answer your questions," he said. The glorious resonance of his voice sent a wave of shivers down my back. What questions? Why did he want to take me out of my hypnotic state into the world of journalism?

His mother and father seated themselves on the couch beside him. I could feel it! They all knew I was not a real journalist. But I just had to go on with it!

Somehow I forced my lips to open so that a sound that must have been my voice escaped. "How long will you be in Little Rock?" I asked.

"I'm just here for a few days before I start my next picture. It's been quite awhile since I've seen Mom and Dad. I really came to invite them out to Hollywood. I'd like to buy them a little house out there." He reached for his mother's hand and gave it an affectionate squeeze. "Mother hasn't felt well lately."

Mrs. Powell laughed. She knew I was trying to overcome my nervousness. It was woman helping woman now! "If we go," she said, "you'll have to come see us in Hollywood someday."

"Oh, I will," I answered—and thought, *even if I have to walk!* As we talked, I began to relax a little. What kind people they were! I began feeling like the most remarkable of all Hollywood columnists, and a beautiful one at that! I drew in a deep breath, sighed and blurted out another question: "Mr. Powell, do you think I could have your autograph?" I just couldn't resist. I knew a famous columnist like Louella Parsons wouldn't have done it, but how else would anyone ever believe I had met Dick Powell if I didn't have proof? No one back in Houston would believe me—and probably not even my relatives here in Arkansas! I waited breathlessly.

He scrawled his name on a piece of paper from the desk, handed it to me, and patted me on the head. "Come to see us again, Betty," he said. Then he opened the screen door for me and waved to the frozen statues on the sidewalk—my friends. I smiled, and ambled casually down the walk. Surely, I concluded, this must be Heaven.

Oklahoma Blizzard

by

Dorothy Rose

It is Sunday in January
We 5 kids huddle on low stools
In front of the fireplace
A big black pot of beans simmers over the
  fire
Mamma sits on a chair behind us
She reads to us from our Bible
We wear three pairs of wool stockings
And our heaviest clothes and coats
We each have a quilt wrapped around us

Outside the wind howls and swirls
The dry powdery snow
Comes through the cracks in the house
The doors and windows rattle

Last night the wind tore a door off the
  barn
Our three cows and a calf got out
This morning Daddy bundled up
And went to look for them

We have little to eat because
The dust and hailstorms
Ruined our crops last summer
And our hogs died from cholera

School has been closed for a week now
The last day we walked down to catch
 the bus
My sister Mary's hands and fingers
Froze around the books she was carrying
We went into Smith's Country Store
Mrs. Smith pulled off Mary's mittens
She got some icy water
Had Mary put her hands in it for a while
Then she changed the water many times
Each time she used warmer water
Being very careful not to thaw out
Mary's hands and fingers too fast
In about an hour her hands straightened
 out
Until she was able to move her fingers
Mrs. Smith saved Mary's hands from
 damage

Daddy comes back home
The wind blasts through the door as he
 enters
His wool knitted cap coat and boots
Are crusted with ice and snow
Icicles hang from his nose and beard
His eyes are bleary and swollen
Daddy takes off his snow-covered clothing

I run to get him a quilt
He shakes and shivers and says
Mandy and Baldy have frozen to death
But I brought Queenie and her calf back
to the barn

Mamma starts to read the Bible again
Daddy snatches it out of her hands
Throws it in the fire
He yells Vallie stop reading that thing
No place in that book
Tells a man how he can live
And take care of his wife and children
Through years of droughts in the summer
And blizzards in the winter

Mamma jumps up quickly grabs the
poker
And rakes the Bible out onto the hearth
She yanks a dish towel from a hook
And beats the fire out
Then she goes over to Daddy
She puts one hand on his cheek
And she pats his back with the other
Says now now Lester
We've got a cow beans cornmeal
And none of the children are sick
We'll make it someway
Everything is going to be all right
You just watch and see

Afternoon Delight

by

Nancy Climer

The minute my husband told me he was going out of town overnight, my heart began to race. He didn't travel all that often and so the opportunities that I'd been daydreaming about were few and far between.

Once I knew when he'd be gone, I could barely keep from taking a crayon to the calendar and physically marking off the days, the way I do as Christmas nears, or Easter. But of course my husband, to whom I've been married for more years than I care to publicly count, noticed that something was awry.

"You're acting awfully strange," he said, his head tipped, his eyes narrowed.

"I am?" I was all innocencc on this, the eve of his departure.

In the morning, however, I was barely able to contain myself. I was practically hyperventilating.

His suspicions continued. "You seem awfully anxious to get me out of the house," he said.

I laughed carelessly, the way Lana Turner had in one of her steamier movies. "Darling, don't be silly," I said, moving his overnight bag closer to the door.

"You've never called me 'darling,' " he said.

It's true, I call him Bear. "Hahahahahaha," I said lightly, with a gesture that suggested affectionate dismissal. That had been in the movie, too.

And then I puckered for our usual goodbye.

It worked! Still, I held my breath and tried to peek through the draperies without being seen as I waited for his car to start.

So far so good. I watched the puffs of exhaust as he warmed the vehicle up. *All right, already,* I felt like shouting, thinking that, if he took any longer, we'd remain like this, frozen in a limbo-like tableau, with him *almost* gone and me, inside at the picture window, starving, literally starving for . . .

But then he was backing down the drive, and, with a brief squeal of the tires, he was hurtling toward the airport.

I leapt in the air the way I used to on the pep squad back when pep squads still existed. Then I bounded into the garage, flung the door aloft with so much force that it almost took me with it, and prepared to make my own little getaway.

Within twenty minutes I was at the supermarket, trying to decide between burgundy and Chianti and . . . well, I won't bore you with the details of something so mundane as *shopping.*

Suffice it to say that a little over an hour later I was about to take a sip of said wine when the door clattered open to reveal none other than my husband, his wagging, accusing finger looking larger than life.

"Aha!" he said. "I knew it. I knew it."

I lowered my eyes and nodded solemnly.

"Well," he shouted theatrically, "Don't let me interrupt." And then he turned on his heel and headed for his study.

Shameless creature that I was, I continued, biting lustily into my inch-thick patty of chopped sirloin, its juices oozing seductively even as I hoisted it toward my mouth. I ought to say it didn't taste very good, but the fact is, it did, it did.

You see, my husband has been on a low cholesterol, low sodium, low everything diet these many months and I, not to rub his nose in my own rude good health, have dutifully observed it along with him. But the austerity had gotten to me. Ever since he'd announced his proposed jaunt, I'd been fantasizing, among other goodies, *this very burger,* its exterior charred, its interior red and dripping grease. I'd even lavished salt upon its bubbling surface as it cooked, luxuriating in the naked pleasure of it.

Still, I know where my bread is, uh, margarined. So, "Forgive me?" I asked later, as my husband told me about the last-minute cancellation of his meeting.

"Sure," he bear-hugged me as he spoke. "It was just this once."

With that remark the guilt set in. I knew what I would have to do. I would have to get rid of the incriminating but nonetheless yummy rasher of bacon and the half-dozen Jumbo eggs and the block of sharp cheddar that I'd stashed away for tomorrow's breakfast. And then, too, there was the matter of that pint—or was it a quart?—of chocolate chocolate chip.

Friends, Lines, and Sinkers

by

Lucille Bellucci

It's not easy to like your friends all the time. Take Bill Carpenter. He has a great sense of humor, he's generous, kind, and always returns anything he borrows. But he has one trait that drives me crazy: Bill knows everything, or else he's done it better than anybody else.

Some evenings we'll be having a quiet beer in the I-80, a tavern east of San Francisco where lots of truckers like to go and swap stories. We talk about tough stretches on the road and good or bad places to eat. A guy told us about ice on a mountain grade where no warning was posted. We look out for each other.

Then one of the guys says to me, Did you hear about Jack Morelli catching a big striper on Sherman Lake?"

"No, how big was it?" I ask.

"As big as his wife. I saw it. There's enough to feed them for weeks."

Bill cuts in. "What'd it weigh?"

"Maybe thirty-five, forty pounds."

Bill smiles. There's a tilt on one corner of it that

tells me what's coming. Bill has told us about hunting bighorn in Wyoming, taking rattlers by hand in Texas, and landing record skipjack tuna on the East Coast. I think he once told me he'd had a pet baboon in the Sahara Desert someplace, but I could be mistaken. I was busy doing my income tax in my head at the time.

But then I remember him coming over to our house at two in the morning last week, scared to death for us. He'd heard on the radio about a fire on our block and drove ten miles to save our lives. Last Christmas he made presents for our kids that showed a lot of thought. His own kid is in another state with her mother.

Now he's saying, "A little baby like that I'd throw back. I've hooked stripers that went to fifty pounds on a slow day."

"Yeah," the guy says and turns back to the TV over the bar. He knows Bill too.

"Hey," Bill says to me. "Have you ever fished Point Pinole?"

"Never been there," I say. "I hear it's a good pier, though."

"One of the best," Bill assures me. "You don't need to go out in a boat to catch the big ones. Want to give it a try?"

I think about it, and decide it *would* be nice to spend a day out in the fresh air. We agree to go at eight o'clock next morning, and I give him a ride home. As I let him out at his place, I ask if I can take his tackle box home with me because I have a feeling some of my stuff must be rusted solid. The last time I've done any fishing was five years ago. Later I'll replace anything I take.

He says sure and gets the box. It's a beauty, with three giant retractable drawers loaded with hooks, spare swivels, leads in all sizes, and a whole line of spoons, spinners, plugs, and even some fancy streamer flies. It's a toy shop. "This is some rig," I say.

"Professional." Bill nods, offhand. "Uncle Bill will show you some tricks tomorrow so's you can take home a *real* fish to Sally. Leave the bait to me. You amateurs mess up from the start."

At that, something snaps in my brain, but I keep my mouth shut and drive home.

In the morning I pick him up and drive to Point Pinole, a pier nearly a quarter-mile long on the south shore of San Pablo Bay. San Francisco is just a smudge southwest of us. We take the shuttle from the parking lot and I enjoy the ride, the whole morning. A clean breeze—with just a hint of fish in it is fanning our faces. I'm feeling good, on top.

We are nearing the pier when it appears everybody has gone berserk. Then we see the flocks of screeching gulls diving into the water, which is churning with anchovies. *Below* the anchovies, chasing them ashore straight onto the rocks, are huge striped bass. We can see them. Several as big as gasoline drums are already flopping on deck. People are throwing lines all over the place.

Bill whoops and jumps off the shuttle, with me following. We ease into a spot at the rail, next to a lady who's got two big stripers lying at her feet.

He's so excited he's panting while he puts his rod together. We finish at the same moment, slap on bait and cast, but the lady's elbow knocks his arm and our two lines go *whing whing whing* as they snake around each other. Bill glares at the woman but she doesn't even look at him—she's hooked into a monster. He shrugs, and we start unfouling our lines.

"Harold," hollers the woman. "I got another one!" Next to her a man wearing a cowboy hat shouts back that he has one too. I am ready to cast again but hold back because the rail is getting too busy and I'm afraid of an accident. But Bill throws his and neatly hooks the woman's striper in the tail as it's coming up. Now it's *her* turn to glare, and Bill smiles apologetically, puts down his rod, and moves to help pull up the fish. It's the first time I've ever seen him look uncomfortable.

"Its my fish!" yells Mrs. Harold.

"I know!" yells Bill.

"Then let go of it!" screams Mrs. Harold.

"All right!" Bill lets go of her line and the fish tears loose from both hooks and disappears.

"Aaaargh!" goes Mrs. Harold, looking at her empty line. Her face swells up, her eyes turn maroon. She takes a deep breath and opens her mouth. As if we are one person Bill and I pick up our gear and walk away. He hasn't even reeled in his line; it drags behind us like a tail.

Further up the pier, we set up again. Bill doesn't say a thing, but he's acting dislocated, makes three tries before he has the bait right. It's like he never baited a hook before. Finally we both haul back and cast. Then a queer silence falls over the bay. The birds are gone, the anchovies have left, and Bill has cast his hook into my sweatshirt.

I keep my face straight as he works it free, *his* face like something you could barbecue a striper on.

Since that day, I haven't heard him say one word about what a swell athlete and sportsman he is.

I'm still ashamed of what I did, even if he never did get his hook in the water. It's all in the past anyway, finished, fixed up. I told him I wanted to clean the things I'd used and put them back properly in his tackle box, so he let me take the box home when he dropped me off.

And that's what I did. I oiled the gears on the reel I'd used and shined it, rewound the line nice and even and put everything in the correct slot in the box. Then I did something else. I replaced all his hooks with new ones. The others, the ones I'd filed halfway through in a place he couldn't see unless he looked really close, I threw away. After what I did to them, those hooks wouldn't have held onto a three-inch minnow.

Traces of the Past

by

Leona Nogues

The first thing I remember as a baby was looking up at three smiling faces peering down at me: my mother, my dad, and my grandmother. Since my grandmother lived only two blocks away, she helped my mother with me a lot. After all, she'd had five children of her own, mostly all grown, so naturally she had most of the answers. Also, she was fat and soft (to a baby) and she laughed a lot. I loved my grammy very much, and when she passed away, I was only three. I remember crying at my great loss. I just felt so alone.

My dad bought a half acre out on the edge of Enid, Oklahoma and built us a small shotgun house on it. I wasn't aware of my parents' indifferences at that time, but an old neighbor lady sure did, and she took the opportunity to convert my mother to her religion. And that changed our lives forever. My parents divorced, and we kids were sent to this religious school which was three miles away from home. I was the first to go, and all alone, after I learned the way. I've always held it against Mother for making me walk all that way to school in the ice and snow and cold north winds when there was a perfectly good public school with lots of kids and much better teachers about three-quarters of a mile away from us on the same route. But we were not exposed to anything public, like the library or museums, and so remained woefully ignorant of the world.

A bunch of us kids were sitting in Uncle Sterling's two-seated touring car with no windows as it was a warm day. We were just passing time, like kids do, when suddenly, up popped a stranger on one side of the car, and on the other side was Uncle Sterling, shooting at the guy who was running. He was trying to get into the house when Sterling shot him in the leg. I guess the guy lived, but we never heard of him again.

Now Mama was always angry at us over any little thing, and she would take her anger out on us kids. It got to the point where we were afraid to come into the house after school, because she might grab us and whip us till we were black and blue. I think she was mad at the world because times were so hard back in the Depression. Sometimes we would go over to Aunt Alma's and pull down our pants and show her our black and blue marks. One time, Alma got so mad at our mama for whipping us, that she went over to our house and pulled Mama out of the house and really mopped up the ground with her. To this day, my sister claims that we were battered children. I do know one thing, it broke our hearts. But Mama never apologized for anything.

Once, when I was about in fifth grade, one of the girl students took a tube of lipstick and wrote four-letter words all over the basement walls. When asked about who did it, she said, "Leona did it," pointing right at me. (Heck, I didn't even know what the words meant!) But being poorer and uglier, I was forced to stay after school and scrub the walls, crying the whole time. No one would believe me, not even my mother, who probably didn't even hear me and cared less. She just knew the teacher wouldn't punish me without a reason. So I just bore it all. It's no wonder I hated that school and all it stood for.

Aunt Alma came over and stayed with us some, and she told me all about becoming a woman; and sure enough, she was right. Just naturally.

That fall, I became fourteen and all filled out. My hair grew naturally wavy and I had my first boyfriend. We were very bashful, so we wrote sappy love notes and smuggled them to each other. I'll never forget handsome Joey. One day a mean kid intercepted our mail and the teacher made him get up in front of the class and read one of them out loud. Of course we were very embarrassed, and that was the end of that affair. (I heard, many years later that Joey's family moved to Oregon, where he married and had twelve children. Wow!)

Sometimes, when the weather was sunny and bright, with new snow a foot or two deep, the teachers would turn out school and let us slide across a frozen pond, or ride sleds down a steep hill. One time a man came with a horse and sleigh and took us all for a ride.

We heard that we could go to Oregon for the summer, and all work together picking strawberries and beans and all kinds of goodies. So we loaded up our clothes, blankets, and our old black iron dutch oven, and hit the trail out Route 66. We would go as far as we could in a day, then we would stop beside the road and make camp for the night. Out would come the old dutch oven and Mama would make some biscuits and sugar syrup and we lopped up every bit.

When we finally got to Oregon, we stayed at different migrant camps and worked hard every day; but we sure enjoyed that summer. The Japanese owned the loveliest strawberry fields (before the war and confiscation), and we worked hard all day and slept in a tent; we saved our money, and when the summer was over, we had enough to buy a thirty-four Ford two-seater, with a hard top, no less. We used to fight over who was gonna drive the car and not one of us had a driver's license.

I had gone as far as the school went—I think through the tenth grade—so I and my sister enrolled in a public school several miles away. We would walk down to the main road and catch a school bus. If we were one minute late, the driver wouldn't wait for us, even though we screamed our heads off. We considered that pure meanness. Then we would have to turn around and go back to a lifeless house and dawdle away the day because Mama always had to work to support us. Mama had to walk a mile to catch a ride to Springfield; she left the house before daylight and would walk down the fence row to keep from getting lost in the dark. Then out of the dollar she earned, she had to pay ten cents for the ride, both ways, leaving her with eighty cents to buy flour, sugar, Crisco, and peanut butter. We bought milk and eggs from neighbors, I think.

My first real date and I had seen each other at a local country store. We sorta sized each other up from a distance, then I left with my family, and he asked the store owner all about me and who I was and all that stuff. Then he found out where I went to school, and where I lived. He was seventeen and I was sixteen, and we thought that was about right. His family encouraged him to ask me out, and my Mama didn't object, so we agreed to go to a movie one Saturday night. He came and got me right on time. He had the cutest black Model A roadster coupe, and it ran like a top, all spit and polish too. He drove carefully, as we had thirteen miles to go. We were both very bashful, so we went indoors to a movie, bought some ice cream and ate it on the way home; but we never said a word until he got me home, and then it was probably goodnight. It seems strange now that we never talked about one thing all that distance. But we did date each other exclusively after that, so we surely must have spoken sometime.

Once more we loaded our belongings (necessities) on the old car and came to Texas and a new life. We had to stop in the small town of Bowie and ask the druggist the way to our newly rented establishment. So on we drove south on the Briar Creek Road. After about five miles we turned left up a one-horse trail, and Whoopee!! There we were! We were looking at a three room weather-beaten shack, sagging front porch, no electricity. We all got out of the car, sat down on the front porch and *cried!* Here we had left a beautiful springtime in the Ozarks to come to this drought-riddled, hotter-than-hell spot in Texas! The grass-hoppers were three inches long. Everything that hadn't dried up, burned up or just gave up and died, was consumed by the hoppers. It was a nightmare to us. Heck, we thought it was hot in Enid when we had to carry a bunch of big leaves to step on because of the parched ground; but it was nothing compared to this 120 degree heat (in the shade!). No wonder we bawled our eyes out! The only redeeming quality we could see was a nice windmill, with lots of water running into a big metal tank.

There was nothing left to do but unpack and try to make it.

I heard about a job at a drive-in cafe. It was a pink-painted place out on Ninth Street, and they gave me my first real job waiting on cars outside. This place sold lots of beer and sandwiches and we had lots of soldier customers, as Shepherd Field was just north of town.

I had always heard that I had pretty blue eyes,

so I made them up to a fare-thee-well. I kept my dark hair clean and long and wavy. The place furnished us with red and white checked uniforms, with a nice little white apron.

One evening about nine or ten o'clock, in came a nice, blue convertible with the top down full of airmen from the base. At the wheel sat the cutest guy I had ever seen, and when he flashed those limpid green eyes at me, I was hooked. Even though his mustache was red and didn't match his dark blonde hair, he was a doll. Apparently he felt the same way about me, because after a few weeks, we drove over to Waurika, Oklahoma, just over the Red River, where they didn't ask many questions. We both were underage, so we lied (and they knew it!) but they gave us a marriage license, and we tied the knot right there.

Soon after, he received his orders to go to Kelly Field in San Antonio, so off we went. Smokey was to become a pilot and I was to become a mama. I lived for a while with an officer's wife and Smokey would come to town whenever he could get away. But I was homesick for my own mama, so we decided I would go back for the big event while he would finish flying training. Graduation and Birth-day would be close together. So I took a train back to Bowie to wait it out. But it just so happened that Smokey graduated first, so he took a leave and came up to Bowie for the big arrival of Mister T, as we called our son, Tommy.

I had a nice neighbor girl who took care of Tommy during the day for me. He was a nice, happy baby, and was not any trouble. I believe I got in three months of typing, shorthand, bookkeeping, etc., before we got the telegram saying that Smokey was lost in action. So I quit school right there, and grieved long and hard, although the Army said they would look for him for a year, and they did. Also, his father sent a couple of detectives over to the area to search for him. But his plane had gone down in the Adriatic Sea, over by the Mediterranean Sea.

When we accepted the fact that Smokey would never return, I burned all his letters and stuff.

Tom quickly met a neighbor boy, Don Underwood, whose mother Eunice just as quickly became our good friend. She knew all about everyone in town. She was a cute little blonde, though she had five kids and a bum of a husband who couldn't support them the way she wanted. So she used to date the town bootlegger, who gave her lots of money to buy clothes and keep the girls' hair all permed. They all seemed happy with the arrangement.

Eunice's husband always threatened suicide when he got to drinking. In fact, he once walked over the railroad bridge via the hand rails on the side, and we all laughed and thought that was very funny. But Eunice got sick and tired of his threats, so one morning at breakfast, she had all the sharp knives and scissors and rat poison and an ice pick all lined up at the table and she told him to take his choice, as she was tired of waiting. Well, he jumped up from the table and ran out the door and just disappeared.

After we had moved back to Bowie, maybe two years later, my new husband George was riding out the fences over in the back pasture, and he saw something move, so he jumped off his horse. It was a fawn, so he grabbed it up and held it across his saddle and brought it home. Under the kitchen table became its home for a few days. It had never nursed, so we got hold of a nipple and taught Bambi how to suck out of a bottle. I've forgotten the formula, but George built him a pen out behind our calf shed and we protected the fawn from the cold until he grew bigger. Also we got some calf meal and hay for him.

It was against the law to hold a wild animal prisoner, but what else could we do? So the sheriff came out to have a look see, but he didn't say anything. So we raised him, and he grew up to be quite big, and we were afraid he would become dangerous, so one weekend I took the boys and went down to Pat's and Betty's. Bambi became meat that weekend. Darn good, too.

It was now January or February 1951, and I had contracted a cold and wasn't feeling good at all, so I decided it was time to take out the old appendix that had bothered me so long. I went back to Dr. Harris and told him and he said that he wanted me to have some repair surgery done while I was so young. That was when they discovered that I was diabetic. (That explained the dark cloud hanging over my head that would never leave.) So I had to stay in the hospital for two weeks to get the sugar down to normal. Then I had the surgery, and they tied my tubes at the same time.

One day, a man knocked on my back door, and asked if he could do some work for me in exchange for a meal. So I let him clean out the garage and then I scrounged up a nice plate full of food for him and a cup of coffee. He was very pleased, as was I with his work; so he thanked me kindly and went on his way.

I thought no more about it, but when George found out, he didn't like it very well. It got to where this same thing happened about once a week, and I heard that these guys have a way of marking your house so others would know you were an easy target. I couldn't ever find the marks. When the next fellow came by, I could tell he was either drunk, or suffering from a terrible hangover, and he just looked scroungy to me. I wasn't feeling up to par that day, so I just dumped some used coffee grounds into a bread wrapper and handed that to him and he ambled on.

About that time, around four in the afternoon, George came home, and he wasn't feeling any pain himself, and I told him what had happened; he got back into his car and went around the block until he found the drifter. He drove up beside him and stuck his arm out the window, and said, "Do you see this fist?" and the guy said he did. Then George said, "I'm the law around here and I say that you had better get along fast."

Well, the guy said, "I'm going, I'm going as fast as I can."

Well, that was the last time I ever saw a hobo around here. I wasn't afraid, because at that time, there wasn't as much meanness and crime as there is now. We laughed about it a lot.

George's old buddy, Ike Wolf, said he knew where I could get a puppy. So we went out north of town to this lady's house. Her name was Thena Trout and she was Ike's girlfriend. She had a border collie mama dog who had some pups. And I could have any one I wanted. So I picked out a black and white spotted short-haired pup and we took him home (over the mama dog's great objections). And I named him Brutus, I don't know why.

I fixed him a bed in a box beside my bed so I could reach in and pet him when he cried. Then I figured out that he was used to nursing in the middle of the night, so I kept a cup of milk on the nearby table, and when he cried, I would hold the cup down level so he could lap up the milk and he would go back to sleep.

Brutus grew quickly, and Daniel, my son, had a lot of fun teasing him. When Brutus got big enough, he would wait at the end of the lane for Daniel to get off the school bus, and come home with him.

Well, Daniel had made the dog so mean by then

with his teasing, that when folks would drive into the yard, they would be afraid to get out of their car until I scolded Brutus and made sure they wouldn't get bitten. That darn dog would bite anything Dan told him to, including the chairs on the front porch.

One Sunday afternoon, when I was still in my thirties, and we lived on the lower forty, I received a phone call from Dorothy asking, "Lee . . . Did you know George has been shot?" Of course she informed me that he would live, that he was in the Bowie Clinic and was shot in the hand, and they wanted me to go to the clinic and go with them to take him to a hospital in Wichita Falls, pronto.

Well, I jumped in the car and went to the Bowie Clinic, and found him on a table out in the hall. All his clothes were removed except his dirty shorts, which I spotted right away.

The doctor had told me that he was too full of alcohol to do any surgery, and would put it off until the next morning. So, we put him in the back seat of the car and Marvin, Dorothy, and I all took him to the Bethani Hospital.

So we entered him in the hospital, and he was in great pain. So the next morning, after the alcohol had worn off, they operated on his hand, which was full of an exploded bullet. Seems he was out rabbit hunting with a friend (and having a few drinks), and the friend, who was driving, turned a wide swath out in the pasture wherever they were, and the door on the passenger's side swung open. Of course George grabbed at it, and the gun exploded into the side of his hand.

So the next day, I took him some clean shorts and he told me how the fellow in the room with him the day before, asked, "What happened to you, fellow?"

And George said, "You oughta seen the other fellow. They are burying him today."

Well, this guy called the nurses, and said, "I want out of this room, right now!" So they moved him elsewhere, and we all got a big laugh out of that.

Another time, when Tom was about sixteen, he was driving home with his dad. Tom had never learned to drive the pickup that George brought home one day. It was brand new and Tom got stopped by a policeman right outside of Bridgeport. The cop told him that he was driving 125 miles an hour. George said, "Well, fella, the speedometer only registers 85." But Tom got a ticket anyway.

When Willie Mae and Laird were first married, Willie Mae wanted to ride a horse in the parade they had each year at Bowie, at the Jim Bowie Festival. So Laird got her a black horse to ride, and she bought herself a black saddle, a complete black outfit, boots, hat, and all. One day she wanted to practice riding her horse, and as she was so large and had never been on a horse before, Laird saddled up the horse and brought it up beside a big box and ladder, so she could straddle and ride. Well, she just kept right on going over the side, and spooked the horse. Laird just about died laughing. She got so mad that she never tried being El Rancho Grande again. So she sold her saddle and trappings, and that was the end of that.

We had a neighbor about three or four miles down the county road whose name was Mrs. Davis, and she tried to be Mrs. High and Mighty, and her daughter was better than anyone else's, and so on. I never knew the lady and didn't want to know her, but one day she showed up at my front door in a wig (but I recognized her) and claimed that my boys had broken into their house and robbed her of a lot of candy and stuff. Well, my boys were 500 miles away going to school, and I told her that. Then she demanded to see George. I became furious and told her to get the hell out of my house and never come back again. So she left, but she cornered George somewhere and he told her where the boys were, so she never bothered us anymore.

We had a local sheriff who was butchered up by two or three guys who caught him out parked one night. They swore he was hanky-pankying with their wives. The sheriff ran a big ad in the local paper saying he was hospitalized with hernia surgery, but everyone knew better and he soon resigned. He was in a wheelchair for a long time. Ever after, when he was seen, he recognized no one, and was a completely different person.

Not long ago, we had a *really* popular sheriff

who was arrested on the Post Office steps, and jailed for possessing pornography. He was tried and convicted and is now in the Huntsville state prison if the inmates haven't killed him by now. He was really good-looking.

A problem I had with Dan was getting him to take a bath or shower; he liked the smell of sweat and he imagined flies flying all around. He was just trying to be repulsive, and he was doing a good job. So one time when he was stretched out on the red carpet in the living room right in front of the television, I decided to pull him into the bathroom. I grabbed his arms and shoulders, pulling him head first. Then he simply turned his big feet sideways and locked them onto the door frame, and there was nothing I could do. He just laughed at me, so I gave up, saying, "Okay. Just stay dirty. I don't care."

Another time, when we first moved back to Bowie, George and his friend Marvin decided that they would castrate a bunch of small bulls, and while they were at it, they would dehorn them, and vaccinate them. They needed someone to keep the fire hot and the branding irons ready. Since I was the only one available—the boys were in school and Dorothy wasn't about to do anything like that—I was drafted.

I never again in my life would be a party to that operation, I tell you! I never saw such a hurt little bunch of dejected animals in all my life. Of course, they recovered in a few days. But usually, after that, George would catch the babies a few days after they were born, grab their legs and throw them down, and do all the necessary doctoring while they were very young.

Dan was always threatening to leave home, and when he was a real young kid, I would say, "Wait a minute and I'll help you pack." And we would laugh and it would pass over quickly. But, when he was a teenager and had his own car, it was another story. So when he announced that he was going to Las Vegas come hell or high water, he put everything he owned and cared about into his car, filled it up with gas, and announced that he was leaving the next day. So I tried cajoling, bribery, threatening or anything I could think of to get him to stay, but to no avail.

The next morning I received a phone call from him saying, "Mother, would you come and get me? I just ran out of gas, and I'm up the road about three miles." So, what else could I do? I hopped in my car and went up the road to where he was standing beside his car, loaded him in and went to town and got some gas in a five-gallon can. I parked right behind him, and when he poured the gas into his car, a stream of gas shot out at an angle and it was no use putting gas in *that* car, so we turned around and headed back towards home. When smoke started pouring out of his hood, he jumped out and hopped over the fence.

As soon as we got back home, George got into the tractor and went up and pulled Dan's car home. Dan swore that Pop put that hole in the gas tank to keep him from going to Las Vegas. George vehemently denied it, but I'll tell you that I would have myself, if I had known how, and dared. To this day, we don't know the truth, and probably never will.

The Virgin of Polish Hill

by

Carolyn Banks

The section of the city was called "Polish Hill." It consisted of narrow streets and row houses, brick pavements gradually being replaced by concrete sidewalks. A few slat fences were left, but these too, were going. In their stead, chain-link fences were being raised.

There was a hospital on the hill that loomed over the rest of the neighborhood. Its psychiatric ward, on the top floor, was commonly referred to as "the crazy house." Children used to line up on the street to stare at the top floor, waiting to see one of the patients. At the slightest sign of movement on any of the floors, they would run, screaming happily, home to safety and normalcy.

Normalcy meant the smell of kishka or kielbasi reaching from the kitchen to hall and all through the house. On Mondays, bleach and ammonia welled up from a hundred whitewashed cellars. Beyond the hospital, enemy lines. Names like Carrozza, Damiano. Pizza houses, not our own.

Most of the people in our section spoke Polish, and all of the older children understood the language when they heard it, although they didn't speak it. In the market on Saturday morning, over the smell of fruit and fresh-killed meat, a steady chirrup of Polish arose.

The market was a favorite gathering place. It was the only store in the three-block shopping district that still covered its floors with sawdust. The older children would slide in it, and the little ones, hanging onto a coat sleeve or hem, would make tentative marks with their shoes: circles, lines, little ditches. My own dream when I was small was to storm and slide up the aisles, a whirl of chips flying, the dust clouds in my wake falling evenly on every bottle, every jar, every tissue-wrapped lemon and apple and orange.

Secular pleasures, even those only imagined, were few. The real center of the neighborhood was the church. Everyone, even the drunkards like Diana Kapinski's father, went to church on Sunday mornings. The ones who went earliest were considered saintliest, while the ones who went to the noon Mass were virtually atheists. My parents went, usually, to 6 a.m. Mass with my grandmother and Aunt Clara, while I went to Children's Mass at 8:30.

All of my classmates were there, unwilling but kneeling starch-straight because of the nuns who had been stationed every third row. Sometimes I pretended to be sick so that I could sit, but during the sermon we all sat, and I would read almost all of the gospels in my missal before the priest had finished preaching.

Even though we went to church every week, few of us seemed to know when to sit, stand, or kneel. We always had to look at each other or to the nuns so that the movement never happened all at once. I always promised myself that I would learn the routine so thoroughly that the class would look at me before rising or before kneeling or sitting. And yet it was always the good girls, like Maryann Wrobleska, the girls who never talked in school and who never got their hands hit with the ruler by the nuns, who were never slow to decide what to do during mass. Despite my promises to myself, I was always off in daydream or in the midst of reading one of the gospels.

May was the cruelest month, the month of Mary. It began with a procession through the neighborhood streets. The boys carried a large plaster statue of the Virgin and the girls followed, emptying baskets of rose petals along the way and singing over and over again, a long, strangely sad Polish hymn called Podgura Dolina.

I hated the whole thing. I think it was a safe guess that all of us did, the boys in crisp navy suits, the girls in starched white dresses and knee-length white socks.

Old tapestry banners recalling miracles were held high, usually by the older men in the Sacred Heart Society: Lourdes, Fatima, Guadalupe. The smell of incense in the streets was fleeting except to those of us in procession. We grew dizzy as we walked and sang, casting the petals into the warm spring streets.

The neighborhood people would come down from their porches and stand at the curb. Some would lean out of upstairs windows. The old women would cry a little and try to sing with us, but always much too slowly.

Except for May, evenings in the church were given over to these old women, who would go in groups to say the rosary. Since few of the babkas had even attempted English, it was said in Polish. In any language, the words would have been indistinguishable. When the priest had hurried through his part of the prayer, the tired, soft, hiss-chirp would begin, all at once, dwindling slowly, with each of the women praying at a different pace. Wrinkled and sad, most of them fat and dressed in dark colors, they huddled over their beads down at the small side altar. My grandmother was one of them.

The only occasion in church that I enjoyed (although I managed to look every bit as put upon as my friends) fell on the Saturday before Easter. The girls would come in wearing babushkas and light jackets carrying baskets of food to be blessed for the Easter morning meal. We would kneel close to the center aisle with the baskets on the floor beside the pews. Filled with the sweet smell of Polish sausage and home baked raisin bread, the church seemed less forbidding; perhaps, too, because the agonies of Lent had passed and we no longer had to spend each Friday afternoon making Stations of the Cross and because the purple shrouds that covered all of the statuary had at last been taken up. Absent, too, was the regiment of nuns, so that we could sit or slouch as we chose.

And then the priest would appear, heralded by two altar boys waving censors, filling the air with the familiar church incense, covering, temporarily, the warm and alien kitchen smells.

We would kneel as straight as if the nuns were yet behind us, and up the aisle the priest would walk, swinging a silver shaker, splashing the baskets and the company with tepid holy water. We would regain ourselves, shuffle out, complain together in the churchyard, and swagger home to beg the now sanctified raisin bread, eggs, or sausage. Each family kept a store of unblessed food, too, though nothing could equal the share in the baskets. But never once would our parents permit us to touch, let alone eat, the food that had been blessed until Easter morning.

The younger women, a group that included our mothers, did not go to rosary, nor did they participate in our devotions. Instead, they played bingo in the church basement. I went only twice and, although I was bored by it, I was jealous of the girls who went regularly because they seemed so much more grown up than I. And so I always wheedled and whined to be able to go.

My mother never won anything except an Aunt Jemima cookie jar, but my Aunt Clara won almost every time she played: towels, doilies, and a salt and pepper set. Once, on one of the two nights I had been allowed to go, Aunt Clara won the $50 jackpot.

She told me to place the red see-through chips on her card, but I was too slow, and eventually she took over. I was almost asleep, my head pressed against the narrow table, when she called out, "Biiiiiingo!" We danced the polka in the streets that night on the way home, and the next day my aunt bought a turkey and we had a huge family dinner at my grandmother's, just like Thanksgiving, to celebrate.

Aunt Clara told all of my aunts and uncles and cousins that I had brought her luck and I got to pull the wishbone with her, although, as usual, she won.

She always won at everything. She even won a toaster once in the church raffle. It wasn't first prize, but still. Each of us had to sell five books of tickets, which was pretty easy since relatives usually bought a whole book. But Aunt Clara won her toaster and was the only one in the whole family who had bought a single ticket.

It was she to whom the Blessed Virgin once miraculously appeared. It was, in fact, the Virgin's only appearance in Western Pennsylvania.

My Aunt Clara had never been my favorite. I remember her sitting on the front steps in the summertime drinking beer, setting the bottle on the steps beside her after every swig. I used to worry that my friends would see her, but if they did, they never told me, never teased me about it, which they would have, I am sure, had they seen.

She was a loud woman, and her teeth were laced

with gold. She laughed a lot, throwing her head back so that all of the fillings would show. When she hugged me, she squeezed too tight and her breath smelled of beer and her cheeks of powder. I would squirm to get away from her, but she always managed to hug me more than anyone else. At least it seemed so.

Her rooms were next door to us, small and cluttered with her winnings and her handiwork. All of our sheets had been bordered by Aunt Clara, and she made my mother's finest tablecloth, reserved for Christmas and Easter dinners. Most of my aunts and uncles bought doilies from her to give as wedding presents and to use in their homes. My parents did not use doilies, except for one long one across the dining room buffet, and so, in our house, all of the doilies that Aunt Clara had given us were upstairs in the third drawer of my parents' chest of drawers, wrapped in white tissue and smelling faintly of lavender sachet.

But Clara's rooms had lots of doilies and long crocheted strips with tasseled edges hanging from the window frames and on the door between her bedroom and sitting room. There were many religious statues—the Infant of Prague, the Virgin in her various guises, a small wooden statue of St. Joseph—with sanctuary candles burning red and blue before them. And on the wall at the entrance, a white enamel holy water font. Her rooms were hot, and the holy water was always lukewarm. I loved to dab it on my forehead when I came in, and so I never really minded having to make the Sign of the Cross when we went there, even though we didn't do it at home, only at church or at my grandmother's and Aunt Clara's.

On the day that the Virgin appeared, my aunt had finished a blue tablecloth. Every year on that day, June 12, she used that cloth and uses it today. "It was blue, and blue is her color," my aunt told everyone later. "I should have known, because I'd never made a blue one before."

When she called on my mother that night, she did not behave as if she knew the Virgin was coming. Instead, my aunt came an hour before the bingo was to start, as she always did, settled in the green armchair with a loud, deep sigh, as she always did and, pulling off her shoes, began to rub her feet, which she did only when she had spent the day delivering her needlework.

"Please can I go?" I asked my mother.

"Not tonight, Kotka," my mother said, and before they left, they each kissed my cheek for luck.

May devotions ended, I had nothing to do that night. My father worked a crossword and listened to the radio, and I went to bed early. In a fuzzy way, I remember hearing my nickname, Kotka, being called in my sleep. This had happened only once before, on a New Year's Eve four years back. I heard my name, and then, over bells and shrieks that sounded like the noon whistle at the mill down the street, I heard my mother say, "It's 1946!" She told me that I said, "Oh," and rolled across the bed, never really waking. This time, though, she didn't allow me to fall asleep again.

Instead, she stood me upright beside the bed and switched on the overhead light. I started to snivel and she handed me a pile of clothes.

"No, don't cry," she sat on the bed and began unbuttoning my pajama top. "You must get dressed," she told me. "Your aunt has seen the Virgin." Then she shouted down the stairs, telling my father, in Polish, that he'd better hurry.

My mother only spoke to my grandmother in Polish. To my father and to my aunt, she spoke English, except when she said something that I was not supposed to know. Now she'd had this relapse. She turned to me and said something still in the mother tongue.

"It's still night," I whined, gesturing at the blackness through the window, but she ignored me. She went into the bathroom, came out with a wet washcloth, and began rubbing it across my face.

By the time she finished, I realized what had happened. The Blessed Virgin Mary had come to Polish Hill.

My father opened the front door and I was startled to see the street filled with people, all hurrying toward the hospital. I had never seen so many people, not even during the day. At night it was unthinkable. I could remember waking at night and going in the darkness to the window. It would be stone quiet and no one was ever out. Now it looked as though all of Sunday's Masses had all let out at once.

I called to the many children I knew as they were

hurried along. Loretta Mozdien waved to me and her mother smacked her. Maryann Wrobleska walked as though she were about to take communion, her hands folded in prayer, eyes uplifted. I am reminded of that night now when I see movies involving the evacuation of villages, war movies, science fiction movies.

We walked up the hill as quickly as we could without leaving my grandmother behind. She began to recite the rosary out loud, matka boska, swieta boska, those soft chirping phrases. My parents joined in and the people behind us joined in and soon the street was a moving, murmuring mass of people praying. Then someone began singing the May Day hymn, and the May procession was enacted there on the hill, but with no need now of the plaster statue and the banners.

"Aunt Clara saw her?" I asked my mother when we stopped to let my grandmother catch her breath.

My mother whispered, as if speech were forbidden. "I would have seen her too, but I left before Clara did. I won a cookie jar. That was the Virgin's way of appearing to me."

"A cookie jar?" But we were on the move again and my skeptical question was lost in the singing, louder now as we neared the hospital.

There must have been a thousand people at the top of the hill. Some of the men wore sweaters over pajama tops and trousers. Women were there in housecoats and pincurls, and some of the children still wore their pajamas entire with a shawl or coat thrown over them. Though it was June, it was cool and a wind had been lifting the dust in the streets all evening, as though it might storm. The wind had died now, or perhaps it had been trampled in the crowd, but it was chill.

We sang and stared up into the night sky. Now and then a voice would break through and shout, "I see her!" in Polish or "There she is!" and all of the people would clap their hands and sing louder and faster and then make the Sign of the Cross. I looked for our priests, expecting to see one of them in the crowd, his trouser legs peeping out from under a hastily donned cassock.

Inside the hospital, people were silhouetted against the windows. We could see nurses in white, standing with the crowd for a time, but usually they would go back inside, I guess so others could come on out. The children who customarily taunted the crazy people were neither laughing nor afraid.

"Maybe," I said to my mother, "one of the crazy people got out up there." Suddenly my grandmother's arm darted out and grabbed my own. She shook me, shook me until my mother made her turn me loose. Even then, she gave me an evil look and spat upon the ground before crossing herself with great indignation and resuming her song.

"Well, maybe one of them did," I said, and my mother led me away from my grandmother, who was now beating on her breast and begging forgiveness for her errant grandchild.

I looked up beyond the building, trying to find my first star. I could find none to wish on. No, I told myself, I must gaze upon the Virgin, gaze the way Maryann Wrobleska might.

I tried to focus on the building, but saw the building only, with people black against the light within, people on every floor, even the top.

Perhaps I was possessed by the devil. The nuns had told us of such people and of others as well. Of those who turned to stone for eating meat on Friday, or those who swallowed their own tongues for taking communion in a state of mortal sin. Perhaps I was in a state of mortal sin. Perhaps the Virgin had come to all but me.

I sang louder and louder, raised my voice until it grew thick in my throat, but still did not see her.

A fire engine appeared. It came slowly, as fire trucks are driven in parades, but with its headlights on, the fire bell clanging. A man called through a megaphone, "Go home, go home. There is nothing here to see." And someone from among us shouted, "Protestant!"

The crowd laughed and cheered and applauded. But the singing had stopped. The fireman trained a huge light on the building and it ran up the side like a roach. The light hovered at the rooftop, then began to creep along the edge. The roof was indeed empty. "You see? There's nothing there," shouted the man with the megaphone. "There is nothing there!"

My Aunt Clara's voice came shrill through the

crowd. I could not see her, but her voice was clear as she explained what had happened away. "It is a miracle," she shouted. "She would not let the Protestants see her. She would not let them shine their lights upon her. It is a miracle."

Her opinion of the Virgin's departure was immediately accepted. The Virgin was Catholic. The Virgin of Guadalupe, of Lourdes, of Fatima, was Polish, too. Of course the Protestants would not be able to see her. Nor would the Italians, nor the Irish. The Virgin was ours.

My grandmother translated all of this to two of her friends who spoke no English. They nodded, grave with knowledge. They, and then everyone, took up the cry again: "Miracle, miracle," in English so that the firemen would know.

"Okay, folks," the man, whose voice had taken on the huskiness that my own had when I'd try to sing too loudly, tried again. "Take your miracle home with you. Go on home." The light still shone on the empty roof.

Then my mother's voice grew loud at my side. "I won a cookie jar!" she shouted, as if to say, "Explain that away if you can."

"That's right," my father hollered, shaking his fist. "That's right, she did."

"Okay, people," the fireman had not heard. "Okay. You can see she's gone now, so go on back. Go back home." The huge truck began to move, turtle-slow, down the street, and everyone began to back from it, from the man with the megaphone, from the building.

We backed too, like all the rest, not turning our eyes from the hospital, but shuffling backward, staring at the spot where She had been, trying not to trip or lose our balance, not to shove or he shoved, but trying, most especially, not to relinquish that which was especially ours, the Virgin of Polish Hill, my own Aunt Clara's Virgin.

Up, Up and Away

by

C. G. Segre

I'm an early riser. Like Superman, I believe in "up, up and away"—or so I tell myself. I like sneaking around the house at five o'clock—or so I tell myself. I crave the dawn's gloomy light; I cherish those hours with the phone mute, the TV screen blank. In that clean, quiet, orderly world, I write wonderful sentences, pick good stocks, plan brilliant lecture—or so I tell myself. Maybe because I'm still dreaming.

I prefer dreaming to waking up. In fact, I often dream of how I'd like to wake up. First I see myself as one of Homer's epic heroes enjoying the glow of Aurora's rosy-fingered dawn. But when I open my eyes, digital numbers on my alarm clock greet me. I try dreaming again. I picture myself at Fort McHenry by the "dawn's early light." Mentally I hum a few bars of the "Star Spangled Banner," but the only things "bursting in air" are those fiery red numbers.

These are not ordinary digits. They burn and glow and glare. They are numbers that do a number on me. Another day has passed, they remind me. A new day is beginning and for the past eight hours I have done nothing to remedy the crises of my life. By the digits' red glare I see clearly what I could be doing now, what I could be doing in ten minutes, what I could be doing in half an hour. I see also that what I am *not* doing now will keep me from doing what I could be doing in ten minutes, which will stop me from doing what I could be doing in half an hour.

As the numbers count down toward the hour, I feel like a space shuttle on the launch pad, loaded with emotional fuel. At 5:00 sharp we blast off. At least space shuttles are free to soar off in a glorious window-shattering burst of flame and smoke. However, neither my softly ratcheting spouse, nor my sleeping offspring care to witness my launch into the new day. Kennedy Space Center, yes; me, no.

Silent launches are my mission. Over the years, I've perfected them. The first part is simply getting off the pad. My standard technique is one I've offered to teach the Marines or the Special Forces. First, on my tummy, I slither ever so subtly to the edge of the mattress. Then, with my hand, I cautiously search the floor for possible booby traps like yesterday's newspapers or my seven year-old's construction toy. With the field clear, I drop silently into the void which ends abruptly two seconds and twelve inches later. I'm on the floor. From there it's a simple matter of sucking in my tummy, pulling my knees up to my chest, rolling onto my haunches and standing up at the ready.

A more advanced technique is what I call the Cybill Shepherd sit-up—silky, smooth, sophisticated. In one sleek continuous movement, I sit, slide my legs off the side and stand. No joints cracking, no mattress squeaking, no sheet rustling. I execute this maneuver so beautifully, so perfectly that on my best days, in gymnast's scoring, I have given myself a nine and even a perfect ten. My spouse, of course, is the ultimate judge. Undisturbed ratcheting rates a nine. Any increase in volume deserves a nine-and-a-half or ten.

Off the pad is only the beginning. Pulling on my sweatshirt and sliding into my slippers without a sound, I negotiate the dark obstacle course through the house. I dodge the avocado plant, I slide around the vacuum cleaner, I skip over shoes or a skateboard until I reach the safety of the kitchen. There, behind closed doors, I dare switch on the light in the pantry. I boldly fill the coffee pot, I fire up the stove, I inhale the heavenly aromas—and I listen. From the nether regions, not a sound, not a peep. The silence of the vast interstellar spaces. I'm in orbit. Mission accomplished.

A couple of hours later, my family shuffles into breakfast. Yawning and stretching, their faces warm and rosy from a full night's sleep, they sometimes make random comments like, "Boy, was I out of it. You could have launched a space shuttle and I wouldn't have noticed." I ignore them. I know they are speaking only metaphorically.

Once Is Enough

by

Dorothy Rose

John Thomas is our neighbor
He is not a very good farmer
"Triflin" is what they call him

Doesn't raise cotton corn pigs
Has lot of kids dogs
Hunts possums wild honey
Plays banjo

Visits everyone
Even while they are working

One day John Thomas was
Visiting my father
They were sittin' and whittlin'
Talkin' about the weather

Suddenly J T Junior
Rushed up to our house
Runs to his father

Says Pa come home quick

Ma just died

John Thomas stood up slowly
Scratched his head
Said my goodness
She never done that before

A Need to Get Away

by

J. Madison Dads

When I returned Stateside in 1946, I did not know how to react to being home. When I climbed off the train in Gordonsville and embraced my sniffling mother, father, and sisters one by one, then in a great swaying huddle, I felt as if I were watching the scene from above. As if I had been adopted by a kindly couple who had mistaken me for their boy. They flattered my size and fussed over me. I said all the right things, even forced the right smiles, but I didn't feel as if I belonged there. Pop drove slowly along Main Street, probably to show me off, but I hunched down in the back seat between Betty and Irma. Shifflett's Hardware, the First National Bank of the Piedmont, the Woolworth's, the post office: everything was exactly the same as it had been in 1942. And yet, everything was strange, different in some secret way.

They never mentioned the war. When we sat around the kitchen table eating biscuits and gravy, Betty and Irma would recall when we went to Grandpa's farm and picked blackberries. Pop replayed my one-hitter against Louisa High, batter for batter. Mama talked about people and events I did not remember and I would nod to pretend I did. I'd wander around town, drinking Cokes in my father's drug store, handing Lem Turner wrenches as he tried to keep his pre-war Chevy running. Betty and Irma tried to entertain me. We listened to radio dramas starring Barbara Stanwyck and Joseph Cotten. I went to the same picture show twice. I bought a Victrola with half a dozen records and played the Kay Kysers over and over. Irma fixed me up with Susan, a friend of hers, but I treated the girl like a French woman who was dating for nylons and chocolate. I danced with the poor thing for hours without saying a word to her.

People stopped me on the street, shook my hand, and asked how it was in the Medics. They knew I had been at Palermo and Monte Cassino and was nearly overrun at the Bulge. I had bandaged the wounded for days on end, I had powdered dying men with DDT to keep the lice off them, and I had cried like a baby when we were bombed for fifteen minutes by our own air corps. I had seen the inside of my friends' heads. What was there to say? I hated people for asking. "They kept me busy," was what I usually answered. No words could explain anything I had gone through, and nothing else was important enough to say.

I figure it took about a month of this to get Pop fed up with my shiftlessness, but he was a patient man who knew that most of the medicines he concocted wouldn't really cure any illness that didn't want to be cured. His hint came quietly one afternoon as I lounged in his swivel chair behind the counter smoking Chesterfields. He was mixing a bottle of cough syrup. I was squinting at the fibers in the cigarette paper. He spoke as if thinking aloud. "You know, boy, you ought to think about what you are going to do."

I lowered the cigarette. He was not facing me.

"Maybe you could go to college," he suggested, "learn to be a doctor or go to pharmacy school. It's a fair living."

I glanced at a teenage couple up front sharing an ice cream soda with two straws. For them, there'd never been a war. I hated them for it.

Pop put down his graduated cylinder and peered over his glasses at me. "Hey, boy, you know what? Why don't you spend the summer with Grandpa? He could use the help. The old cuss won't admit the farm is just too much for him since your grandma died." Pop considered this and smiled. "You can do a lot of thinking while you're pulling weeds."

"It'll be lonely out there," I said, watching the couple noisily suck up the bottom of the soda. Pop poured the red liquid into his bottle and didn't seem to hear.

Grandpa's farm was only about fifteen acres of arable land. The rest was a tree-covered mountain. He truck-farmed, mainly corn, and said he had no interest in any crop like tobacco that you couldn't eat. I took on most of the heavy work when he let me, carrying the big buckets of slop to the hogs while he gathered eggs, digging a new outhouse pit while he milked the cow. "You know," he'd say, "hogs get most of this milk. I cain't drink it all and there just ain't the kids around here there used to be. I'm right popular with the kitty-cats, though." Even with me there the days were full, so I talked him into hiring Zeke, an old black man, to give me time to paint the house and patch the loose boards on the barn.

Pop had been right, there was a lot of time to think as I yanked the morning glories from the corn and edged the paintbrush along the windows. Neither Grandpa nor Zeke ever had much to say, so there was even thinking time as we sat by the spring eating the first watermelon. But I did not think. I let the timelessness wash over me. There was no future and no past, only the smell of weeds ripped out of the earth, the buzz of the wasps under the eaves, and the cold nose of the cow when it kissed me on the cheek. I began to whistle as I walked between the corn rows and talked to the hogs as I fed them.

Grandpa noticed. One evening after dark, I stretched out on the porch swing. In the rocker beside me, he silently listened to the crickets for some time. Then, he slapped at a mosquito and said, "You like it here, don't ya? You find yourself a woman and this could all be yours. There's a lot of empty places for sale around here. You could triple the place in no time. Your daddy's done good, don't get me wrong, but I ain't got nobody to pass this place to. If you'd take it, it would be just like the old days, with a woman, and children to drink up the milk. It'd be like the war never happened."

"The war happened," I said.

He paused. "You know what I mean. Same thing in 1919. Everybody thought they was too good to grow food and they run off to work for factories in big cities. They'd tell you they wasn't going to waste their lives in the dirt like I did. There's only twenty-five members of my church, now. What'll they do when there ain't no need to make *aeroplanes,* huh? They'll envy us our farms then. You wait." He slapped at another mosquito. "It burns me up. Nobody likes to be told he wasted his life. You say the word and the deed is yours. I mean it, boy."

I hesitated, trying to grasp the largeness of this gesture in the old man's mind. I was on the verge of taking his offer, but the words didn't come out. "I don't know," I said. "I—well, I appreciate it, but maybe we need to think about it more."

I looked, but I couldn't see his face. He was nodding, but what he felt, I couldn't tell. We said nothing more about it and went in to bed.

The corn was sold; the stalks were heaped. My staying for the summer had stretched into autumn. The maples on Grandpa's mountain had begun to turn. I was leaning against a fence post smoking a cigarette and listening to the leaves rustle. Next to me, Grandpa had his foot on the lower rail. I could smell the salt of his sweat. "The coming of winter is scary for a lot of farmers," he said.

"I think it's that kind of scariness that drives them off, you know. You're just in the hands of nature. You got no control. To me it seems right. It gives you a chance to rest. Many a winter I been hungry, but it's right. It's what makes summer good."

"Like war makes peace good," I said. Where the remark had come from, I don't know. But I stood there squeezing the fence as if understanding it would clarify everything.

Two weeks before, my father had driven away from the farm in a huff when he found out I hadn't done anything with the pharmacy school application. Grandpa had grinned as if I had made up my mind to take the farm. I hadn't. The rest of my life stretched before me and I could not decide what to do with it. Each decision seemed too final. Choose this, or that, and I would be like a locomotive, trapped between two rails, unable to turn around, rushing only where the tracks led me. I wanted to be out of this body and this mind that had seen too much, that had felt too much in places like Catania and Lige and Cologne.

"Looky there," said the old man. He pointed across the corn stubble to the brush line at the base of his mountain. He hurried into the house and emerged with his enormous old rifle.

I was stunned by the sight of a rifle barrel and gaped as if I needed an explanation.

"Groundhog," he said.

I glanced across the field. "I don't see anything," I stammered.

"There," he said calmly. "His head just popped up." Grandpa propped the rifle across the fence, hugged it tight to his shoulder and squinted. I turned away and automatically covered my ears like a ten-year-old afraid of the noise. The report went through me as forcefully as if it were the thunder of a howitzer. I may have cried out, but Grandpa tugged my arm. Let's go see if we got him!"

We stumbled across the field. I hadn't seen the groundhog. How could he be so certain? What if he had shot a man by mistake? I had seen too many men killed by mistake. I found myself walking halfbent over, as if I expected the groundhog to return fire, and I nearly called out to warn the old man to watch out for mines.

He spread the weeds with the rifle barrel. "It was right around here. You go along that way." I hadn't gone very far when he called out. "Here. Blood." The browning weeds crunched as he moved further into them. He lifted the dead animal up by its hind legs.

"Why you crazy old coot!" I laughed. "There really was a groundhog."

He turned the limp creature, inspecting it. "I didn't get him clean, though."

I saw the groundhog's bloody wound, but I was giddy with the wonder of the shot. The blood was not a man's blood. The groundhog would not call out in the night. He wouldn't leave a half finished letter for his wife or mother or sister. For the first time since I had been home I felt amazement, happiness, exultation. I had survived. It may not have been as important as destiny. But I had, and for the first time, selfishly, I reveled in it.

"In the old days," said Grandpa forlornly, "I woulda got him in the head."

"It was incredible!" I said. "Incredible!"

"I shouldn'ta shot him," he said. "They taste all greasy. You ever eat one?"

The old man's eyes were moist. "I remember your grandma cooked one once, roasted it, I think, and we was pretty happy to get it. That was long ago. You don't see so many groundhogs now. I shot him for nothing. It's too bad. Maybe Zeke'll have some use for him."

He walked away carrying the animal high and cradling the rifle in his arm. I watched him recede toward the house and for the first time in months, maybe years, felt a connection to another human being. Everyone carried sorrow and horror in them. Sometimes it was war, sometimes the loss of loved ones. Sometimes it was the loss of the world you grew up in. But you weren't a human being without the sorrow. Somehow, being alive, enjoying the world, meant knowing that you could lose it.

I ran up to him and put my hand on his shoulder. "That was a great shot, Grandpa."

"Ah!" he snorted. He stopped suddenly and glanced at my hand on his shoulder. I hadn't shown him any real affection since I had come to the farm. He looked me in the eye. "Boy," he said, "you don't want this place."

I wanted to protest, but I lowered my head slightly and said, "No. I'm sorry."

"What for?" he said grumpily. "You don't belong here. You better get out in the world and find some work. If you think that was a great shot, you really don't belong here. Hmmph! It should have been a head shot."

"Okay," I said.

He put down the groundhog and stretched his gnarled fingers behind my neck. "My life ain't your life, boy, and this place, well, I can't make it your life. But, listen, I want you to believe there's *something* certain in the world. You understand me?"

"I think so," I said.

"Even if there ain't nothing certain in the world, I want you to believe this place is always here for you, always the same. And when it all gets too much for you, I want you to come here. Even if you have to imagine it, come here whenever you need to get away."

"I will, Grandpa," I said. "I will."

I pulled him close and smelled the sweat in his old hat. We might have stood there for more than five minutes, I don't know, but when he said we'd better get the animal over to Zeke's and pushed me away, my eyes were full of tears. I had come home.

A New Life

by

Janis Rizzo

"Sit," Julia ordered as she sharply tugged at the leash in her right hand and patted the rambunctious puppy's behind with her left. He sat, but only for a second, his tail wagging with more energy than his owner had felt in years. "Sit," she said again as she repeated the tug on the leash.

I'm too old for this, she thought as the puppy cheerfully jumped on her leg. But what could she say when her favorite granddaughter, Kelly, after dropping her two young children off at school, unexpectedly appeared at her doorstep several months ago with the surprise package?

That day, the chubby eight-week-old German Shepherd puppy was trying frantically to scramble out of Kelly's arms. "Grandma, this youngster told me he needed a special home and I couldn't think of anyone more special than you." As Kelly handed the eager whelp over to her grandmother, he squirmed and wriggled, stopping just for a moment to run his wet tongue across Julia's hand. Julia slowly stooped over to put the pudgy fellow down, but he leapt to the ground before she got halfway there, throwing her off balance and nearly knocking her over.

"Now, Kelly, I'm almost seventy years old. This little guy needs a young family like your own to grow up with." The words seemed the right thing to say, but Julia was entranced as the puppy dashed off after a butterfly, pirouetted, then dropped to the ground before scooting away in the opposite direction. "With all his antics, he's apt to drive me to an early grave," she laughed.

"Nonsense, Grandmother," retorted Kelly, "he's just what you both need. He's a little sweetheart, so affectionate and full of fun. I'd say he's a lot like you." Kelly grinned as she gestured at the dog's face, "You two even look alike. His big brown eyes, with a hint of mischief, are a mirror image of your own. And from what Grandpa told me, you were quite the mischief-maker yourself."

"Rumors, pure rumors," Julia replied with a feigned air of innocence. "Besides, who is going to teach him some manners?"

And so here they both were—Julia and Lancelot working in an obedience class—Julia fighting her natural inclination to let the young dog get away with everything, and Lance exuberantly ignoring what little discipline his owner enforced.

"All right, everyone make a large circle and tell your dogs to sit," the middle-aged instructor declared after a short break.

Lance was settling down now. At seven months old he was still a pup, but certainly not the round little brown ball of fuzz that had entered Julia's life. There was no question that he was gradually maturing into a fine example of his breed. His sable coat was of medium length, with black hairs scattered along his back and on his chest. His ears were still struggling to stand upright, with the right one leaning in and the tip of the left bent slightly to the outside. He would have appeared quite comical if it weren't for his intelligent and soul-searching dark eyes.

Julia said, "Lance, sit," and this time he responded by dropping crisply right next to her left leg. "Stay." Julia leaned over to pet her companion, but was careful not to get him too excited again. "Good dog. I guess we're finally getting the hang of this."

The next direction from the instructor was to walk on the circle. Almost in unison, the twelve trainers commanded, "Heel," as they started to move. Chains jingled as the owners worked to keep their dogs close to them. "Halt," came the next command. Four of the dogs sat immediately, while the others took several seconds or more to obey.

"Okay," the instructor called, "one at a time, please walk your dog toward the door, turn, and let the dog sit."

The exercise took awhile, but Lance's turn finally came. "Lance, heel," Julia directed as she stepped off on her left foot. The dog jumped forward in front of Julia, and she responded with a quick correction, battling his already substantial weight with her frail frame. "Heel," she repeated as they moved on. At the door Julia made an about-face turn, and Lance slipped into position and sat, not perfectly square, but good enough. "Good boy, Lance."

But the teacher didn't seem pleased. "Julia, walk him some more," she said. "Something's not right." Julia and Lance headed toward the group again, then reversed and walked another thirty feet or so. "It's his hind end," the woman decided. "Let's discuss it after class. Now return to your place. Next dog."

Three more dogs performed the exercise, but Julia was too distracted to watch with any real interest. What could be wrong with Lance? He was only seven months old, certainly too young to have physical problems. She glared at the seemingly insensitive instructor as if it were the woman's fault.

After the other dogs and owners had left, the trainer walked over to Julia and said rather coolly, "I've been watching Lance closely for three weeks now. It looks like he has hip dysplasia."

Julia, surprised at the woman's bluntness, was confused.

"Hip dysplasia," the instructor explained, "is very common in German Shepherds. The ball and socket joint of the hip does not function properly." Trying to keep the description simple, she continued, "The dog may walk with a swaying gait, like Lance does, and may 'bunny hop' when he runs. However, I've never seen a case this severe in so young a dog." She hesitated a moment, "I don't think this dog will be able to get up and walk by the time he's two years old. You should spare Lance the pain and put him to sleep now." She turned and left Julia standing there, unable to move.

At ten the next morning the telephone rang as it did daily. Kelly's cheerful voice rang out, "Good morning, Grandma. How are things going today?"

"Oh, Kelly, you know, the mind is willing, but the body, ah, the body . . ." Julia's voice trailed off.

"Well, one of these days you're going to have to quit skateboarding with my brother," Kelly laughed. Julia blushed, thinking of the one time she had challenged thirteen-year-old James to a contest. She would have won, too, if she hadn't hit that rock and fallen in an unladylike sprawl to the hard pavement. But that was several years ago and she knew that a fall like that now would cause a lot more damage than the ugly black, red, and purple bruise that had taken a month to disappear.

"And, by the way, how's Lance's training coming along?" Kelly asked.

"Lance still wants to play, but we're keeping at it. I must admit I adore the little character." Despite her attempt to sound cheerful, Julia's voice darkened noticeably. "But, Kelly, our instructor says there's something wrong with the way he walks." Finally giving in to her feelings, she related the previous night's events. Tears began to slide down her wrinkled cheeks. Her voice started to shake, "She said I should put him . . . to sleep. I'm taking him to the vet clinic at two o'clock today. Do you think the woman could be right?"

Kelly, trying to reassure her, said, "The way he jumps around on those pogo stick legs? No, I'm sure he's just fine."

Five minutes before their appointment, Julia and Lance arrived at the veterinarian's office. The receptionist filled out the appropriate paperwork and escorted them into an examining room.

Julia sat on the lone homemade bench, while Lance sniffed and explored the room at the end of his leash. The small room contained an old-fashioned enamel cabinet, a small refrigerator, a simple round clock, and the shining stainless steel table. The countertop next to the sink was uncluttered, but the overhead cabinets were filled with multi-colored apothecary jars.

After a few minutes the doctor opened the door and came in. He squinted at Julia, "You're Kelly Anderson's grandmother, aren't you?"

Julia nodded, "Yes, I am."

The vet turned to Lance and knelt beside him. He let Lance sniff him as he petted the dog and spoke quietly, "Hi there, mister. You look like a spunky chap." His sharp clear eyes contrasted with his soft features and gentle manner. "What seems to be the problem?" he questioned.

"My trainer says there's something wrong with his hips and legs," Julia relayed.

"Let's take a look," the doctor said as he moved out of the way. He directed Julia to walk with Lance. Julia told Lance to sit, then heel. They walked back and forth across the room three or four times.

The doctor bent over and spoke to the dog in low tones, constantly reassuring the pup. His hands tenderly and unhurriedly slid along the dog's back until he reached Lance's hips. The vet felt around the area for several seconds, then straightened. "It looks like he does have a problem, but we'll need to take X-rays just to be sure. And to do that we'll need to knock him out."

Julia winced. "Is that absolutely necessary?" she queried. "I've always heard such terrible stories about anesthesia."

The vet explained, "Lance needs to be asleep to get good X-rays. There are always risks, however. Sometimes an animal has a paradoxical reaction, in which the body does not react to the anesthetic the way it should, but that is *extremely* rare." There weren't any guarantees, he said, but there was also no other choice.

As the door closed behind the doctor, Julia called Lance to her side and gave her buddy a long affectionate hug. "Don't worry, I'll be back tomorrow," she told him as she fought back the tears. "Nothing's going to happen to you." She hoped.

The hours passed slowly. Julia had a restless night and awoke feeling depressed. She got dressed, made a cup of coffee, and tried to read the newspaper until it was time to leave.

At the veterinarian's office an assistant informed Julia that the doctor was out on an emergency. When Julia asked how Lance was doing, the young man replied that he hadn't seen any German Shepherds in the kennels that morning. He escorted the increasingly frightened woman to the examining room.

More waiting . . . waiting . . . waiting. It became unbearable. Julia's eyes were fixed on the clock. Five minutes. Fifteen minutes. She could hear the trainer's voice. *I don't think this dog will be able to get up and walk by the time he's two years old.* Twenty-eight minutes. *You should spare Lance the pain and put him to sleep now. You should spare Lance the pain and put him to sleep now. You should spare . . .* Forty-three minutes and 32 seconds.

"Good morning," the doctor began. "Lance . . ."

Julia was so totally startled when the vet walked in that she all but toppled the narrow bench. "Where's Lance?" Julia interrupted, desperation in her voice. "What happened to Lance? Why isn't he in the kennels?"

"Just a minute, he's fine. He's out in one of the exercise areas," the doctor said, trying to calm Julia down.

"I'm *not* going to put him to sleep, I'm not,"

Julia shrieked, now on the verge of hysteria. "He's just a puppy; he's too young to die. It's not fair; I can't . . ."

"Julia, nobody's going to die," the vet finally managed to say as he took the delicate hand of the sobbing woman. Julia looked up with tears streaming down her face. "Really," he continued, "Lance definitely does have severe hip dysplasia, but we don't have to put him to sleep."

"But," Julia said, "I . . . I don't understand."

"Now, don't get me wrong," the vet smiled, "Lance is never going to win a blue ribbon at Madison Square Garden, but he'll live a full and happy life. We'll just treat his symptoms. There'll be plenty of time for you both to grow old together."

As Lance entered the room and recognized Julia, the overgrown puppy bounded into Julia's arms. Julia beamed. "Lancelot, heel," she ordered. She left the office, one hand on his leash, the other patting his head.

Pies Sagradas:
Praying at the Feet of the Saint

by

Barbara Lau

It is whispered
that the Spanish priests had to place their
  saints under glass
to save the few remaining toes. Not
  because
their embalming methods failed; *claro,*
   the bodies stayed
fresh and white as gardenias. And for years
  the candles werc lit,
the tombs unlatched, and the patron saints
  put on view
for the annual pilgrimage of the knees.

Everyone came. They washed the dust and
  manure and corn flour
from their hands and dressed in their
  fiesta clothes. Then they
joined the long line of waiting and hoping
(which in Spanish is the same word,
  esperando).
At the cool marble entrance, they dropped

to their knees and
crawled, one-by-one, toward the sandaled
feet of their saint.

The men bowed and prayed, *por favor,*
for a good harvest
and many healthy children. But the
women needed miracles.
One begged for the life of a dying child.
Another for deliverance
from a *diablo* of a husband. Another for the
cure to a frozen womb.
Under the shadow of their veils they
murmured and yearned and ached
with such fervor it made their men shiver.

What the priests discovered made them
shiver, too. Faith
was not enough for the needs of their
flock.
Some needs were so impatient that the
sacred toes snapped
like crisp green beans under the weight of
those prayers.

Cook's Choice

by

Barry Bauska

Back when I was a kid, one of my truly great and abiding interests was the weekly school lunch menu. This was always taped to the wall right at the entrance to the lunchroom. We were supposed to line up there, just outside the door, in scruffy rows of disintegrating tennis shoes, fading Levis, and imitation letterman jackets. Then, at some mystical signal, a mechanism was tripped, the door lock unlatched itself, and we would propel ourselves between the tubular steel runners that carried us through the lunch line. As we lurched inside, we each had about nine seconds to take the message in.

Actually, the lunch menu would stay up all week, but Monday was the real day of discovery, the day the list was first posted. None of my gang ever went so far as to *buy* hot lunch on a Monday; that was far too risky. But it was Mondays that we got the word, saw our immediate gastronomical futures laid down in living purple and white on those dittos that always smelled like iodine.

Each of us, in our nine-second burst of speed-reading, would review the chart, studying it with all the devoted absorbtion of a frenzied gambler probing his racing form in search of a desperately needed winner. Like the gambler, we started with a recognition of certain realities. First of all, Friday was a known throwaway, reserved for "Catholic Lunches" like fishwiches or grilled cheese or tuna noodle casseroles. And since Monday gave us no warning, we really had three choices for the week: Tuesday, Wednesday and Thursday.

We knew we could count on having hot dogs or spaghetti somewhere along the line, and both of those were eminently eatable if nothing better turned up. The hot dogs, to be sure, were not quite like hot dogs anywhere else. Certainly they bore no resemblance whatsoever to the hot dogs sold at baseball parks. Nor, though we couldn't have known this then, would they have anything in common with certain wonderful frankfurters to be bought at fairs or circuses in summers to come. No. School hot dogs were definitely something else. They were, for one thing, very definitely Cafeteria Hot Dogs, bearing indelibly the strange but unmistakable taste of waxed paper, whether from the buns or the weiners we were never sure.

The spaghetti was better; in fact I was just about ready to go for spaghetti at any offering. True, it was closer to Franco-American than to Mama's home-cooked, but then your average ten year old is rarely a true gourmet. The only real drawback to cafeteria spaghetti was that it came, always, with something called "mixed veg," a loathsome concoction useful only for flinging out of precisely leveraged spoons in the general direction of Carol Honneycutt or Sally Hunt.

In a way mixed-veg flinging was a genuine art. It required delicately balancing one knife across two others, then setting the spoon (loaded with a deadly payload of mixed veg) across the fulcrum. Finally, while at least three sets of scouts watched for lunch monitors and vice principals, the artillery expert of the day would drop his fist squarely onto the handle of the spoon: *Spronng!*

All eyes would jerk heavenward, fixed upon the wad of mixed veg arcing its way along a preprogrammed path, then hanging at some point like a tiny paper moon, and plummeting earthward: a silent, deadly missile homing-in. *Splatt.*

Ah, the looks on the faces of the victims or near-victims! The girls did a great job of pretending to be disgusted with us, but we knew better. We knew we'd just scored major points in the perpetual coolness derby.

Our school tended to feature a wide range of what might be called ethnic meals. It is highly unlikely that these dishes were authentic replications of actual ethnic food, but they all bore impressively convincing names: tamale pie, ravioli, lasagne, chili, chop suey, crepes. Since we never had any ethnic kids in our school—or at least we didn't know that Jerry Coriani, Steve Kaspari and Ricky Kozinak qualified as ethnics—I suppose we didn't know what we weren't getting. Still, we did have a pretty fair hunch that the people in Italy or China or France would never have eaten this stuff voluntarily.

The worst of the ethnic lot was unquestionably the tamale pie, a sort of breaded bread loaf, topped with bread crumbs and exactly three olive halves. Those olives were often the only portions of this particular delicacy actually consumed by human beings. Tamale pie contained, for some unknown reason, bits and pieces of macaroni and spaghetti and corn. Good, solid, balanced starches. The very appearance of this ersatz Spanish melange was enough to strike terror into the bravest hearts and strongest stomachs. What it looked like was what in fact it often turned into: somebody's regurgitated nightmare.

The chop suey ran a close second in the barfo brigade. I can still remember, and not with pleasure, the feeling of biting into those hard brown noodles coated with some kind of gooey sauce. What chop suey amounted to, basically, was mixed veg in an MSG paste. Most of this stuff, we assumed, was ultimately fed to the unfortunate pets belonging to the kitchen staff.

One especially sharp reality recognized by all students of hot lunch was that there was no such thing as a "good" lunch, nothing one could look forward to with genuine, unalloyed anticipation. Still, beginning with the hot dogs and spaghetti, there *were* possibilities—dishes that stayed in the running, generally on the basis of some sort of gimmicky accoutrement. Take meat loaf for example. The meat loaf itself was pretty awful, a gray-brown conglomeration of shredded carrots, beef and gristle. But it invariably came with a small dish of canned peaches and with celery stuffed with peanut butter. Those bonuses insured that the old meat loaf would sell pretty decently in spite of itself. The same thing was true of the hamburgers. They were only vaguely edible (again there was that faint taste of waxed paper), but what made them worth buying was that they always came with tater tots. I can still remember jamming a pair of those babies into my cheeks, then chewing away mindlessly, in a slow, circular motion like a cow, while a mishmash of hamburger and bun blended themselves lovingly into the mass. The overall effect was about as close to heaven as one was likely to get in the school cafeteria.

Applesauce was big too. The cafeteria crew could unload a lot of otherwise unapproachable crap if they would only lob a dollop of applesauce on the plate. The same was true for carrot and raisin salad. And chocolate pudding.

But there was one item that could not be peddled at any cost. That item was called Cook's Choice. The brains behind school lunches obviously knew that this one was a marketing challenge. To start with, they'd only dare to dump Cook's Choice on us once or twice a term. More than that and they'd have a riot on their hands. Second, since Cook's Choice was a guaranteed financial loss, it could only be sold on a Monday, and only to those poor suckers whose mothers had somehow failed to rally up their lunches in time. This was another reason that we always played it safe on Mondays. We knew where courage passed and foolhardiness strode ahead.

Exactly what a Cook's Choice *was* was never clear. There were a lot of pretty gross rumors in circulation of course, but nothing that was ever confirmed. Probably it was just a random collection of the previous week's leftovers, scraped into a single pot, cooked up with some powdered gravy and jammed into a pastry shell. But whatever went into it, the effect was clear: it was the most deadly meal laid before innocents since the Borgias hung up their aprons.

Every cloud has its silver lining though, and the silver in the great Cook's Choice cloud was watching some poor new kid in class take his first bite. That was a moment to savor.

Now, a kid couldn't simply plow into a Cook's Choice. He would have to fight his way manfully through the tough and crusty pastry shell first. Only then, once he had penetrated that outer perimeter of defense, would he come upon the first casualties of the war: clotted bits and pieces of mixed veg dripping out and down the sides of the shell. No question about it; it was a sight to give one pause.

Still the human child is seldom daunted, and the new kid especially tends to expect that life is meant to be hard on him. And so, regardless of those horrors *we* all knew lay just ahead, that first fateful bite would yet form itself upon the fork. As forty pairs of bulging eyes looked on in gleeful anticipation, the fork would be raised up, up, up toward the waiting mouth. The lips would begin to part! They would open! The fork would enter the waiting cavity! And then . . .

"AAARRGHH!!"

Cook's Choice had struck again.

I had pretty much forgotten about hot lunch in the decades I've gone without it. It is, I suppose, the sort of thing from which one usually graduates although I do have a friend who has spent the better part of his adult life in one jail or another. He reports that hot lunch as we knew it is still very much alive (or dead) behind bars.

Anyway, I hadn't give the old chow much thought until the other day when I was doing my laundry in a laundromat. I had read all the old *Reader's Digests* in the place and had pretty well come to terms with "Life in These United States," "Humor in Uniform" and "My Most Unforgettable Character." The only reading material left was the Wednesday food section of the newspaper, something called "Dimension." I picked it up, and began turning the pages mechanically when suddenly I stumbled upon a large square box with a picture of Somebody's Mom bearing a tray of steaming cookies. The caption over the box proclaimed to the waiting world: School Lunch Menus.

And that's exactly what they were. District by

district, the article reviewed the week's delights and *next* week's too. If a kid or mom read this thing, they wouldn't have to wait until Monday. My God, I thought, a kid could even eat on Monday if he wanted to. What a find; it was Paradise in print.

I didn't read the piece right away. Instead I checked the laundromat for spies, saw I was safe, then folded up the paper and tucked it inside my jacket. When my laundry was done to a degree of dampness that promised not to turn into mildew, I took my socks and treasure home.

That evening, after dinner and after I'd folded the laundry, I dragged out the article, a bag of Fritos and a bottle of Pabst Blue Ribbon beer. Then I sat down to savor the listings.

And oh, what a trip it was! Tuna fish casserole, turkey á la king, Sloppy Joes, grilled cheese, cheese zombies. Over and over again the words on the page brought my childhood rushing back to me. I could see kids lining up. I was with them, a kid again myself, set loose in the cafeteria, my quarter hot and sweaty in my palm.

As it turned out, reading the menus was a three-beer affair, the pearls of delight transporting me back across time and space to blowing the wrappers off straws and watching them float airily through the lunchroom skies, dipping and rising and finally settling down right smack in the middle of somebody's Cook's Choice!

Holy Cow! There it was for God's sake! Right in the family newspaper! Cook's Goddamned

Choice! At Wilson Junior High School—and on a Monday too! Oh, those sneaky bastards! Oh, the poor new kid in town. And oh, to be there to watch him.

I wonder . . . Naah.

West Texas Photograph

by

Patricia Lewis Sackrey

A girl of eight stands in front of a stone house next to a windmill. Her stringy blonde hair hangs limp. It is afternoon, the sun is high, she is squinting, frowning and standing sway-backed, staring into the camera. Two other smaller children are next to her, a blonde girl with plaits tied over her head, who grins somewhat impishly, and a dark-haired boy who flashes laughing dark eyes at someone next to the photographer.

The girls wear matching dresses. The taller one, the scowler, does not like to have her picture taken, or at least she pretends not to. What she actually doesn't like these days is being agreeable at all. She likes the way the dry, hot dirt feels under her feet, standing there in front of the house where Aunt Dony and Uncle Charles live. She likes helping to feed the chickens, holding her skirt out for Aunt Dony to pour in some corn from the burlap bag. She holds the skirt like a sack in one hand and feels the weight of it with the other, calling out "here chicky, here chick" like Aunt Dony and scattering the corn ahead of herself in a big fan, being careful not to drop the corn too near her feet for fear a hen might peck her toes. She likes all that.

But she doesn't like her sister, because everybody likes her sister. She doesn't mind her brother too much because he's funny, but she doesn't like to be his "little mommy," as their daddy sometimes says. She doesn't like her momma because she always says stand up straight and smile and be nice. She's mad at her Aunt Ruby for telling her so loudly to say thank you in church this morning. And she's mad because she gets more attention this way.

After the awful moment when her mother insists on taking the picture, the child will run to the big, corrugated metal barn and go inside. Uncle Charles is in there sharpening knives on the grinding wheel. It is dark and cooler in there. The old stone wheel will whir as Uncle Charles pushes steadily and rhythmically on the foot peddle, throwing a little water on the top edge of the wheel to keep it cool against the metal blades.

She will watch for a while. Uncle Charles rarely speaks and he won't speak to her. The child will say nothing. She will sit down in some old hay next to the empty horse stalls. Maybe she will never leave.

Outpatient

by

Rosalind Warren

The waiting room is crowded. Mothers watch fidgety children, couples sit together on drab sofas, adults talk in soothing voices to elderly parents. Everyone in the waiting room has someone with them. Luisa has come alone.

"New patient?" the receptionist asks. Luisa nods.

The receptionist hands her a clipboard that holds a form. "You'll have to fill this out," she says. When Luisa returns it a few moments later the receptionist looks it over. "You haven't filled in your occupation," she says.

"Hypnotist," says Luisa.

"Oh?" The receptionist meets Luisa's eyes. They're unusual eyes. Clear blue, almost violet. They often remind people of deep bodies of water.

"It's the family business," says Luisa. "Both my parents were hypnotists. As were two of my grandparents."

"How lovely," says the receptionist.

"The doctor will see me right away," says Luisa,

still looking into the receptionist's eyes. She enunciates each word slowly and carefully.

"But we call people in the order they arrive," the receptionist says.

"I arrived first," says Luisa.

"You arrived first," the receptionist agrees.

Luisa has barely glanced at *Life Magazine's* special Winter Olympics issue when a nurse calls her name. She follows the nurse down a corridor to a small examining room. The nurse hands her the usual skimpy garment, telling Luisa to remove her clothes and put it on. When the nurse leaves, Luisa strips, puts the thing on, and sits down on the edge of the examination table. It's cold. Almost immediately, she has goose bumps.

Luisa doesn't look great in the drab shapeless garment, but she looks better than most. She is of an indeterminate age. Certainly past forty. She would probably be described as "well preserved." She is tall and strong-looking and has longish red hair. Not beautiful but striking.

The nurse comes back in and smiles when she notices that Luisa's fingernails and toenails are painted cherry blossom pink. "Stand on the scale," she instructs. Luisa gets on the scale and the nurse adjusts the indicator back and forth, minutely, until it finally rests on 130. "One hundred thirty," she says.

Luisa turns to look at her. "What about my eyes?" she asks.

"Hmm?" the nurse says, writing. She looks up and meets Luisa's eyes. "Oh!" she says. She gazes at Luisa for a moment. "They're such a nice color," she says.

"Really?" asks Luisa. "Tell the truth."

The nurse hesitates. "They're a little weird," she says.

"Scary?" asks Luisa.

"Nope." The nurse smiles. "I like them.

Luisa smiles. "I weigh 157," she says. The nurse glances down at her clipboard and frowns. She erases the 130 and writes 157.

"But I carry it well," says Luisa. "Don't I?"

"You certainly do," says the nurse. "Now I have to take your blood pressure." She straps the arm band on, pumps it up, and looks at it. "One hundred ten over sixty," she tells Luisa.

"One twenty over seventy," Luisa says. The nurse gazes at her blankly. "I'm sorry," Luisa explains, "but these silly games are quite harmless and they're crucial if I'm to stay in practice. I'll stop if it disturbs you."

The nurse smiles. "It doesn't disturb me." She writes one hundred twenty over seventy on Luisa's chart. "I think it's interesting."

"What happens now?" Luisa asks.

"You wait for Doctor Heller," the nurse answers.

"I probably don't even need Doctor Heller," Luisa says. "I'm ninety percent sure I've got bronchitis. Everyone in my family has bronchitis. Everyone on my *block* has bronchitis. But I can't just write myself out a prescription for antibiotics, can I?"

"No," says the nurse. "You can't."

"What's Doctor Heller like?" Luisa asks.

"He's very nice," the nurse says.

"Tell the truth," Luisa demands.

"He's a complete jerk, " says the nurse. Then she looks startled and they both burst out laughing. "But he's a very competent doctor," the nurse says. He can diagnose your bronchitis as well as the next doc."

"Thanks for putting up with me," says Luisa. "You will feel happy for the rest of the day. You will walk around thinking life is a piece of cake."

"I certainly look forward to that," says the nurse.

Luisa snaps her fingers. The nurse blinks, then moves quickly to the door. "Doctor Heller will be right with you," she says as she leaves. She has left the clipboard with Luisa's chart on the table and Luisa quickly changes her weight and blood pressure to the correct numbers.

Time passes. Ten minutes. Twenty minutes. Nothing happens. The nurse had left her with the impression that the doctor would be right in. Clearly, he won't be. There is nothing to distract her. She should have brought her magazine with her. She considers parading out into the waiting room dressed as she is to retrieve her copy of *Life*. She decides against it.

She looks around the room. It's a generic examination room. No windows. No pictures or photos. Nothing interesting or unusual to hold her attention. Luisa hasn't much interest in things anyway. Things rarely hold surprises; people do.

Another twenty minutes pass. Luisa is beginning to think they've forgotten all about her. She's starting to feel woozy. It angers her. Sitting here half dressed is the last thing she needs. She knows that in examining rooms up and down this hallway sick people sit in skimpy hospital garments waiting for the doctor. It's more convenient for him this way. She tries to calm herself. *This treatment may be dehumanizing and demoralizing,* she tells herself, *but it won't kill you. They only do it this way because they can get away with it.*

Finally, the door opens and a big man in a white coat breezes in. He's in his mid-thirties, large and bearded. He looks like a lumberjack. His blue eyes are intelligent but not particularly kind. He moves in a rush.

"Well Luisa," he says loudly, glancing down at the clipboard, "I'm Doctor Heller. What's the trouble?"

"Sorry to keep you waiting," says Luisa.

"Hmmm?" he says, scanning her chart.

"I said I was sorry to keep you waiting," Luisa repeats.

He looks up at her. "Symptoms?" he asks.

"Fever," she says. "Sore throat. Bad cough. I think I have bronchitis."

"I'm the doctor," he says, making notations on her chart. He places his stethoscope on her back. "Cough!" he barks.

Luisa coughs as he moves his stethoscope about

on her back and then her chest. His movements are all precise and quick and his touch is firm and cold. He looks into the distance, concentrating. He doesn't look at her.

"It began two weeks ago," Luisa says. "I woke up with a bad sore throat. Three days later I began running a slight fever." She stops. He isn't listening.

"How much pain have you caused your patients by not listening to them?" she asks quietly.

"Hmmm?" He takes a thermometer from a drawer. "Open," he says, angling the thermometer toward her mouth. Luisa pushes it away.

"Listen to me!" she says.

He stops and looks at her. Their eyes meet. It's a struggle. But Luisa is angry. "You will slow down and give me a good thorough examination," she says finally. "You will take your time, pay attention and explain the reason for each procedure. You will listen to me when I speak. Not only am I older than you and deserving of your respect for no other reason, but I live in this body. I may know something about it that can help you."

The doctor gazes at her unblinkingly.

"I'm not just a body with an illness," says Luisa. "I'm a person. You care about my feelings."

"I care about your feelings," he says. He sounds doubtful. But he continues the examination at a much slower, kinder pace. Luisa is surprised at how good he is. His cold hands even seem to warm up slightly. Still, it's clear that he's fighting the impulse to race through the exam and get on to the next patient.

"Why are you in such a hurry?" she asks.

"I have so many patients," he says. "I hate to keep them waiting."

"You don't care about that," she insists. "Tell the truth."

"You've got a fabulous body," he says. "I love older women with big breasts."

"Not about that," she laughs. "Why are you in such a hurry?"

"This way," he says, "I stay in control."

"What if you aren't in control?" Luisa asks.

"I have to be in control. I'm the doctor," he answers.

"And you're the doctor because you have to stay in control," says Luisa. "Right?"

"Yes," he says. "I do like your eyes. They're . . ."

"What?" she snaps.

He thinks, then says, ". . . calming."

He finishes the examination. "You have bronchitis," he announces. "I'm writing you a prescription for 500mg of ampicillin."

"What would make you listen to your patients?" she asks. "What would make you care?"

"Nothing," he says. He is writing the prescription. "Take this four times daily with plenty of water." He hands it to her and turns toward the door.

"Wait," she says. He stops. She considers him. "Take your clothes off," she tells him. He turns around and stares into her eyes. He begins to unbutton his shirt.

As he removes his clothing, Luisa puts her own

back on. By the times he's naked, she's fully clothed. He stands there looking very pale. He has goose bumps. She hands him the hospital garment. He puts it on.

"You will sit here and wait," she says, "until the nurse comes looking for you. You'll see what it's like."

He sits down on the edge of the examination table and sighs.

She pauses at the door. "When the nurse comes, you'll forget about me."

"I'll forget about you." He sounds happy about that.

"But you'll never forget the next half hour," she says.

As Luisa leaves the room she sees the nurse heading toward her with a clipboard. "Doctor Heller is in the examining room," she tells the nurse. "He asked not to be disturbed for at least a half hour. But he wanted you to explain to the patients who are waiting that there'll be a delay. And to apologize."

"That's new," says the nurse.

"That's right," says Luisa. She meets the nurse's eyes. "Have an interesting day," she says.

The Man Who Shot Bats

by

Mary Connor Ralph

We never figured out what Josh had against bats. The crowd at Smitty's was ripe with theories that got tossed around when Josh wasn't there, but none of them ever bore fruit. He wouldn't talk about it.

Maybe he'd seen too many horror movies when he was a kid. Or maybe it happened when he was much younger. Eddie Phelps said he'd heard a bat had flown into Josh's mother's hair when he was suckling and she went wild and it soured her milk. Maybe he'd been bitten and was actually a little rabid.

Whatever the reason, Josh was more than a little weird when it came to bats. "Monsters," he'd mutter, "stinking devils." Then he'd go get his gun and shoot bats. He owned several different guns and it didn't matter if he landed on a Browning over and under or a handgun, or something in between. Josh grabbed what was closest to hand and made it do the job. Once I saw him knock a bat off the chimney of his Aunt Sadie's farmhouse with a Luger. It had to be rabid, he told me.

We saw it flying circles like a hawk, at noontime, above the barn, which is now a garage. Sadie's farm was grabbed up by a big outfit after her husband died. All she has left is the acre her house is planted on. The main buildings, with all the equipment, were sold with the land, so Josh turned the small barn into a garage for Sadie's old pick-up.

He spied that bat when we pulled up with Sadie's groceries spilling around in the bed of the truck. When he hit the brakes, cans crashed against the sides, and a box of spaghetti jumped overboard. He swung the door open and leaped out with the keys still in the ignition. I leaned across and switched the engine off, climbed out and scooped up the spaghetti. Then I hopped into the back to rebag the rest of the stuff. Next thing I knew, Josh was up beside me, taking aim over the roof of the cab.

"What the heck?" I said.

"Bat!" Josh howled in my ear.

His first shot sunk into the big elm beside the garage. "Tree was sick anyway," Josh said. He'd spent the early part of the summer taking down all the elms around the house after the tree doc had declared they all had Dutch Elm Disease. Josh figured the last one standing must be in the early stage. A tiny branch with three brown-yellow leaves still clinging to it, floated to the ground beside the pick-up.

The bat squealed, like it had been hit instead of the tree. Then it high-tailed out of there. Josh wasn't giving up.

He disappeared behind the garage and I couldn't tell where the next two shots landed, but he'd clearly missed the bat, which made a dash for the housetop. I stayed put, watching the show.

Aunt Sadie came to the back screen door and hollered what was all the fuss about? Josh pointed up and yelled again, "Bat!" Sadie nodded as if she'd seen it all a hundred times, then she turned and shuffled back inside. A minute later, as Josh was putting the ladder against the side of the house, she came and slammed the heavy wooden inside door.

The bat rested upside down from the top edge of the red brick chimney. Josh climbed the ladder and poked his head over the corner of the roof above the clogged gutter. He yanked a small oak sprout out of his way and took aim. He steadied his firing arm with his other big paw and squeezed the trigger clean, no shake. The bat dropped like a turd and hit the roof with a small sound like dry leaves scraping your windowpane at night. Josh scrambled up onto the roof and stood over the furry corpse, then sunk another bullet into it.

"Gimme a bag," he yelled down to me.

"A bag?" I said.

"Yeah, a bag, stupid. One of them," he said, and pointed the empty gun at the groceries I'd just finished rebagging.

"Aw, not one of these," I said.

"Quit belly-achin' and gimme a bag," he shouted.

“No,” I said, folding my arms across my chest like Sitting Bull. “Get it yourself, you jerk.”

Aunt Sadie has hearing just like a bat. She appeared at the back door with an empty brown grocery bag at the same moment that Josh came off the ladder and lunged for me. “This what you want?” she asked.

At the sound of her voice, Josh got this look on his face like butter wouldn’t melt in his mouth. “Thank you, Auntie,” he said, and planted a wet kiss on her sunken cheek before he climbed back up to bag the bloody mess.

It was shortly after that Josh made up his mind to rid the countryside of those rabid little vermin, as he called them. He announced his intentions to the whole gang at Smitty’s. The guys started rattling off places where they’d seen bats come out just after sunset. Now don’t get me wrong, nobody hated bats like Josh did, but there hadn’t been much excitement since Anna-Lee went off to the nunnery with her father’s shotgun in her back. A one-man war on bats looked pretty darn good. Especially to Eddie Phelps. He swore he knew the main cave where the biggest lot of them holed up. He drew Josh a map on the back of one of Smitty’s Budweiser placemats.

It took us most of the morning and some of the afternoon to find Eddie’s cave. If it wasn’t such a steep climb, and I wasn’t loaded to the gills with all Josh’s extra weapons and ammo, I might have felt like apologizing to Eddie Phelps for my doubts about the cave’s existence. When we hit the mouth, I dropped everything and grabbed the knapsack with the food in it off Josh's sweaty back. I wasn't stepping foot in that cave without chow.

"Chew faster," Josh prompted.

I took tiny bites and swished them around in my mouth with long pulls on my beer.

"Heck with you. I'm goin' in," Josh said.

He took a few steps into the shadow of the cave before he turned around to look at me again. I just sat there, chewing. "Sissy," he said, and trotted off into the cave.

I waited ten minutes, and then picked up the gear and followed. The sun was still high, but the cave was black as pitch a few feet in. Josh had disappeared like a puff of smoke in a night sky. I almost turned on the flashlight, then I remembered why we were there. If the place was full of sleeping bats, I didn't want to be their bad dream.

I stumbled on for awhile, then all of a sudden I heard Josh roar. I thought the vibration would bring down the rock walls, or wake the dead, and at the very worst wake the bats. I waited. Nothing. Then Josh howled again. Then came the strangest whooping and hollering I'd ever heard.

That was it. I turned on my flashlight.

Up ahead I saw Josh down on one knee, cradling his head in one paw. Behind him, laughing up a storm, stood Eddie Phelps and all the guys from Smitty's. Dangling above everybody, were dozens of baseball bats, suspended from the roof of the cave by wires or ropes, I couldn't tell which from where I stood.

With his free hand, Josh reached into his belt and pulled out the Luger. The cave thundered, and baseball bats rained onto the hard-packed dirt floor. I thought I heard Eddie Phelps squeal as he and the guys high-tailed past me and out of the cave, but then, in the beam of my flashlight, I saw the first furry body land at Josh's feet.

Grandpappy and the Indians and a Bear

by

John H. Lambe

"The old man was a wanderer. He had a family, but I guess they were used to him being gone. Some folks are better loved that way anyhow, and he was probably one of them. He sent money home every now and again.

It was August of eighteen fifty four. He'd been settled into an old cabin which had known a long line of occupants, some human, some not. It was the legacy of some forgotten trapper long returned to the earth.

He was panning for color on Passway Creek, not far from the headwaters of both Yellowstone and the great Snake Rivers. Beautiful, high country, dropping off from the mighty Tetons up above the bubbling cauldrons of the Yellowstone plateau.

He'd been there long enough to find a few flakes of yellow which he could point to as a reason for being there. But I reckon his main reason was just to fill his life with days he could live with. His real gold was all around him.

He'd noted four things in a descending order: First was the beauty and the soul-filling thrill of just being there. Second was Injuns. He hadn't seen any, but there was enough sign to give even a fella with sunset eyes a pause.

The third was bears. Great silver-tipped monsters that lumbered down out of the spruce and across the park. They fished the trout creeks and occasionally exploded with speed and blinding force to bring down an elk or moose. And they lived with him in this world.

The fourth was gold. This was the least of all things.

Late one evening, when the red of rubies played across the skies of a sundown world, he looked up into the twenty-four eyes of twelve warriors. He was a good enough judge of men to know they weren't friendly and this would be entirely their show.

He sighed a little and figured there was no better place to die than right here on the mighty backbone of this great continent, the roof of his world, in the company of twelve warrior-men of another slowly passing world. So, Grandpap looked south at the endless waves of peaks washing down to that high sagebrush desert of the Green River country. There around behind at the notch of Two Pass Creek and far beyond it, was his family . . . fire, home, and safety. Then, he faced west. The sky was aflame over the blue-grey Teton peaks. The reds and purples reflected off the timeless glaciers woven on their rocky shoulders.

The men tied him to an old snag, the brave survivor of a long ago forest. First, they ate, then they talked it over. They'd dispatch him, of course, never any doubt about that, just the method.

When the proceedings began, one man, then another would dash at him, shaking a spear at his belly or a club over his head. They'd shout their fierce words and contort their faces. He suspected he was getting a good preview of their future intentions. Leather clad and tough, he was just as glad that he couldn't understand the lingo.

The preliminaries went on for over an hour. But, Grandpap was resigned to dying from the start, so it never really worried him as much as it perhaps should have. Then the moon, full and orange with a halo, rose.

Yeah, that moon was a sight. Big and round, it looked like the Mama of all the stars, fixing to add a few more just for good measure. And as he looked at it's hallowed wonder, hoping it would be the last thing he saw, an old silver bear caught the corner of his eye and all of his attention. And the bear walked into camp.

Well, that bear spoiled a good little party. And Pap felt a little let down at this abrupt change in plans. The Indians made a strategic retreat in a mass of flying legs and dusty feathers, leaving Pap to face Mister Silver by his lonesome.

Superstition over bears is a thing all Indians shared. They decided right quick that this one had a message. They delegated Grandpappy to make note of whatever wisdom was about to be revealed.

The old bear ambled over and plopped, whump, down on his bohunkus in front of Pap, his big silver back to him, looking at the departed parties. They could be seen silhouetted in the moonlight at a respectful—very respectful—few paces. Their eyes glistened from the abandoned fire, like coyotes waiting for the scraps.

That furry monster was fed up on fish. Pap could smell the lingering aroma, he was that close. And the bear was doing a little talking to the Indians. It couldn't be heard, just a low rumble in his throat only he could understand. Pap felt it vibrating way down deep in the pit of his own stomach. Probably the bear was telling them what he would do if they really wanted to play.

Directly, Silver pivoted all nine hundred-odd pounds around and looked over at pap, as if to say, "You poor dodger, what ever am I going to do about a dreamy-eyed bugger like you wandering around my mountains?"

Then his little huckleberry eyes noticed the sweat pouring off Pap's face and down his chest. The Children of Nature had shredded his shirt, probably with the intention of a little job of tattooing with a hot brand. Now, in the cool air of a high mountain night, Pap sweated enough to make a water hole for two mules and a burro under his knees.

His legs gave out when Silver turned his laconic attention on him. Loosely tied to the snag, he collapsed, or collapsed as far as he could get that way, to his knees.

To an Indian in that country—the high recluse of the all powerful Grizzly—that bear was an age-long object of worship. A direct link to the Great Spirit. The Earthly messenger of such memos as Heaven directed to men. And here was their prisoner in a worshipful position before just such a divine runner.

Well, Ol' Silver ran that massive bundle of bone and muscle which served as his head out on his long neck and snuffled the sweat on Pap's chest. What he smelled was salt, of course, and salt is a mighty valuable commodity in the wilderness. In fact, salt is just the thing to top off a bountiful feast of mountain trout.

He could have used his great yellow fangs to rip off the salt and thirty pounds of meat, blood and bone along with it, but he didn't. What he did do was to daintily lick the sweat off. The big, sandpaper tongue swiped chest, face, even Pap's ears.

I don't know what went through Grandpappy's head right then, he never told. But the Indians were figuring that it was about as direct a message from the Last Hunting Ground as they would ever get. And it didn't take any medicinc man to translate or diagnose it for 'em.

When the bear vamoosed, they undid Pap's ties. Then they got on their shaggy ponies and rode out of the park, up the side of the valley, through the spruce and aspen, and over the mountain. All the way to their lodges.

And over many a winter fire burning at the center of the lodge-poles, the story was told of how they had almost killed a Small Spirit. Until the Great Bear had shown them their mistake.

The Quarry

by

Christopher Woods

Margaret was an artist who made things from stone. She was almost seventy years old, and she lived in Mexico. She lived in a house that stood in the middle of an old quarry, the place where stone comes from. The quarry was grey and dusty, like a dream on the moon. It was an unusual place to live, but Margaret loved the quarry. It was so very plain, it made her imagination come alive.

On this night, she lay in bed, listening to the wind and the cries of coyotes. Living in the quarry was like living in a desert, away from the noises of other people. Still, she never felt alone there.

Margaret's house was only a few miles from Taxco, the silver mining town. There was more silver in Taxco than anywhere else in Mexico. Now, listening to the sounds of the Mexican night, Margaret had an odd feeling. As if she were expecting something, but she didn't know what it was.

Outside, the moon was full. It glowed with a light that made the sheets on her bed shine like silver. In the next room, the studio where she worked with stone, was a statue of a young Mexican girl. The statue was almost finished. In that room the moonlight played with the shadows. Light danced on the Mexican girl who was coming out of the stone that came from the quarry.

Margaret could not sleep, but she was not afraid. She had lived by herself for many years, so many that now she was afraid of nothing. She decided she was sad because of what she'd had to do. Earlier that day, she had fired her gardener, Ramon. She told him to leave, and not to come back again. Ramon had worked for Margaret for twenty-five years. He was the closest friend she had. Margaret was not so close to her own family, who lived very far away.

Sometimes, a relative would travel to Mexico to visit Margaret in her house in the quarry. They came from places like Baltimore and Boston. Margaret felt that when they returned home they would tell the other relatives how strange she was. And they would laugh about her. But the truth was this. None of them knew Margaret. Only Ramon, who had worked for Margaret so very long, really knew her. Now, sadly enough, he too was gone.

Here is how it happened. Margaret was in her studio, working on the statue of the Mexican girl. As she worked, she felt that someone was watching her. In the corner of her eye, she saw Ramon standing in the open window. He was watching her work, but she didn't know why. She didn't say a thing to him. Instead, she turned the face of the statue away from the window. It was not ready to show to anyone, not even Ramon. After she had done this, Ramon turned and walked away.

Ramon went to work in the garden again. He was always working there, trimming bushes, watering flowers and weeding. He loved the garden. Margaret could see that he knew it as well as he knew himself.

Not long after this, Ramon began coming to work late. He didn't seem to care about his job. He didn't pull the weeds when they reached through the dirt. He forgot to trim the bushes. He did not water the flowers. The garden looked terrible, as if no one cared if it lived or died.

All this worried Margaret. She didn't know what to do. After so many years, she was afraid that anything she might say would hurt Ramon's feelings. She wondered if he had problems, if one of his children was sick. But when she asked if anything was wrong, Ramon only shook his head and looked away. His brown eyes looked very sad.

Things went from bad to worse. It wasn't long before the garden was overgrown and full of weeds. All along Margaret had tried to busy herself with the statue of the Mexican girl, but now she had to say something.

"Ramon, what has happened?" she asked. "The garden looks terrible. Everything is dying."

"I'm sorry," he said. "I promise, it won't happen again."

Margaret decided to give Ramon another

chance. Still, she could not understand what was wrong. In all the years she had known him, he had never acted in this way. One day, when her own work was done, she went for a walk in the garden. It was worse than before.

Margaret stood in the garden, both sad and angry. Then, a little at a time, she tried to pull the weeds from the earth. She carried buckets of water to the thirsty plants. Then, when she stopped to rest and wipe the sweat from her forehead, she saw something in the distance. Someone was walking up the road. It was Ramon, coming to work at the very same hour he usually went home. In a few minutes, when he was close enough, Margaret called out to him. "You must leave, Ramon. You have forgotten how to care for the garden. Everything is dying here."

Ramon, knowing this was true, said nothing. Margaret watched as Ramon, his shoulders low, walked away on the road that led out of the quarry. When he had walked some distance, it looked like he had walked into the stone itself. This reminded Margaret of the Mexican girl in her studio. The statue was half outside the stone block now, one foot stepping free into the world.

Now, on this night, Margaret lay awake, thinking about Ramon. She wondered what had made him change so. It came to her that perhaps Ramon had finally come to see what she herself had seen all along in the quarry. She had seen it when she first arrived in Mexico. She saw that the quarry was full of people, all waiting to be set free.

She got out of bed. She went to the kitchen and made tea. Then she walked into her studio to look at the stone girl. The statue's eyes were wide open.

"So, we are both awake," she said to the stone girl. But the statue, which was almost finished, said nothing. How could she? She was only made of stone from the quarry, made to look like a real Mexican girl. "Soon, child, you will be free," Margaret said, and started to work.

A week later, at dawn, there was a knock on the door. Margaret, who was still asleep, got up to see who it was. She feared bad news, that maybe one of her relatives in Baltimore or Boston, was sick. She had all kinds of terrible fears as she opened the door.

There, on her doorstep, stood Ramon. In his hands he held a small cloth sack. "I told you not to come back," Margaret said. She could not believe he had come. She looked over Ramon's shoulder and into the quarry. The first light of day had begun to shine on the sleeping stone.

"I worked in your garden a very long time," Ramon said, "nearly half my life. I made something, and I want you to have it."

He handed her the cloth sack. When she opened it, Margaret could not believe what was inside. It was a wood carving of the Mexican girl. And she also noticed something. Ramon's carving was not yet finished. The face of the Mexican girl had not yet been carved. It was only as finished as her own stone girl had been, the day she turned the statue away from the window where Ramon had stood watching her.

"After you sent me away," Ramon said, "I didn't know how to finish it. I couldn't watch you through the window anymore."

"But it's a beautiful carving," she said. "You must finish it, Ramon."

Ramon went on: "At first I didn't see the people in the quarry. Then, one afternoon, I found this piece of wood. I looked at it for a long time, until I was sure there was someone inside it. After that, I knew I couldn't be happy just taking care of the garden."

Above them, night stars were fading. But Margaret knew that, even in the day, stars remained. They were always there, whether she could see them or not. This is why she never felt alone, living in the quarry. It made her happy that Ramon felt the same way she did. Sbe was getting old, and she didn't know how much longer she could work. She knew there were many more people still waiting in the quarry.

"Come with me, Ramon," she told him, opening the door wide. "We have so much work to do."

Ramon followed her into the house. Margaret was smiling because Ramon had returned to help her. Ramon's eyes, before so sad, now sparkled like stars on a very clear night.

Going Home

by

Dotte Shaffer

It was early summer. The sun shining through the trees was hot upon his face and the air smelled of green grass and clean water. Martha, his young wife, trailed her bare feet in the gently flowing brook, tilting her head to listen to the symphony of the wild birds who shared this wooded paradise. She laughed in delight at a pair of chipmunks scrambling over a piece of apple left over from lunch. Oliver Dotson's heart overflowed with love and he moved eagerly to her side. She turned her face to him and he bent his head to meet her waiting lips.

But the young aide interrupted: "Mr. Dotson. Wake up. Nap time's over. The doctor's waiting to see you."

And with that, it was gone, all gone. Martha. The warmth. The feeling of youth and vitality. Oliver was back in the real world, otherwise known as the West View Nursing Home, where the nurses were overworked and underpaid and the doctors didn't like to be kept waiting.

"I'm really sorry I had to wake you, Mr. Dotson. You looked as if you were having a real good dream." The girl spoke kindly as she helped him to sit up on the bed.

"It's all right, Debbie," he lied, accepting her help gratefully. "What doctor is it this time?" Some, he had noticed, were more impatient than others.

"Doctor Graham," she said, holding Oliver's arm to steady him as he stood up.

Doctor Graham was the worst of the lot. He was cold and uncaring, in it for the money, Oliver thought. He didn't like him and didn't pretend to. Oliver muttered a mild obscenity at the news.

The girl stifled a giggle as she took a dark blue cardigan from a drawer and held it out. "This will look nice with those grey slacks, Mr. Dotson. This is your day out with Bob Martin, isn't it?"

"Why, yes. Yes, it is." That information served to speed up the process necessary to get him down the hall and to the examining room. The thought of Bob Martin and the afternoon's activities negated the distastefulness of the upcoming encounter with the clinical Doctor Graham.

"You go on now, Debbie. I know you've got things to do. I'll just be a minute in the toilet, then I'll go on down." He shook his head. "Won't hurt Graham to wait. Keeps me waiting often enough. What's he doing here so early, anyways? Usually stops here on his way home, doesn't he? Must have a golf game coming up."

"I don't know, Mr. Dotson," the girl said, smiling. "I do have Mrs. Lacey waiting, so if you're sure you can manage, I'll go."

"I can manage. I'm just old. I'm not helpless." He returned her smile, raising his hand to wave her off.

At age ninety, Oliver was in good physical shape, all things considered. He had arthritis and some trouble with his heart, but pills and common sense kept them under control. He slept well, and, when there was anything fit to eat, ate well. And he could see and hear as well as age permitted. He did use a cane to walk with, but all in all, he was probably the healthiest patient in the home. At least, that's what he thought.

He moved as quickly as his arthritic body would permit, tucking his shirt into the waistband of his baggy pants on the way to the bathroom. There, he rinsed his mouth with something that tasted minty and tried to brush some order into his hair.

His full head of snow white hair contrasted sharply to Doctor Graham's premature baldness. Oliver smiled, unable to squelch the smug pleasure that the irony afforded him. Still smiling, he grabbed his cane and started down the hall.

"Good morning, Oliver." The young physician greeted him noncommittally as he came through the open door, seemingly unconcerned that his patient didn't return the greeting. Accustomed to the routine, Oliver automatically sat down and began to unbutton his shirt, wincing with the pain in his swollen, arthritic fingers.

Doctor Graham studied the chart on his desk as if he'd never seen it before.

Playing a little power game with me, Doc? Oliver

wondered silently. *I kept you waiting. Now I can wait? Okay, Doc whatever turns you on, as Debbie would say.*

"You know, Doc, I saw something on TV the other morning. Might interest you." Oliver's mouth twisted in an effort to hide his grin. "It was on a new cream they got out that grows hair. Guaranteed. You oughta look into it." Oliver was pleased with how sincere he sounded.

"You're probably watching too much television, Oliver. Should be taking more exercise. Your heart's not going to hold up, you know." Nothing showed in his voice or in the cold grey eyes. There was no tightening of the lips or creasing of the suntanned forehead, no sign Oliver had touched a nerve. Unwillingly, Oliver was forced to admire the man's ability to give the impression of complete indifference and wondered, as he had so often, if there was a person at all behind that cold facade.

Perhaps he is only like this with me, thought Oliver, flinching as the cold ear of the stethoscope touched his hairless chest. Though he sat rigidly silent, his mind raced, studying the man who examined him with smooth, uncaring fingers. He tried to picture the doctor making love and couldn't.

"Are you taking your heart pills regularly, Oliver?"

Bah! What was the use of taking heart pills? When a body's lost its reasons for living, why should a heart keep on beating? Then Oliver's mind flashed suddenly to his earlier dream. There had been no heart trouble with Martha beside him and the two of them in their own special paradise.

The doctor continued, "Have you been exercising as I told you? You remember. If you can't get outside, then up and down the hall several times a day, all right? Dr. Graham's pen moved rapidly across Oliver's chart. The doctor's long nose was twitching, no longer able to conceal his impatience to be gone.

Gets to you, doesn't it, sonny? Oliver taunted soundlessly. *Guess you can't wait to get out on the golf course, out in the fresh air. Bet you don't draw a deep breath all the time you're here. I should walk up and down the hall, you say. Easy for you, you with the cold hands and even colder heart. You can turn a deaf ear and a blind eye to me, to everyone here, those who were once as alive as you. More alive, I'd say. But they're just statistics to you, money in the bank.*

"What you are, I once was. What I am, you will be," Oliver spoke up suddenly, his voice crackling as he quoted from a now forgotten source.

Dr. Graham's mask dropped and a look of surprise crossed his facc. He regained his composure too quickly for Oliver to be certain whether or not he had actually caught a glimpse of a real human being. The doctor's voice was unchanged, and he advised, "Exercise. Take your heart pills. I'll see you next month." Duty done, fee earned, the doctor took his leave. Oliver buttoned his shirt, tucked it in, smoothed back his hair and went back to his room to wait for Bob Martin.

It was not long before he recognized Bob's footsteps coming down the hall. The young man who came into the room radiated a feeling of such wholesome goodness that it was almost tangible. His wide smile was real and his manner reflected sensitivity and caring. Oliver couldn't help but compare him to the antiseptic, self-serving Doctor Graham.

"Mornin', Mr. Dotson," Bob said. "All ready and waiting, I see."

"Yep. Been looking forward to this ever since the last time," Oliver confessed with a smile that lit up his watery blue eyes. There was an almost youthful spring in his step as he walked with Bob down the hall and out into the fresh air of a warm summer day not unlike the one he'd dreamed about.

He paused to take a deep breath as Bob waited patiently, viewing the old man with a look of tenderness and compassion. His visit was a monthly event that had been taking place ever since Bob bought Oliver's farm and Oliver had come to live here at West View. Bob was well aware of how much these visits meant to Oliver.

In the car Oliver sat quietly, gazing out the window and enjoying the view. His pleasure was marred by his resentment of the changes in the once familiar countryside. "What're they putting in there?" he asked, pointing to a group of newly constructed buildings.

"Another shopping center," Bob answered. "Progress, Mr. Dotson. Progress." Bob shook his head in sympathy with the old man's feelings.

The ride continued in a companionable silence. At the house, Sally, Bob's wife, greeted Oliver warmly. He admired the turkey roasting in the oven, which she prepared in his honor several times a year, always sending a generously filled 'doggie bag' back to the nursing home with him. Today, however, her manner seemed strained. He wondered what the problem was, but didn't feel he should pry. He hoped it was nothing serious. He excused himself, returning in time to hear Sally ask, "Did you tell him, honey?"

"Not yet," Bob replied solemnly. "I thought I'd wait 'til . . ." he paused when Oliver entered the room. "Going to walk down to the stream now, Mr. Dotson?" This, too, had become one of Oliver's rituals.

"Why, yes, Bob, believe I will," Oliver said casually.

"You go slow now, Mr. Dotson," Sally advised. "Rest along the way. A mile can be pretty far in the noonday sun." Sally patted his arm in a friendly, caring gesture.

"Will do, Miz Martin. I'll be back in time for turkey and a piece of that apple pie you've got cooling on the window sill." He smiled in acknowledgement of the effort she had made to please him. "Sure smells good," he added, anxious to be gone, but not wanting to show it.

The couple walked out the door with him and

stood watching as he made his way through the yard and out the gate toward the meadow. He turned and waved, concerned with the look of sadness on both of their faces. He would talk with them when he got back, he decided. Maybe he could help if it was financial. He still had a little money put away and, if the State didn't get it before he died, he had willed it to them anyway.

He walked slowly, placing his sturdy wooden cane firmly in front of him with each step. The midday sun was high in the sky and the sharp, pungent smell of wild grass was heavy in the air. The old man didn't linger in the meadow. His destination was the woods. His damaged heart lightened and his steps quickened as he approached the gnarled old oak that signaled the entrance to 'Dotson's Paradise', the name he and Martha had given this piece of their property over sixty years ago.

Breathing heavily, his chest hurting with each labored breath, he leaned against the tree, drawing strength and comfort from the familiar landmark. Too late he remembered that he'd left his heart pills on the dresser back at the nursing home.

"It's okay," he said calmly. "It'll pass. I'll just take it easy for a minute." He gazed across the meadow at his home. Not his home now, he reminded himself sadly. Not any more. He was grateful that Bob Martin brought him back here once each month. He hated to think of never being able to see or visit this spot again. West View would really become a prison if that were to happen.

Terrible, he theorized somewhat resentfully, that one has to get old and dependent on others for help. He was never one to seek help from anyone, least of all strangers. Oh, the nursing home wasn't so bad, he reckoned begrudgingly. The nurses were nice, most of them anyway, though they did tend to treat you as if you had no more sense than a pup. The other patients were all right, too, except they were so blasted old. All they wanted to talk about was their aches and pains and going home.

The way Oliver saw it, he had his own aches and pains, so who needed or wanted to hear about anyone else's? And as far as going home, well, that was the biggest ache of all. Because the nursing home *was* their home now.

Oliver never thought much about dying. As a farmer he was accustomed to seeing birth and death and took it as a part of life. Lately he was plagued by a series of do-gooders pestering him to get ready for the Lord. It didn't sound to him as if they really knew anymore about what to expect than he did. He began to pretend he was deaf as a post and they soon stopped preaching, settling instead for a wave and a smile as they passed by his room on their way to some other captive.

It would be nice, he admitted, if it were true that a person saw his loved ones after death. He'd be awfully happy to see his Martha again. This morning's dream flashed in front of him and he pulled himself to his feet, rested and eager to continue his journey.

He walked quite briskly down the well-worn path to the creek, spurred on by the anticipated pleasure awaiting him. Finally, his goal in sight, his tired old eyes lit up with joy. His bent back straightened imperceptibly and he took on the stature of a much younger man. Here it was, his own private paradise. It was a corner of the world that held all of the memories he treasured.

Leaning on his cane, he ignored the persistent pain in his chest and stood drinking in the beauty that surrounded him. The little stream rippled and danced over the stones worn smooth by time and water and the sun filtered down through the great leaf-laden trees, speckling all with flecks of gold. On either bank the moss grew thick and green and an abundance of wild flowers filled the air with their fragrance. Red geraniums, white and blue violets, delicate Queen Anne's lace, trilliums with their three petals of waxy white and leaves like green umbrellas intermingled in a gala display of color. It was a sight for the soul.

Music was provided by the bobolinks, meadowlarks, catbirds and redbreasted robins. A hummingbird, like a miniature buzz saw, flew in and about the heavily scented blossoms. Two small chipmunks scurried up a tree, chattering excitedly as if scolding Oliver for trespassing. Was it the pair he had seen in his dream?

Funny, he mused, until Martha's death he always felt it was she who was dependent on him and all the time it was the other way around. Here in this place he could pretend she was with him, that she had never left his side. Sixty years of Martha were here; her gaiety and laughter, her warmth and passion.

He smiled and patted his stomach, recalling the picnics they had enjoyed here—the fried chicken and potato salad, the baked beans and homemade bread. And Martha's dark chocolate cake. It made his mouth water to think of it even now. Strange how food was uppermost in his thoughts these past years. He supposed it was because he never quite got enough to eat at West View. He figured those in the know had decided that a person lost his appetite along with everything else when he got old.

Now he realized that it wasn't food he hungered for. It was the love that went into the preparation and the sharing of it with Martha.

He could see her now. Her long skirt held daringly high, wading in the stream. She would kick water at him and scream with delight when he threatened to splash her. They made love here often. The lush, green moss was their bed, the trees protected their privary and the songs of the birds contributed to the magic and wonder of it all. He felt a surprising stir of desire at the memory. What a mixture of angel and devil his Martha was, teasing and pleasing in a way that kept him in her thrall throughout their life together.

Suddenly very tired, he gingerly lowered himself to a knoll beneath a large elm tree. Leaning back against the tree, welcoming the support and familiarity of this old friend, he reflected that maybe ninety years was damned old for bones and heart. Reluctantly he admitted he wasn't as healthy as he liked to think. Well, he shrugged, when my time comes, I hope it happens right here.

He got up and moved closer to the stream, leaning over so he might cup his hands with water and splash the cool clear liquid on his face. Abruptly, a knife-like pain stabbed his chest, causing him to gasp aloud. He fell back in the grass, panting, the pain holding him. He wondered if his time had come. He stared up at the sky. Would God reach down His hand and raise him up? But the pain subsided and he drifted into a light sleep.

He awoke within the hour feeling rested and strangely disappointed to find himself still alive. He rose slowly. It was time to leave. Funny, he mused, how Father Time who moved so slowly at West View, seemed to acquire an unexpected agility here.

The path back to the house seemed longer and Oliver stopped often to lean against the larger trees along the way. When he finally reached the big oak, he sat down gratefully, more tired than he had ever been. As he leaned back against the rough, sun-warmed bark, it seemed he could hear a pounding in the old tree like that of a beating heart. *Well why not?* he reasoned, *A tree is God-made. Why shouldn't it have a heart?*

He would like to linger drawing strength from the oak but he had no wish to keep Sally and Bob waiting. They apparently had worries enough already. He wouldn't want to add to them.

He had just gotten to his feet when he heard Bob Martin's voice. *He's come looking for me, I reckon,* he said to himself. He opened his mouth to call to him when he heard a stranger's voice. The words that reached the old man's ears were painfully clear.

"We should be able to get a real good price on this, Mr. Martin. This is choice property. You don't find real estate like this any more." The realtor's voice rang with excitement as he added, "In fact, I'm sure I already have a buyer for it. I can almost promise you a check for the full amount by this time next week. How does that sound?"

To Oliver it sounded like the death knell. He stumbled and would have fallen if the oak had not been there to catch him.

"That's fine," Bob said, the tone of his voice making a lie of his words. Oliver knew how hard it must be for the Martin family to give up this property. Didn't he go through the same thing himself? No wonder they had looked so sad. He leaned closer to the oak. The pounding in the tree sounded weaker and he pressed even closer, straining to hear it. Somehow it seemed of the utmost importance that he be able to hear it.

"I'll show you the woods and the creek tomorrow," Bob was saying, his voice growing fainter as he and the realtor moved back towards the house. "The previous owner is down there now and, since this will probably be his last visit, I don't want to disturb him."

Oliver felt dazed, his mind accepting what he heard but his stubborn heart refusing to. He closed his eyes. He could hear the wind in the trees and the faint, sweet music of the running brook. Oliver's heart seemed to swell with joy. Then, suddenly, the sharp, now familiar pain enclosed his chest like a breath-stopping vise.

The need to hurry became all important. He pushed away from the now silent oak, scorning the ever increasing pain that was making its way down his left arm. Stumbling, and cursing the aged limbs that slowed him, he once again stood beside the little stream.

Panting with exertion, he lowered himself to the grass beneath the elm. Unexpectedly, from the depths of the forest, a bird burst into song. The pure loveliness of it brought sudden tears to Oliver's eyes and seemed, somehow, to lessen the raging pain in his chest.

"Ah," he sighed with pleasure, "Martha, my love. Did you hear that? Sounds like the one we used to hear, remember?" Closing his eyes to more clearly recapture the memory, he felt the presence of his beloved wife so strongly he reached out to touch her and was surprised to feel only the cool grass.

An intense longing filled his being and he trembled with emotion. He struggled to his feet. Again the searing pain cut into him and he cried aloud. He fell back against the moss-covered tree and lay there helpless. The pain in his arm was excruciating now and his vision was blurred.

He rubbed his eyes as if to clear them and there was Martha, standing on the other side of the stream, beckoning to him. Her long dark hair was blowing free and one slender hand held her full skirts high. She smiled happily and called to him, "Oh, Oliver. Come now, dear. And do hurry. I've been waiting such a long time."

The pain fled his body and in its place was a joyous feeling, a feeling of such magnitude that he was able to cross the little stream with no effort at all.

No Butts About It

by

Ruth D. Langston

Recently the sight of military personnel carriers loaded with troops brought back the memory of an encounter I had with one of those vehicles during World War II. For a few magic moments my gray hair turned brown, wrinkles faded from my face and my waistline measured the same as my age: 23 inches and 23 years. Waiting for the convoy to pass by, I was filled with the same sense of adventure and anticipation I had felt the day I set forth on an assignment that would take me around the world.

It came about like this: In 1944 I received a Civil Service appointment to an office of the State Department in India. Two of the job requirements were that applicants be 25 years old and male. Halfway through a six-month training course at the University of California an alert government employee noticed that I was neither. A waiver was requested. Since the War Manpower Commission had approved my transfer from a defense job with Boeing Aircraft Company and I had passed all the tests—including a visit with the in-house psychiatrist and a security check by the FBI—the waiver was granted.

Thus, shortly afterward, I was one of a covey of thirty young women, all Red Cross workers and Civil Service employees, about to set sail for Bombay, and thence be scattered over the CBI theater.

Breakfast at dawn had been lavish. We filled our trays from an assortment of ham, bacon, hash-brown potatoes, scrambled eggs, cereals, cinnamon rolls, hot biscuits, fruit juices and fresh fruit. As we were finishing breakfast the mess sergeant came to our table and invited us to help ourselves to the fruit still in bowls on the serving counter. With a grin and a wink he told us he thought we just might be hungry before lunch. Sick jokes were made suggesting the possibility that this might be our last meal.

A few minutes later those sick jokes took on an aura of reality. We were told that our ship would have an escort of three destroyers carrying depth charges. Our route would take us through waters thought to be infested with Japanese submarines. Another ominous note was sounded when we were issued ID cards stating that the bearer had the assimilated rank of Captain in the U.S. Army in the event of capture by the enemy. One by one we went silently back to the counter and filled our jacket pockets with fruit.

Anxiety levels were high as we lined up behind the personnel carrier that would take us to the port of Los Angeles and the U.S.S. General Randall, which would be our floating home for the next six weeks. The day before, we had completed the last of the exercises designed to test courage, determination and physical stamina. We had learned how to put on a gas mask in five seconds in a mustard gas-filled room. We had climbed up, over and down a twenty-foot tall wooden wall by means of a swaying rope ladder. We had warned each other, "Don't look down!"

There we stood, slightly apprehensive and physically tired from staying up most of the night before making last phone calls home, writing documents headed "Last Will and Testament" and promising each other that no matter where we were sent we would keep in touch forever.

Now we were ready to travel. The Red Cross girls wore official uniforms jacket and slacks and sturdy shoes. The Civil Service employees wore khaki shirts and pants and GI combat boots. Each of us wore an Army field jacket, pockets now stuffed with fruit, and carried a backpack loaded with gas mask, first-aid kit, emergency food rations, and a canteen full of water. We also carried medications for dysentery, malaria and other tropical ailments, as well as chemicals for purifying water. A shoulder musette bag held a collection of official documents, passports, medical histories and those articles of personal hygiene, religion or sentimentality we thought we could not live without. Altogether we had added about thirty pounds to our stripped-down weight.

Three enlisted men were assigned to accompany us in the carrier to the dock. The first girl in line stepped forward, placed one foot on the high step and tried valiantly to raise her backpack-burdened body into the truck. Impossible. After several tries, one of the soldiers got in the truck and tried pulling her up by her hands. No luck. She lost her balance and staggered to one side. Then the other two men tried boosting her by the rear end. This brought forth a yelp of pain because the day before we had received the last of our cholera shots. Nervous giggles broke out. The tension was broken when a dignified Red Cross supervisor said, "How are we going to help win the war if we can't even get in this damn truck?"

Finally one of the soldiers called the other two aside for a conference. We heard him as he announced his plan. "One of us will get in the carrier and grab the passenger by the jacket collar and pull up. The other two will stand on the ground and lift these ladies up by their elbows. *Do not boost 'em by the butt!"*

Despair fled as laughter restored our spirits and our energy. He continued, "Now girls, on the count of three, give it all you got. If you can get both feet on that first step you got it made! Ready? One . . . two . . . THREE!" Cheers arose as one by one we were launched upward into the truck.

Off-loading at the dock was quick and easy. The three soldiers stood on the ground at the rear of the carrier and steadied us as we jumped into their outstretched arms. Mission accomplished.

I had just stepped off the gangplank and onto the deck of the General Randall when I saw a police officer directing traffic and walking toward my car. He blew his whistle and beckoned for me to cross the highway. Instantly my hair turned gray, lines crept back on my face and my waistline stretched the elastic in my sweat pants. Horns honking behind me signaled the end of my journey into the past. "Okay, old girl," I muttered. "All aboard. All aboard for Wal-Mart."

Old Women

by

Barbara

Old women
wrap scarves around their necks
to hide their wrinkles,
and flatter their bosoms
with bold beads and brooches.
In dresses buttered with flowers
they billow over pictures of grandchildren
passed round and round like hors
  d'oeuvres
like jewels they plant on each hand
to occupy the spaces once held
and warmed by husbands.

Now twined around each other
arm in arm down the sidewalk,
defying the dark grave
with their colors and perfume,
old women.
Tending time more fragile than youth:
poinsettias in the snow.

Everybody Has a Snake Story

by

Kathleen Hoffman

Snakes. As the poet Ogden Nash said about fleas, Adam had 'em.

Here in a still rural part of Virginia, we have 'em, too.

Culpeper, Virginia, is a town of maybe 8,000 now. It's just over an hour from Washington, D.C., but it's in a county made up of farms and small villages, very country in a lot of ways. The inhabitants of the town, villages, and county vary from five-generation farm folk to city refugees. They have their differences, but one thing they all have in common is that they are apt to have to deal with snakes.

There is almost no one around here, in fact, who doesn't have a snake story. To stay here you have to learn to deal with the slithery things—in basements, under porches, sometimes in the kitchen or bedroom, in pickup trucks.

Pickup trucks? Yep. Even pickup trucks are not off-limits to snakes. Dewey Joe Hearl, who lives in Rapidan, shudders just a bit when he recounts his pickup truck story.

Now Rapidan is kind of a snake capital, because it is at the confluence of the Rapidan and Robinson rivers. It's damp, and rocky, and cozy for snakes because there are only two little roads that form its streets, no sidewalks, and almost no commercial buildings if you don't count the Rapidan Trading Post because of the uncertainty over whether it'll be open on a given day.

Dewey Joe says he doesn't really have a tremendous snake story, full of impact and terror but rather a "mini-series of snake stories."

One involves a reptile which insisted on bothering the nestlings in the Hearl back yard. Hearl and his family are fond of birds, and really didn't like watching growing families in nests or birdhouses suddenly disappear. After a number of appeals from his wife, Hearl snatched up the snake villain as it crossed the yard one afternoon. He flung it into the back of his pickup, rapidly started the motor and headed out before the snake could recover from the unexpected change of location.

The bird-killer was, after all, a black snake, and therefore theoretically harmless. Dewey Joe figured he was doing it a favor by hauling it away down the road. Put down somewhere away from its accustomed prey, maybe it might decide to go straight—if a snake can be said to do that—and change its diet to moles or something.

Not far from his driveway, though, the snake, an obvious ingrate, made its move. It eased gently up the back of the truck cab, coiled around to the window on the passenger side, dropped to the floor inside and whipped under the seat.

Dewey Joe had to take the seat out to get rid of his unwanted and uninvited rider. It wasn't easy, he says, "working around the seat, moving it back and forth, and all the time looking for the snake."

Another black snake turned up wrapped around the stair banister inside the Hearl's house, unnoticed by everyone until they were heading for bed. The creature had to be peeled from the railing before anyone would go to sleep.

While Hearl, who has country ways going back a few generations, ordinarily deals with reptile intruders by snatching them up by hand, this hasn't always been a good idea. Once, heading outside to feed the dogs at night, he found another snake, also black. "I was gonna take it in to scare the kids," he recalls, apparently still thinking that taking snakes lightly had merit. But the prop for this practical joke crossly refused to play its part. Instead it bit him smartly on the hand.

The victim can now attest that indeed, black snakes aren't poisonous. The hand was only sore, as if from a bee sting. "There are no giant anacondas in Rapidan," Hearl has concluded, and few really poisonous snakes. But there are plenty of snakes, enough to go around. Rapidan people also have lots of pickups, but they figure they could fill the beds of all of them with squirming reptiles and have some left over to lie in wait over doorways and along garden paths.

Our family has its own snake-and-pickup-truck tale. Our collie, Ben, generally a very silent dog, began a fierce barking in the basement one afternoon. When we went to check, we found a huge black snake literally cornered—it was sort of packed into a corner of the cinder block basement walls, clinging there while just below it the dog circled cautiously.

Our approach to snakes is that they're all right in their place, but not our basement. With a rake, we maneuvered it down, across the floor a few feet, and into a handy plastic garbage can. It was a full-size can, with one of those tops that fits tightly over a five or six-inch lip. We weren't the sorts to toss a snake into the bed of a pickup to await hauling away, so we not only put the lid on tightly but secured it with baling twine.

We went to get car keys and sunglasses to take the thing for a nice ride to freedom in some less inhabited place. Returning in perhaps two minutes, I noticed the lid looked a bit swollen on one side. A dread thought occurred. I checked it. There was maybe a half-inch clearance. I shook the can. Nothing. Our captive had split, having no problem scaling the three-foot interior and snaking his way out of a lip that did bend.

Hurriedly we checked the basement, and then reconnoitered the yard. Nothing. Never underestimate the resources of a scaley captive.

Bob Apperson, who retired recently after years of running things down at the Agricultural Stabilization and Conservation Service, harks back quite a few years to come up with his favorite, or non-favorite, snake story. Bob and his wife had gone down to Gloucester to do some serious fishing. To really hit the fish at their most cooperative, they had to get up really early when the tides were right.

When they turned on the light of their cabin bedroom, very early on that summer morning, a snake was revealed stretched across the headboard of their bed. "It wasn't ten inches from us," Bob recalls. Pretty frightening, huh? He said they weren't scared until they turned on the light.

Then there is a reptile report from Richardsville, another town on the river. When Bill and Virginia Trible were married, back 35 years ago, he wanted to come to the country. She considered herself a city girl, and set terms. She explained very firmly to Bill that if anything crawled, she would point to the corner or wherever it was, and say *There!* and hc was to get it out.

On a summer evening, the Tribles came home fairly late to find, inside their house, the uncomfortable feeling that something wasn't quite right. Virginia, who takes pride in leaving her kitchen in order, was shaken to find a cabinet door open, a salt and pepper set knocked awry, stacked pie plates separated, and even hanging utensils off their hooks.

Someone seemed to have been looking for something. By the time he, or they, had gotten to the sink, violence had set in. Two glass shelves over the sink had flowers and decorations swept off into the sink. Things were broken, and the Tribles were upset and more than a bit frightened. "I said, 'Something's in this house,' " Virginia recalls.

There were four decorative copper molds on the wall. Lying across all four molds, and then doubled back again, was the Richardsville version of a giant anaconda.

"I started screaming and running," Mrs. Trible admits, with Bill running after her, still not having seen the addition to the wall decor. Eventually she stopped, caught her breath, and called into force the longstanding agreement. Bill dutifully gathered the intruder up with fireplace tongs and took it outside.

Another inside snake story comes from down at Reva, where a daughter home alone after school was beginning her homework in the living room. A small, dry noise, like grass being parted, suddenly alerted her. She looked up to see what some friends had once declared to be a "black racer" slipping quietly along the living room carpet. As she watched in dreadful fascination, it proceeded to the corner fireplace and went up it; the tip of its tail receded from view and there she was with a snake up the chimney.

There seemed nothing to do but wait for it to come down, so she did, but it didn't. When they came home, her parents noted that there was rat wire over the top of the chimney, installed to keep the starlings from nesting inside, so the snake had to come down. It didn't. They waited for it to show up, presumably first peering into the living room with its little snakey eye, but it didn't. They then waited for the smell of dead snake, but there was none. Either it's still there, having lifted the rat wire and found contentment living on starlings, or it exited the bottom when no one was watching—in which case its current residence may be under a bed.

Then, there's John Russell Aylor's snake story. John Russell grew up on a farm partly in Culpeper and partly in Madison, down around Crooked Run. Once, in his youth (he's retired now), he came in kind of tired from planting corn, or maybe, as he recalls it, just a bit tired from being out kind of late the night before.

At any rate, some of his aunts and their children were visiting. A planned, big, midday dinner wasn't quite ready, so he figured he'd take advantage of the time. Contentedly, he lay down on the big front porch that stretched across the front of the farm house, and dozed off in the sun. It beat the corn-planting.

One arm was lying back, under his head, and presently he felt something tug on it. Aha, he thought, it was the most mischievous of his young cousins, disturbing his well-earned snooze. His plan, drawn up on the spot, was to pretend slumber, and then turn on the child and give him a good scare.

Another tug came, and he put his plot into action, whirling rapidly on his tormenter. What he saw, as he swung around toward the still-lax hand, was a snake with his little finger in its mouth, already up past the second joint.

"My mother said I was white as a sheet," says Aylor, many decades later. Still, not even the skin on his finger was broken in the attempt of the reptile to digest it.

The family also had a lattice-work porch on the house, and snakes seemed undeniably attracted by it. They were as common around the Aylor house as chickens—in fact, Aylor recalls, they once had a memorable incident in which a larger snake tried to swallow a full-grown hen. The hen was rescued, not alwavs the case, as in another of Dewey Joe Hearl's mini-series.

Yep, everybody has a snake story, but you have to take some of them on faith. At least one of the above narratives came from somebody considered by a co-worker to be less than reliable. It seems the storyteller once had the co-worker convinced that if you shot the lead goose in a flock and it fell down your chimney, all the rest of the geese would follow it down.

But that's another kind of animal story.

The Leap

by

Louise Erdrich

My mother is the surviving half of a blindfold trapeze act, not a fact I think about much even now that she is sightless, the result of encroaching and stubborn cataracts. She walks slowly through her house here in New Hampshire, lightly touching her way along walls and running her hands over knickknacks, books, the drift of a grown child's belongings and castoffs. She has never upset an object or as much as brushed a magazine onto the floor. She has never lost her balance or bumped into a closet door left carelessly open.

It has occurred to me that the catlike precision of her movements in old age might be the result of her early training, but she shows so little of the drama or flair one might expect from a performer that I tend to forget the Flying Avalons. She has kept no sequined costume, no photographs, no fliers or posters from that part of her youth. I would, in fact, tend to think that all memory of double somersaults and heart-stopping catches had left her arms and legs were it not for the fact that sometimes, as I sit sewing in the room of the rebuilt house in which I slept as a child, I hear the crackle, catch a whiff of smoke from the stove downstairs, and suddenly the room goes dark, the stitches burn beneath my fingers, and I am sewing with a needle of hot silver, a thread of fire.

I owe her my existence three times. The first was when she saved herself. In the town square a replica tent pole, cracked and splintered, now stands cast in concrete. It commemorates the disaster that put our town smack on the front page of the Boston and New York tabloids. It is from those old newspapers, now historical records, that I get my information. Not from my mother, Anna of the Flying Avalons, nor from any of her in-laws, nor certainly from the other half of her particular act, Harold Avalon, her first husband. In one news account it says, "The day was mildly overcast, but nothing in the air or temperature gave any hint of the sudden force with which the deadly gale would strike."

I have lived in the West, where you can see the weather coming for miles, and it is true that out here we are at something of a disadvantage. When extremes of temperature collide, a hot and cold front, winds generate instantaneously behind a hill and crash upon you without warning. That, I think, was the likely situation on that day in June. People probably commented on the pleasant air, grateful that no hot sun beat upon the striped tent that stretched over the entire center green. They bought their tickets and surrendered them in anticipation. They sat. They ate caramelized pop-corn and roasted peanuts. There was time, before the storm, for three acts. The White Arabians of Ali-Khazar rose on their hind legs and waltzed. The Mysterious Bernie folded himself into a painted cracker tin, and the Lady of the Mists made herself appear and disappear in surprising places. As the clouds gathered outside, unnoticed, the ringmaster cracked his whip, shouted his introduction, and pointed to the ceiling of the tent, where the Flying Avalons were perched.

They loved to drop gracefully from nowhere, like two sparkling birds, and blow kisses as they threw off their plumed helmets and high-collared capes. They laughed and flirted openly as they beat their way up again on the trapeze bars. In the final vignette of their act, they actually would kiss in midair, pausing, almost hovering as they swooped past one another. On the ground, between bows, Harry Avalon would skip quickly to the front rows and point out the smear of my mother's lipstick, just off the edge of his mouth. They made a romantic pair all right, especially in the blindfold sequence.

That afternoon, as the anticipation increased, as Mr. and Mrs. Avalon tied sparkling strips of cloth onto each other's face and as they puckered their lips in mock kisses, lips destined "never again to meet," as one long breathless article put it, the wind rose, miles off, wrapped itself into a cone, and howled. There came a rumble of electrical energy, drowned out by the sudden roll of drums. One detail not mentioned by the press, perhaps unknown Anna was pregnant at the time, seven months and hardly showing, her stomach muscles were that strong. It seems incredible that she would work high above the ground when any fall could be so dangerous, but the explanation I know from watching her go blind is that my mother lives comfortably in extreme elements. She is one with the constant dark now, just as the air was her home, familiar to her, safe, before the storm that afternoon.

From opposite ends of the tent they waved, blind and smiling, to the crowd below. The ring-master removed his hat and called for silence, so that the two above could concentrate. They rubbed their hands in chalky powder, then Harry launched himself and swung, once, twice, in huge calibrated beats across space. He hung from his knees and on the third swing stretched wide his arms, held his hands out to receive his pregnant wife as she dove from her shining bar.

It was while the two were in midair, their hands about to meet, that lightning struck the main pole and sizzled down the guy wires, filling the air with a blue radiance that Harry Avalon must certainly have seen through the cloth of his blind-fold as the tent buckled and the edifice toppled him forward, the swing continuing and not re-turning in its sweep, and Harry going down, down into the crowd with his last thought, perhaps, just a prickle of surprise at his empty hands.

My mother once said that I'd be amazed at how many things a person can do within the act of falling. Perhaps, at the time, she was teaching me to dive off a board at the town pool, for I associate the idea with midair somersaults. But I also think she meant that even in that awful doomed second one could think, for she certainly did. When her hands did not meet her husband's, my mother tore her blindfold away. As he swept past her on the wrong side, she could have grasped his ankle, the toe-end of his tights, and gone down clutching him. Instead, she changed direction. Her body twisted toward a heavy wire and she managed to hang on to the braided metal, still hot from the lightning strike. Her palms were burned so terribly that once healed they bore no lines, only the blank scar tissue of a quieter future. She was lowered, gently, to the sawdust ring just underneath the dome of the canvas roof, which did not entirely settle but was held up on one end and jabbed through, torn, and still on fire in places from the giant spark, though rain and men's jackets soon put that out.

Three people died, but except for her hands my mother was not seriously harmed until an overeager rescuer broke her arm in extricating her and also, in the process, collapsed a portion of the tent bearing a huge buckle that knocked her unconscious. She was taken to the town hospital, and there she must have hemorrhaged, for they kept her, confined to her bed, a month and a half before her baby was born without life.

Harry Avalon had wanted to be buried in the circus cemetery next to the original Avalon, his uncle, so she sent him back with his brothers. The child, however, is buried around the corner, beyond this house and just down the highway. Sometimes I used to walk there just to sit. She was a girl, but I rarely thought of her as a sister or even as a separate person really. I suppose you could call it the egocentrism of a child, of all young children, but I considered her a less finished version of myself.

When the snow falls, throwing shadows among the stones, I can easily pick hers out from the road, for it is bigger than the others and in the shape of a lamb at rest, its legs curled beneath. The carved lamb looms larger as the years pass, though it is probably only my eyes, the vision shifting, as what is close to me blurs and distances sharpen. In odd moments, I think it is the edge drawing near, the edge of everything, the unseen horizon we do not really speak of in the eastern woods. And it also seems to me, although this is probably an ideal fantasy, that the statue is growing more sharply etched, as if, instead of weathering itself into a porous mass, it is hardening on the hillside with each snowfall, perfecting itself.

It was during her confinement in the hospital that my mother met my father. He was called in to look at the set of her arm, which was complicated. He stayed, sitting at her bedside, for he was something of an armchair traveler and had spent his war quietly, at an air force training grounds, where he became a specialist in arms and legs broken during parachute training exercises. Anna

Avalon had been to many of the places he longed to visit: Venice, Rome, Mexico, all through France and Spain. She had no family of her own and was taken in by the Avalons, trained to perform from a very young age. They toured Europe before the war, then based themselves in New York. She was illiterate.

It was in the hospital that she finally learned to read and write, as a way of overcoming the boredom and depression of those weeks, and it was my father who insisted on teaching her. In return for stories of her adventures, he graded her first exercises. He bought her her first book, and over her bold letters, which the pale guides of the penmanship pads could not contain, they fell in love.

I wonder if my father calculated the exchange he offered: one form of flight for another. For after that, and for as long as I can remember, my mother has never been without a book. Until now, that is, and it remains the greatest difficulty of her blindness. Since my father's recent death, there is no one to read to her, which is why I returned, in fact, from my failed life where the land is flat. I came home to read to my mother, to read out loud, to read long into the dark if I must, to read all night.

Once my father and mother married, they moved onto the old farm he had inherited but didn't care much for. Though he'd been thinking of moving to a larger city, he settled down and broadened his practice in this valley. It still seems odd to me, when they could have gone anywhere else, that they chose to stay in the town where the disaster had occurred, and which my father in the first place had found so constricting. It was my mother who insisted upon it, after her child did not survive. And then, too, she loved the sagging farmhouse with its scrap of what was left of a vast acreage of woods and hidden hay fields that stretched to the game park.

I owe my existence, the second time then, to the two of them and the hospital that brought them together. That is the debt we take for granted since none of us asks for life. It is only once we have it that we hang on so dearly.

I was seven the year the house caught fire, probably from standing ash. It can rekindle, and my father, forgetful around the house and perpetually exhausted from night hours on call, often emptied what he thought were ashes from cold stoves into wooden or cardboard containers. The fire could have started from a flaming box, or perhaps a buildup of creosote inside the chimney was the culprit. It started right around the stove, and the heart of the house was gutted. The baby-sitter, fallen asleep in my father's den on the first floor, woke to find the stairway to my upstairs room cut off by flames. She used the phone, then ran outside to stand beneath my window.

When my parents arrived, the town volunteers had drawn water from the fire pond and were spraying the outside of the house, preparing to go inside after me, not knowing at the time that there was only one staircase and that it was lost. On the other side of the house, the superannuated extension ladder broke in half. Perhaps the clatter of it falling against the walls woke me, for I'd been asleep up to that point.

As soon as I awakened, in the small room that I now use for sewing, I smelled the smoke. I followed things by the letter then, was good at memorizing instructions, and so I did exactly what was taught in the second-grade home fire drill. I got up, I touched the back of my door before opening it. Finding it hot, I left it closed and stuffed my rolled-up rug beneath the crack. I did not hide under my bed or crawl into my closet. I put on my flannel robe, and then I sat down to wait.

Outside, my mother stood below my dark window and saw clearly that there was no rescue. Flames had pierced one side wall, and the glare of the fire lighted the massive limbs and trunk of the vigorous old elm that had probably been planted the year the house was built, a hundred years ago at least. No leaf touched the wall, and just one thin branch scraped the roof. From below, it looked as though even a squirrel would have had trouble jumping from the tree onto the house, for the breadth of that small branch was no bigger than my mother's wrist.

Standing there, beside Father, who was preparing to rush back around to the front of the house, my mother asked him to unzip her dress. When he wouldn't be bothered, she made him understand. He couldn't make his hands work, so she finally tore if off and stood there in her pearls and stockings. She directed one of the men to lean the broken half of the extension ladder up against the trunk of the tree. In surprise, he complied. She ascended. She vanished. Then she could be seen among the leafless branches of late November as she made her way up and, along her stomach, inched the length of a bough that curved above the branch that brushed the roof.

Once there, swaying, she stood and balanced. There were plenty of people in the crowd and many who still remember, or think they do, my mother's leap through the ice-dark air toward that thinnest extension, and how she broke the branch falling so that it cracked in her hands, cracked louder than the flames as she vaulted with it toward the edge of the roof and how it hurtled down end over end without her, and their eyes went up, again, to see where she had flown.

I didn't see her leap through air, only heard the sudden thump and looked out my window. She was hanging by the backs of her heels from the new gutter we had put in that year, and she was smiling. I was not surprised to see her, she was so matter-of-fact. She tapped on the window. I remember how she did it, too. It was the friendliest tap, a bit tentative, as if she was afraid she had arrived too early at a friend's house. Then she gestured at the latch, and when I opened the window she told me to raise it wider and prop it up with the stick so it wouldn't crush her fingers. She swung down, caught the ledge, and crawled through the opening. Once she was in my room, I realized she had on only underclothing, a bra of the heavy stitched cotton women used to wear and step-in, lace-trimmed drawers. I remember feeling light-headed, of course, terribly relieved, and then embarrassed for her to be seen by the crowd undressed.

I was still embarrassed as we flew out the window, toward earth, me in her lap, her toes pointed as we skimmed toward the painted target of the fire fighter's net.

I know that she's right. I knew it even then. As you fall there is time to think. Curled as I was, against her stomach, I was not startled by the cries of the crowd or the looming faces. The wind roared and beat its hot breath at our back, the flames whistled. I slowly wondered what would happen if we missed the circle or bounced out of it. Then I wrapped my hands around my mother's hands. I felt the brush of her lips and heard the beat of her heart in my ears, loud as thunder, long as the roll of drums.

The Pontiac Years

by

Paul Estaver

It would not be quite true to say that Luke drove his father's 1931 Pontiac. He *almost* drove it in 1935 when, on his eleventh birthday, he sat at the wheel while his father was doing business at the optical factory. Luke started the engine and inadvertently drove fifteen feet in a wavering line to a large rock that blocked the front wheel and brought the Pontiac to a halt.

Unfortunately for Luke, his mother had been dozing in the passenger seat at the time of this event. It was a bad awakening. She had never mastered the art of driving and was inclined to catch her breath and grip the dashboard in times of crisis even when Luke's father was at the wheel. This time she said, in a terrible voice, "Luke, I don't want to have to speak to you about that again!"

Another black mark was entered onto Luke's record.

When his father emerged from the factory, his first response to Luke's mother's complaint was to investigate the damage to the front of the car.

"Well, it didn't hurt the rock," he said straightening up.

"That is not amusing, Lawrence," said his mother, "under these circumstances. What about the car?"

"I think," his father said, "the bumper has a small mark on the bottom."

"Well, thank heaven it isn't worse," Mother offered as she looked over at the back seat where Luke was in custody. "Consider yourself lucky," she told Luke.

Luke tried to consider himself lucky.

His father started the engine, backed off the rock and drove toward the cottage they had rented.

"What if we had been parked by a lake?" his mother, angry at his father, asked. "Or a highway? What if the baby had been with us?" The baby, Hannie, had been left with a sitter. This was to have been Luke's day once his father's business was done.

"What you have to do," his father said to the back seat, "is be sure the gear shift is in neutral—"

I know that, Luke thought.

"—and then," his father continued, "keep your foot on the clutch just in case."

Luke would remember that for the rest of his life.

The actual start of Luke's driving career was in his father's 1936 Pontiac. They bought it at Healer Motors in Watertown where his father had gotten the 1931 Pontiac. Healer was an Oldsmobile-Pontiac dealer, which was still permitted in those days when the General Motors divisions were less competitive. Mr. Healer's name was actually a translation from something Armenian. His garage was antiseptic. The shop foreman wore a white coat like a doctor, except that it had small Pontiac and Oldsmobile emblems sewn over the pocket.

The fact that Luke's father patronized this particular automobile dealer elevated it to a special class beyond other car places. The principle applied to everything where his father was concerned. If he smoked an aromatic tobacco in a large pipe, those choices were established as the single best way to smoke. If Luke in his twenties found that a heavy pipe made his jaw ache and that aromatic tobacco burned his tongue, then the fault lay with himself for being insufficiently tough and strong about the mouth. It wasn't until he grew to his fifties that he understood that he had elevated his father in this way. Unlike his mother, his father never defined anything. He just did what he did, and it all blended together in Luke's mind, the biography of the man in dimensions that were infinite.

His mother was nothing if not finite. Her life and her beliefs were there like boxes of assorted fruit, like pieces of furniture with shelves and drawers and labels and directions for assembly and dismantling, and the management of one's life from sex to the clipping of toenails.

Sometimes when his mother was giving unnecessary instructions, his father would say, "For Heaven's sake, Clara, leave the boy alone."

Luke hadn't been permitted to wear trousers until he was twelve. Young boys wore shorts in summer and corduroy knickers the rest of the year. Junior-size wool suits for Sunday School came with knickers. When he had finally been given a pair of long pants, his mother took a picture of him wearing them. He was holding a shovela spadein the picture by the front porch of the house on Pleasant Street as though he had been digging a hole. He had no memory of digging a hole for anything. What he remembered was his mother telling him to pull his pants up when he sat down so they wouldn't get baggy at the knees, and his father saying, "For Heaven's sake, Clara, give the boy a little peace. He can't even sit comfortably unless he pulls his pants up at the knees."

Luke's mother didn't say anything, but she hated it when his father disagreed with her over Luke's upbringing when he was in the room. She always tried to discuss him in private so there would be a united front. *Against me,* Luke thought, *like the British and the French against the Germans.*

But on the occasion of the long pants, Luke was trying to decide whether it was really true that you can't sit down in them comfortably without pulling them up and thinking that he would try it later to see. And whether it was true or whether it was what his father had said, Luke never sat down again without pulling his pants up at the knees.

Sometimes he even caught himself trying to do it when he sat down in shorts. It was that automatic.

In the earlier years, Luke's father had been on the road a lot. The times they had alone together were so precious that Luke tried not to think about them, the way you wouldn't risk bad luck by speaklng of good luck without touching wood. But what do you touch when you only think good luck?

They bought the 1936 Pontiac together. Its color was very much like fresh cow manure. The salesman actually gave his father a hundred dollars off for taking that color. The other choice would have been to buy one of the unsold 1935 models that also had the silver streak down the center of the hood. But the shape of the hood itself was reminiscent of the Whippet, and Luke and his father couldn't bear that.

His father said, "Did you ever think of how many choices you make in life, not because you especially liked what you picked, but because you couldn't bear the alternative?"

Luke hadn't thought about it much. "Like going to school?" he said.

"Well, not quite," his father said. "Maybe when you start voting and looking for jobs and dating girls and buying cars of your own, you'll see." This was before they had taken the new Pontiac for inspection by his mother. They were driving around in it, putting off going home.

Partly joking, being a little fresh, thinking the

occasion was so sweet that he wouldn't get taken down for his audacity, Luke said, "When do I get to drive?"

His father thought for a long time, looking at him, measuring his legs and arms by eye. "Okay," he said finally.

Luke couldn't believe it. "Okay what?" he said.

They were coming up the hill to Newton Centre, but his father kept going past Pleasant Street, across Beacon Street and into the Baptist Church parking lot. It was eleven o'clock on a Saturday morning. Only one other car was there. His father stopped the Pontiac in the middle with plenty of space around it.

"When they're doing the final reports," he told Luke, "I want you to tell them I let you drive my car the same day I bought it."

By the time they bought the place in Center Harbor in 1938, Luke seldom had his father to himself because Hannie always tagged along. Hannie was now four, captivating and obdurate. In a world of powerful people, the only way to establish her identity was by refusing to do as she was asked.

They were getting ready for the fall pilgrimage to New Hampshire to check out any damage that the late season tenants might have done and to close up the cottage for the winter. Mother would stay home to teach. Hannie had her heart set on the trip.

Luke had difficulty sympathizing with his sister's needs. The plain fact was that Hannie got away with behavior for which Luke would have been keel-hauled.

"It's the tragedy of first sons, old man," his father said. "You drive your parents like a dog team through the frozen wastes of child rearing, then some kid comes along and slips into your tracks as though the snow weren't there and never knows enough to thank you. It'll make you a more tolerant father some day."

Luke grunted. He asked, "Couldn't we leave Hannie home this once?"

His father answered, "She just wants to be included, Luke. Are you hearing me? If she gets left, there's two of us doing the leaving. Her father and her big brother . . ."

Luke said, "Hah!"

But his father finished, ". . . whom she loves."

Luke argued, "You sound like Mother."

But then Father took Mother's side, "My son, your mother is not invariably wrong."

Irony and self-deprecation were his father's quiet games—catching Luke, catching himself, with motives exposed. Luke savored that line—"your mother is not invariably wrong"—again and again, first, for its recognition of Luke's battles with her, second, for his father's own struggles with her, but third, for his complicity with Luke in mocking her when indeed she was the most devoted mother and wife either of them had ever seen. All these shadings had been caught in their complexity and subtlety in father's one wry phrase.

Of course Hannie went with them to New Hampshire and was a perfect pain in the butt. In 1938 the journey from Newton Centre to Center Harbor was an all-day odyssey. It took three hours to Portsmouth up through Boston congestion and the narrow Newburyport Turnpike with its treacherous hills, then two more hours of country roads to the lowest end of Lake Winnipesaukee at Alton Bay, and nearly another two finally to Center Harbor, driving for most of the trip from town to town, battling local traffic the whole way.

It was the fourth weekend in October, when New England was in its Indian Summer. The peak of the fall foliage color had passed, leaving a sparse dusting of yellow against the black trunks and branches of the trees and, on the ground, a blanket of russet with flashes of yellow. In New Hampshire especially, the air was smoky and warm, its natural autumn haze spiced with the burning leaves in the towns.

But these were delights for grown-ups. To a four-year-old child, any journey over half an hour was confining. Hannie crawled from front seat to back, refused to sit down properly because she couldn't see out, wriggled in Luke's lap until banished, and demanded stops to tinkle every thirty minutes.

They played the cow game, Luke against his father and Hannie, for as long as they could stand it. You got one point for every cow you could count on your side of the road. A man with a beard was worth twenty-five cows. A grindstone, worth fifty. A tandem bike was a hundred. If you passed a graveyard, you lost all your cows. The games always entailed outrageous cheating, cries of foul, appeals to the referee. On this trip, his father was both referee and combatant. Luke lost with poor grace and was shamed into a reluctant apology.

Once they crossed the New Hampshire line, Luke took the wheel and Hannie fell asleep in her father's lap. Until now, Luke's driving had been limited to remote back roads without serious competition, but this was Route 1 and traffic was heavy on a Saturday afternoon. He probably could have done it without coaching, but it was a comfort to have the calm voice at his right offering occasional observations. This was partly because the insights were useful, but far more because he loved having his father talk to him about anything at all.

"Coming up is Hampton Falls. Not much here except the Exeter road to your left. Take one good look . . . that's it . . . keep an eye on that truck . . . always assume the other guy is incapable of rational thought . . . When you follow in line, leave some space. The faster you go, the more you need. Always be looking for escape routes in case disaster comes . . . Okay, this old biddy is never going more than twenty-five. It's time you learned to pass. Can you see ahead? All clear? Okay, go! Get it done quickly. You've got about twelve seconds to get back into line . . . good . . . good . . . Can you see her in your mirror yet? Both headlights? Okay, get back in . . . Wonderful feeling, isn't it? Not that many firsts in a lifetime . . . I love these old haycocks in the marshes . . . Okay, now, slow down a little. Hampton coming. In little towns like this, everyone thinks they own the road, and they hate cars with Massachusetts plates. It would be preferable if you didn't get your first ticket before your fifteenth birthday . . . easy . . . easy . . . try to drive as though you were transporting nitroglycerin."

By the time they reached Rochester, Luke was starving. It was closer to two than one.

"Could we stop for a sandwich?" he said. "Maybe I could bring some out so Hannie can stay asleep."

"I'm hungry, too," said Hannie, instantly awake.

If they'd stopped in Dover there'd have been the diner, but the only visible restaurant in Rochester was a proper place with tablecloths and upholstered chairs and matronly waitresses. Eating here would be serious business.

Luke said, "Okay, Hannie, you've got to behave yourself in this place."

"Mistake number one," his father said.

"I want a hot dog," Hannie ordered.

"This is a decent restaurant, Dad," Luke said. To Hannie he said, "If you start making a scene in here, I'll personally wring your neck."

His father stopped them at the door. "If you play mother to this girl, you will grow breasts," he said quietly, "and Hannie will be four years old for the rest of her life." To Hannie, he said, "Come on, sweetheart. Let's find you that hot dog." He grabbed Hannie's hand and left Luke to follow them to a table.

The restaurant had neither hot dogs nor hamburgers. They settled on a toasted cheese sandwich for Hannie and chicken and dumplings for Luke and his father. "Why don't you bring some milk and crackers real soon," his father said to the waitress. "The little ones don't cope well at a table with nothing to do."

The waitress hurried away smiling. She thought Hannie was a darling. Hannie was turned backward in her chair staring at a group of women two tables away. His father caught Luke's eye.

"This is an order," he said. "Leave your sister's behavior to me."

Luke closed his eyes and sat with his hands in his lap. He could feel Hannie's vibrations in his stomach. He opened his eyes. Hannie had climbed down from her chair and was about to disappear under the table. Luke rolled his eyes.

"Hannie," said his father.

"What?" Hannie said. She was out of sight under the white tablecloth.

"Where did you put your hat?" his father continued.

Hannie reappeared. "What hat?"

"The one you were wearing in the car," he said.

"Daddy! I didn't have a hat." She dived below the surface again. Luke snorted through his nose, avoiding his father's look.

"Hannie," his father said.

"What?" She spoke from below, as before.

"Where did you put your hat?" he asked.

Hannie surfaced, made a fist and punched her father in the stomach. Luke stifled a gasp. He could feel his father's eyes upon him.

Then Hannie submerged again. The water in the drinking glasses shivered from the impact. His father spoke swiftly to Luke, and not kindly. "Would you please absent yourself from this table. Five minutes. I'm serious, Luke. Go. Now."

It was better than being banished to the car, but not much. The crack about growing breasts still burned. What Hannie needed was a good spanking. Luke had been spanked for much less. Now Luke was trying to goad his father into firmer justice and who got the blame? Luke, that's who. He considered staying in the men's room so long his father would have to come after him, but he was hungry. His chicken and dumplings were probably out there getting cold this minute.

There was a knock at the door. Hannie. "He says you can come out now."

When the trip resumed, his father took the wheel. Luke exiled himself to the back seat.

"It's your own choice," his father said.

First he tried to sleep, but he was afraid he'd miss the first sight of the water when they came down the hill to Alton Bay. Then he slept anyhow until they were climbing the heights above The Weirs, hallway up the lake as they headed for Meredith and Center Harbor.

The coming awake that afternoon in the woolly

back seat of a 1936 Pontiac was a moment of such aching beauty that it was fixed forever in Luke's heart and senses:

His father had tossed his sweater in the back seat. Luke's cheek still showed the imprint of the weave where he had used it as a pillow. But now his father's arm was bared, his shirt-sleeve rolled midway from elbow to shoulder, a feathering of fine hair alive in the wind, the skin more ruddy than tanned, faintly freckled.

Luke fixed his consciousness on his father's arm as though it were the only thing left in the universe, as though his sister had ceased to exist, as though Luke's own substance had dissolved, and everything around him had evaporated except that arm.

Below and behind them Lake Winnipesaukee stretched to the eye's limit, beaded with islands that seemed to float on the water's surface. But it was more than lake happiness that welled up. There were, too, the sensations of road motion bowing long tones against the chords of his back and buttocks as though he were a cello, the song of the engine itself in its pipe, the tires singing to the asphalt, the last warmth of the hazy afternoon air spilling in through the Pontiac's open window.

Tale Spinner

by

D. W. Wright

When I was a lad and lived by the sea
A seafarer's widow was a friend to me.
She knotted gray ropes and wove a fine
  basket
And spun me tall tales whenever I'd
  ask it.

Her frail knobby fingers slipped over
  the string
Fashioning lanyards and seafaring things;
She told of fierce storms and foundering
  ships,
Shaping my life with her papery lips.

When I became man and turned to the
  sea
I traveled that world she created for me.
Now I etch my scrimshaw and weave a
  fine basket,
Tell tales to my grandsons whenever they
  ask it.

Sweet Revenge

by

Lisa Fisher

"Come on, Benjamin, name all of Humphrey Bogart's movies. Come on. *Teasure of Sierra Madre, The African Queen, The Maltese Falcon.* Benjamin? *Benjamin!* Are you paying attention?"

Benjamin tried to drown out his father's voice. He pressed his forehead against the icy window and cupped his hands to the sides of his face. The smell of leather filled the back seat of the Mercedes. His breath made Rorshach patterns on the glass. This he found more amusing than the sight of his father's latest girlfriend, who was running to the car and hailing them with bright red enameled nails glistening in arctic sunlight. Benjamin leaned over, reaching for something under his down jacket.

"Just thinking about last night's Bulls game," he said, as he watched his father fix his hair in the rear view mirror.

Benjamin might have chosen to please his father as he had always done before, but today would be different.

For twelve and a half years he had been the star of a crazy dog and pony show, written and directed by his father. Oh but lots of parents take pride in the little feats their children perform: those first wobbly steps, those melodic sounds we force into "Da Da."

Dr. Feingold beamed every time Benjamin jumped through the hoops. Benjamin was an exceptional child. At the age of two, he was reading street signs and at three, *The Wall Street Journal.*

"Benjamin, tell Grandma who the presidents were, starting with George Washington," Dr. Feingold requested when Benjamin was about to blow out the candles on his fifth birthday.

But this day Benjamin had other things on his mind. "So, Dad, did ya know that Mom went out with Deidre Fox's dad last night?" he asked.

"Good to hear it," his father said. "'Your mother needs to get out more."

Benjamin went on. "Mom lost thirty-five pounds. She looks awesome, you should see her."

"Great, great, Benjamin," his dad said. "Please reach over and grab my Tic Tacs, I think they're back there somewhere."

"Here." Benjamin passed the little plastic container. "Where are we going today?"

"Haven't decided yet," his father confessed. "Let's see where Sue wants to go."

"I promised Mom I'd go out to eat dinner with her and Grandma, just as long as we get back in time," Benjamin announced.

"You're awfully jumpy today," his father observed. "Sue's really excited about meeting you. I've told her all about you, how much of a Humphrey Bogart nut you are. See, you guys have something in common right off the bat, isn't that neat?"

Benjamin sighed. "I'm fine Dad. I like most of your girlfriends." Every month, a new girl friend for Dr. Feingold. And before each ritual outing, Benjamin was asked to brush up on a new topic.

Three months ago, it was Dolly, who worked as a lab technician. Her interest was ballet. (A lot of good it did her.) The interest led to a reckless obsession with dieting. You could almost picture her doing pirouettes right into the emergency room at the hospital, where she was being treated for malnutrition. "Anorexia Nervosa," Dr. Feingold had said.

"Isn't it considered unethical to date your patients, Dad?" Benjamin wished he had the nerve to ask.

Dolly was cured by the attention of Dr. Feingold and son, who had offered a trip to the zoo and hot fudge sundaes, as soon as she was fully recovered.

Meanwhile, Benjamin had been prepared. "Benjamin! Nijinsky, Fonteyn, Nureyev, Pavlova? Who were they? Quick. Quick. Quick."

They had strolled around the zoo together, Dolly ruffing up Benjamin's hair, tilting her head, and coming up so close to his face that he could see all of the little blemishes and smell the make-up that tried to conceal them.

"Benjamin! First position-second position-third-fourth-fifth. Now don't forget the arms! *Arabesque.*"

"Yuck!" he said under his breath, as he stood with his back to the giraffes, positioning himself in awkward postures to please the girl of the day.

Dolly was impressed. After going to the zoo, the aquarium and out for hot fudge sundaes, she rested her head on Dr. Feingold's shoulder and played with his earlobe as they drove home. Benjamin sat in the back seat, staring out the window and wondering if she was really cured. After all, he had heard about those anorexia patients. She might be one of those who would go straight to the bathroom to stick her finger down her throat after an ice cream binge.

At the beginning of the month, there was a new one: Mary, the waitress-psychology student with an outside interest in Punk Rock (especially that old timer, Lou Reed). Benjamin got a wink of approval when he reminded his father not to forget the Velvet Underground tape for the drive to the shore.

Mary told Benjamin she wanted to change her name to "Lumen" (whatever that meant). She talked about auras and crystals in one breath and then turned around and asked Benjamin if he wanted to see her knife collection. "I gotta Frog Sticker, that would blow you away, Bobby," she said.

"Benjamin," he corrected her.

"Hey son, do you think my girl here leads a secret life?" the doctor asked as he admired himself in the rear view mirror. "What's a nice girl like you need knives for?"

"'Yeah," Benjamin teased, "she must be a terrorist. I bet she has plastic explosives in her basement. Maybe we should call her Molly Kadafi, Dad."

Dads's girl turned around and forced a phony laugh that sounded something like a cross between a machine gun and a sea lion. "I don't get it, Doc," she said, cracking her grape gum and blowing out a big purple-veined bubble about half the size of her head.

"Kadafi? You know who Kadafi is, right?"

"Yeah," she answered, "yeah—the Italian guy—the designer, right?"

Today was going to be different. Benjamin patted the newly purchased boa constrictor under his ski jacket, which was scrunched up in a ball in the back seat of his father's car. The exhaust billowed up into clouds around his window as the engine idled. He wondered if snakes tucked under down ski jackets could suffocate in a closed Mercedes with the heat blasting. They were waiting in the driveway, as Sue, the latest, approached with those inch-long fingernails.

His thoughts drifted back to a party his father had given two weeks ago. A sardonic grin of satisfaction crept across his face. He bit down on his lower lip to hold back the expression.

Two weeks ago, Sue had been a guest at Dr. Feingold's party. Benjamin stared. Where had he seen that face? At one point, he got up from his favorite chair to go to the kitchen for ice. When he returned, the woman had taken his seat and was acting as if she owned the place. On the table next to her was a bowl of spinach dip, some raw broccoli, radishes, celery, carrots and a wooden oval-shaped plate with an assortment of crackers. Also displayed on that very table were the rare treasures that he had found on a trip to Sannibel Island with his mother and father two years ago . . . before the divorce. They were sand dollars and Benjamin had arranged them into three rows of three. He stood behind the end table, watching the way Sue would dip her vegetables into the spinach dip, pop them into her mouth and then wipe her fingers on the beige leather chair. He wondered if anyone else had noticed this annoying little habit of hers. He also continued to wonder why she looked so familiar.

Sue reached over and daintily picked up one of the sand dollars. Benjamin was on the verge of stopping her. They were quite fragile, and, if she dropped it on the marble tile, it would be the end of his prized possession. She studied the large round wafer carefully. Had no one else been in the room, she might have sniffed it first. But she did something else instead. She scooped it into the dip, and before Benjamin could say a word, he suddenly remembered her face from his mother's lawyer's office. At that point it did not matter whether she ate his precious sand dollar or not. Watching her choke and spit as she asked, "Eeew! What was that?" was worth it.

Sue—Sue Shiller, the secretary of the lawyer that robbed his mother of a happy life. Sue, who had interrupted his parents' divorce. A divorce that may have been reconciled, with a good therapist and a not-so-anxious attorney. Dr. Feingold was taken by that twenty-one year old secretary, Sue Shiller. Batting fake eyelashes, talking about her favorite actor, Humphrey Bogart (whom she claimed once had asked her mother out in L.A.), shown-a-cleavage-at-all-time-Sue, who hoped to go back to school to become a para-legal. Sue, who really didn't have any interest beyond nail polish and shopping malls, but who had one terrible phobia . . .

Benjamin smiled as Sue opened up the car door. He smiled at his father. Yes, Dr. Feingold, today would be the performance to end all performances.

Dad's Wrench

by

Bruce Wick

The wind was blowing pretty hard, but the canoe was making good time on its way downstream. It had been rainy that spring, and the water was high. The eighteen foot white fiberglass canoe bobbed up and down, clean and crisp on the flowing brown water, looking like a handkerchief peeking out of the pocket of a neatly pressed pair of jeans. Martin sat in the back half of the canoe directing its progress with gentle but firm pulls on the paddle. He was intent on the task at hand and if there had been anyone along the muddy banks he wouldn't have noticed. Berto assumed much the same posture in the front half of the canoe, his eyes constantly on the river, flicking from this side to that. He was a good dog and this wasn't his first trip down the river in a canoe. He and Martin spent plenty of time on the water.

Martin liked to get out on the river. It was a good way to get the everyday cares and worries relocated to the back of his mind where they belonged. He remembered lots of weekends with his dad fishing and hunting along the Navasota. That was a long time ago. Dad had been dead almost two years now.

The splash of a water moccasin hitting the water on a nose dive from a tree got his attention. "Jeez, would you look at the size of that one, Berto?"

Berto was barking up a storm in the front of the boat. He never did like snakes that much.

"All right, all right. I'll get him. Don't you worry Berto." He laughed and reached for his 410, took aim, and shot the snake when it was about ten feet away from the canoe. It was a big one, close to four feet long. It gave a death dance, squirming along the surface, and Martin saw blood gushing from its cotton mouth and over its fangs. Then it disappeared in the muddy brown river, where life and death swam side by side. He put the gun down next to the life jacket and leaned forward to get a beer out of the cooler. He threw Berto an ice cube, and popped the top of a cold one. He took a couple of good swallows and looked around.

The river really was high, higher than any other time he could remember. It was really hard to tell just how high unless you had something to gauge it by. He'd be getting to Nelson's Bridge pretty soon, and he'd check the water level then. He sat back and let the canoe follow the currents, making an adjustment every now and then, digging with the paddle one or two times, but, for the most part, just letting the river do the driving.

No one lived out along the river these days, and Martin was sure he was the last person to ever see this part. He hadn't seen anyone out here since before dad died. They used to run across a couple of river rats now and then, old guys running trot-lines, or maybe trapping a few nutria, but probably just looking for an excuse to drink a few beers. He wondered if those old guys had died or just moved on to another river. Since the army engineers had made Lake Somerville, most people camped and fished out there, or, if not there, on the nearby Brazos, which was much more accessible and friendly.

Berto let out a quiet sigh, stretched his eighty-pound frame, and dropped down in the front of the boat with his huge brown head propped up on Martin's sleeping bag, keeping a watchful eye on the river, not wanting to miss anything. Berto's loyalty to Martin seemed to reflect the fact that Martin had probably saved his life when he rescued him up from the city pound six years earlier.

He'd been a funny looking pup, mostly white with brown spots and a brown head, strange blue eyes, and paws that seemed too big for any dog to grow into. He grew into the paws, the blue eyes had turned brown, and, as it turned out, Berto had a special knack for learning. By the time he was six months old he sat, stayed, heeled, fetched, and came every time he was called. He obeyed only Martin. By the time he was a year old, he would get in the front of the car or the back, whichever Martin specified. Martin never locked his car anymore; he didn't even worry about it.

Eighty pounds of dog was a pretty good security system.

Martin saw the old humpbacked sycamore up ahead. They were almost to Nelson's Bridge. When they reached the bridge Martin had to bend over and put his head on his knees to keep from bumping it on the bottom of the bridge. The water was moving faster now; Martin looked back at the bridge, wondering if he should have ended his trip early. But there was no turning back when the river was moving this fast. He looked up at the sky. Big, black, ominous clouds twisted and writhed two hours to the south, threatening to wring out a couple more inches of rain. Somewhere behind, he heard another water moccasin flop down onto the river.

"Jeez, Berto, we may be in for quite a ride here," he said. It was becoming more and more work just to keep the canoe in the middle of the river, and it was also becoming more and more vital to do so. It had rained so much that branches, brush, and other debris lined the river's banks in precarious piles. Martin knew from experience that it didn't take much to tip a canoe over, especially one loaded down with coolers, camping gear, and an eighty-pound dog who couldn't help paddle. The river slung the canoe through the dark mossy bottom lands, weaving and twisting through this tightly banked area. With the trees leaning over the water it felt like being in a tunnel.

Martin saw the logjam about thirty seconds before they hit. He backpaddled hard, his muscles straining beneath the white cotton tee shirt that warned, "Don't Mess With Texas." They smacked a sixteen-foot long section of what looked like cottonwood. The bark was pretty smooth, but the piece of wood hadn't been in the water long enough to get soggy and slick. Martin paddled hard to keep in a straight approach angle and then said, "Berto, get in the back! Come back here!"

Berto cocked his head to one side and looked kind of doubtful, but started toward the back of the boat, gingerly stepping over the backpack. The front of the canoe began to rise as the weight shifted to the back and then the first four feet of the canoe crossed over the log. Martin was kneeling by this time, and he urged the dog, "Come on Berto, a little more, come on boy."

Another two feet of the canoe passed over the log. Then the fiberglass bottom flattened out and threatened to crack. Water started pouring into the back of the canoe. The front of the boat raised upward in response to the added weight of the water. Martin leaned forward as far as he could and told Berto now to go to the front. Berto lumbered back to the front, barking in excitement. Martin put all of his strength into each stroke of the paddle, and the boat moved forward another couple of feet until the mid point was reached, then teetered back and forth as if the man and the dog were playing seesaw on the river. Finally the boat scooted over the log, and they slid easily over the rest and were on their way down the river again.

Around the next bend the river widened and

the waters slowed down. Martin sat back and took a minute to look at the Spanish moss hanging from the branches above. Then he grabbed the rusty coffee can that every canoe seems to carry, and started bailing the water out; pieces of bark and occasional bugs went over the side with the water. He pulled another beer out of the cooler and tossed two ice cubes Berto's way. Martin figured they had two or three more hours of daylight.

The river bent to the left and then it became vast. Martin looked to the east and west and saw nothing but murky brown water. He remembered his father telling him that when the river flooded in the bottom lands, the flood plains were sometimes fifteen or twenty miles wide. Martin looked hard, trying to find the current rippling the smooth surface but couldn't see a sign of it.

"Out of the frying pan and into the fire, Berto," he said. Berto looked back, wagging his tail. He knew that fire signaled the end of the day and the start of dinner. "No, not yet, buddy." He let the canoe go its own way for a good twenty minutes, hoping to latch onto the invisible main current.

He knew there was no point trying to go back upstream. He'd never be able to fight the current or go back over the logs that were blocking the way. He'd barely been able to cross them with the force of the river behind him. He tried to spot the taller trees that lined the river's banks, but all of the trees looked about the same. He could almost hear his father scolding, "Now son, you don't need to be on that river alone. Take somebody with you and leave the dog at home." Dad's arthritis had been so bad that he couldn't make the trips himself. He seemed to resent having his place taken by a dog. Dad just never seemed to realize that Martin wasn't going to let any man take his dad's place at the front of the canoe, so he took Berto. Martin planned to explain this to Dad, but death had intervened.

The water sat lifeless beneath the canoe, without even a hint of the power that had bullied them thirty minutes before. He started paddling south in what he hoped was the direction of the main stream. He pulled hard on the paddle. The canoe was really loaded down. As the sweat started pouring out of him, dripping down his forehead and into his eyes, he sure wished he had somebody to help with this chore. He was getting hot and bothered, the way he felt when it was ninety in the shade and that last lug nut just wouldn't come off no matter how hard he'd turn the tire tool or how loud he'd curse.

The only bright spot was the weather; those black clouds had changed their minds and had gone off looking for somebody else's parade to rain on. He paddled, sweated, and cursed for the next two hours.

It was close to dusk, and the mosquitos were waking up, starting to buzz around looking for tender spots on the night's menu. Martin slapped at a mosquito, leaving a red smear of blood on his arm.

He decided to give it up; they weren't going to

find a dry place to camp before dark anyway. He tied up to an old dead oak tree knowing only that the river was out there somewhere.

He sprayed himself liberally with the foul smelling insect repellent. He hated the way he always ended up tasting the damn stuff, no matter where he pointed the can. He figured that was what shoe polish must taste like.

He scanned the spindly branches above to make sure there weren't any snakes up there looking to drop in for dinner. Satisfied that no unexpected guests would show up, he dug around in the backpack for the dry dog food and Berto's bowls. He filled one with the kibbles and the other with water from the cooler. Berto was giving him one of those sad but demanding looks, the kind he gave when he wanted something but knew he probably wouldn't get it.

Martin stuck a paddle in the water and wasn't too surprised to find that the water was only a bit more than a foot deep. "Berto, if you have to go, you're going to have to do a little wading," he said. "Go ahead, get out." Berto didn't look too happy, but he jumped into the water and went sloshing off. In the meantime, Martin opened a can of stew and ate as quickly as he could. He washed it down with another beer and set about rearranging the gear in the canoe to get ready for a long uncomfortable night. A few minutes later he heard Berto splashing back toward the canoe, and he helped him climb back in.

It had been dark for about an hour when Berto

drifted off to sleep; his long, deep snores would resonate throughout the night. Martin listened for other sounds, but heard nothing besides the frogs belching for their mates and crickets making their monotonous chirps. Martin couldn't hear a car or a truck anywhere in the distance even though he thought FM 30 might be within earshot. He pulled another beer out of the cooler and savored the one cigarette he allowed himself each day. He leaned back against the sleeping bag he'd propped up and tried to get to sleep.

He wasn't sure what woke him up, the sun in his face or the last beer from the night before banging around inside his head. He felt greasy and grubby as he rubbed the sleep out of his eyes. He realized two things right away: Berto was gone and he wasn't lost on the river anymore. During the night the flood waters had drained.

He hollered for Berto a couple of times as he got out of the canoe and stretched his cramped, creaking muscles. They were busy reminding him that he had spent the night in a canoe with about as much extra space as you'd find in a ten-pound potato sack that already had twenty pounds of potatoes in it. He could hear Berto barking, probably chasing a rabbit or an armadillo.

The muck made big slurping noises and pulled at Martin's boots as he tromped over to the tree. This dried up old dead oak was going to solve two problems this morning. He jumped up for the lowest branch and pulled himself up into the tree's arms.

He broke off some of the smaller branches for a cook fire and tossed them down near the canoe. Then the branch under his feet began cracking and he quickly moved in closer to the trunk and safer footing. He looked up and plotted the path he'd take to climb higher in the tree, where the view would be good enough for him to figure out where he was and the best route back to the river. He didn't want to drag the canoe across the mud one step farther than he had to.

He slung his leg up over a sturdy looking branch about four feet above and started to pull himself up when the pain hit the back of his thigh like a hot iron. He couldn't hang on and, as he was falling through the tree, he saw the cottonmouth trailing from his leg like a tail on a kite. Then he saw the ground rising up at him and he crossed his arms in front of his face to take the brunt of the collision. He landed with a huge splat peppered with the crunching of the firewood he had thrown down. The fall knocked all of the wind he'd ever had out of him. He rolled over on his side, gasping for air as the snake slithered away. Berto came and ran after the cottonmouth, barking and darting at it. Then he was back whining and licking Martin's face.

Martin sat up, and the pain screamed through his leg and echoed around in his head, and then found its way to his mouth. He yowled, scaring Berto and anything else within hearing distance. He reached down and felt around his left knee. He cried out in pain as the two shards of his kneecap pinched unseen nerves. One of those crunches hadn't been firewood.

He unlaced his boots and pulled the right one off. He gritted his teeth and with his right foot tried to nudge the left boot off. The pain wouldn't let him. He took his buck knife out of its worn leather sheath and cut off the left leg of his jeans. Then he slid his belt around his thigh and cinched it snugly about six inches above the four holes the snake had left as a calling card. He rolled onto his right side and used the knife to make a slash across each of the four punctures.

His knife was always sharp and it cut through his skin with sickening ease. He made the cuts a half-inch long and a quarter-inch deep the way his dad had taught him. "Hell, the snake's fangs are only half an inch long. Ain't no sense bleeding to death over a snakebite or pushing his poison in deeper for him, son," Martin remembered him saying.

He sat up as best he could and squeezed the skin around the bite forcing a mixture of blood and, he hoped, venom out of the wound. He worked at it about twenty minutes. Then he dragged himself over to the canoe, leaned against it, and started laughing the laugh of a slightly crazed man who knows he's had it.

"Berto! Here I am leaning on a canoe in the middle of someone's lost acres, I got a busted knee, I've been snakebit, I don't know where in the hell the river is, much less where *I* am, and you're probably the only one who's ever gonna hear any of this. And to top it all off I cut the leg off my best blue jeans!" Laughter took over again and didn't stop until tears of fear and frustration found their way down his face.

"What would Dad do?" Berto cocked his head to one side and wagged his tail. He never seemed to understand that dad was gone; he still went to dad's chair looking for him when they went over to mom's for Sunday dinner.

"Well, for starters, dad wouldn't be out here with just a dog, would he, Berto?" Berto stood up as if he expected to see dad walking across the field.

"Come here, Berto," Martin said quietly.

Berto walked over and sat in the mud beside him. Martin pulled his wallet out and drew out one of his business cards. On the other side of "Martin Swift's Custom Remodeling" he wrote with the stub of a carpenter's pencil that lived in his change pocket. "Mom, help! A cottonmouth bit me. Between Navasota River and Highway 30 about 5 miles ? south of Nelson's bridge."

He pulled his bandana out of his hip pocket and carefully rolled it up around the card. He took the lace from the boot he'd kicked off and cut two six-inch pieces from it, which he tied tightly on either side of the card wrapped up in the bandana. Then he knotted the red and white bandana around the dog's thick brown neck and scratched Berto's head right above his eyes, where he always liked it. Berto closed his eyes and groaned in pleasure. Martin sat a minute and hoped that Berto would remember a game they hadn't played since dad died.

"Berto, where's dad? Where is he?" Berto got up and looked around. "Where's dad?" Berto was barking now and dancing from side to side. Martin looked him right in the eye and said firmly, "Go get dad's wrench. Go get it! Go get dad's wrench." Berto took a few steps then turned around waiting for Martin. Martin yelled, "You go boy! You go! Get dad's wrench!"

Martin watched Berto take off like a shot and bound east across the low field and then up the gentle slope that met him a few hundred yards later. When he reached the crest he looked back toward Martin who yelled, "Go on! Go!" Then Berto disappeared over the top. They were a good twenty-five miles and two full days from home by the river, but by cutting back across the land Martin figured they might be twelve miles away.

Martin lived about a mile from his parents' house. Sometimes when he worked on his car he'd find himself a part short or without the right tool to finish the job. He didn't like to bother dad with the phone, so he and Berto would walk over to borrow the tool he needed to finish up. Like lots of people who had dogs, Martin taiked to Berto; that was the way he taught him to understand things. Things like what a frisbee was, what a bone was, the difference between catching and getting, and who "Dad" was. While walking through the neighborhood, Martin would tell him they were going to dad's to get dad's wrench. After a few of these trips, he started telling Berto to go ahead of him, and the dog would proudly trot off on his own. Eventually Martin stayed home and sent Berto over with a note clipped to his collar. Berto would bark at their back door until somebody came out, read the note, and gave the insistent dog something to bring back to Martin.

He loosened the makeshift tourniquet and tried to coax more of the bloody mixture from the gashes on the back of his leg. The skin around the bite felt numb and tingled when he touched it, but it didn't hurt very much, and that was bad. If it didn't hurt like hell, it was probably pumped full of venom. His smashed knee was a different story; sickening white pain pulsated through it in sync with the agitated thumping of his heart. He reached behind and got the plastic milk jug of water out of the cooler and took a drink, then he poured some of the icy fluid over his head. He grabbed the ice bag from the cooler and slid it under his leg. He threw the rest of the gear out of the canoe and tipped it over so its broad white bottom faced skyward. That was all he could do now. The rest was up to Berto.

He imagined Berto running through the grass at a steady gait, stopping once in a while to sniff the air for familiar scents. He would breathe hard but steadily, his big pink tongue jumping from side to side in his mouth. Berto loved to run and had amazing stamina for such a big dog.

Martin cinched up the belt again and sat there as the water dripped silently from his hair and rolled down his face and the back of his neck. He watched the drops plop onto his one-legged jeans and vanish in the muddy blue fabric. The sun was shining bright and hot; the air was thick and wet with moisture steaming up from the mud. Martin drifted off somewhere between the highest levels of pain and the bizarre dream state of venom-induced fever.

Then Martin was falling out of the tree again, but not fast like earlier. He saw how blue the sky was, dark blue like a piece of stained glass in church, no streaks of white from any clouds. He looked over at the tree and saw the pattern of the bark and remembered how it felt rough and scratchy on his arms and legs when he had climbed up into it. He saw the ants at work, dragging a blade of grass up the trunk. The spider web still had a few drops of dew on it and they sparkled and danced in the sun. The furry black spider waited patiently for his next meal to arrive. The snake trailed out from his leg and he saw the grainy texture of its green-brown triangle of a head. Cold grey eyes peered out from black holes. The snake floated free beside him. Its forked tongue slithered in and out of its mouth. In his dream, the snake spoke, "'You can't beat me, Martin, I've already won. I am the strongest, you are the weak one. You'll die today."

Martin saw himself leaning against the tree in the warmth of the late morning, eyes half closed, staring up at the sun. His skin looked greyish and his lips struggled to pull each labored breath out from his lungs. His left leg was swollen and below the knee, it lay at a painfully unnatural angle. Flies buzzed noisily around the cuts the knife had made, landing, probing, then buzzing away.

Martin's hands crossed his chest, then wandered feebly over his face and through the tangle of dirty brown hair matted on his scalp. His drool stretched in a slimy, windblown strand to his chest. A small airplane droned overhead and its shadow crossed his face and then the canoe's exposed white underbelly. But the shadow moved away.

Martin closed his eyes and listened to the breeze flutter around his ears, sounding the way it did when he sat up on his ten-speed and coasted silently down a hill. How nice to just coast down, deeper and deeper, farther and farther. Going home, just going home. Going to see dad again . . .

Something heavy dropped onto his chest. He felt around up on his chest and found the cool, wet, steel handle and held it up. Dad's wrench. He looked up for dad but saw Berto standing over him, whining in anticipation, rump twisting from side to side, his huge tail going in crazy circles behind him. Berto licked his face.

And Martin could hear a jeep coming down the hill now.

Duststorm

by

Dorothy Rose

Dark reddish dust has rolled
Through our farm for a week now
The silt has sifted into our house
Through the windows and doors
When we go outside we wear handkerchiefs
Over our faces
We look like bandits
The baby cries and coughs
We take turns holding her on our laps
So she can breathe better

But this morning the sun is shining
The storm seems to be over
The dust has settled down

We will not work in the fields today
The whole family must clean up the place
The dust has to be shoveled
Away from the doors of the house
The barn and the outbuildings
The floors and windows have to be
 scrubbed

Everything inside the house has to be
cleaned
Including our clothes sheets quilts
Curtains cooking utensils

Inside the house Mary sweeps scrubs
And rinses the floors
Then she washes and dries
The dishes pots and pans
Bob washes the windows and sprinkles
the yard
Royce shovels the banks of dust
Away from our flower and vegetable
gardens
Daddy works down at the barn
Shoveling dust and cleaning
The animals' drinking troughs

In a galvanized tub on the back porch
Mamma scrubs our dirty things on a
washboard
The wash is so dirty with the
Reddish gray dust that it
Must be boiled in the pot
We have a big black iron pot
In the back yard
A wooden fire burns under the pot
Lye soap and water boils in it
I stir the laundry with a clean broom
handle
Then with the stick I lift the clothes out
And drop them into cool rinse water

I wring them out and put them into a
 copper tub
Then Charlcia and I carry the tub
To the clothesline
We hang the wash to dry
It takes all of our lines to hold everything

We work all day to get the job done
At last we go inside the clean house
To prepare our supper

Daddy comes running up from the barn
He yells get the laundry in quick
There's a big cloud back yonder
Coming this way

The swirling powdery silt
Starts to roll in again
The clothes drink up the dust so fast
That before we can gather them in
They are ruined

Bookmark

by

Penny Wilkes

In their primitive stages, fear and puppy love both start at the tip of the big toes and surge upward through the body. Little creatures with electrical charges pin prick the tongue, blind the eyes and race through the mouth drying every tooth. They circulate inside their victim with the rising and plummeting speed of a roller coaster.

Melly first experienced these gremlins while sitting next to Stanley M. Mason. The effect of his blue-gray eyes and big-toothed grin made her toes tingle. Best of all, he smelled like animal crackers and hot cocoa. She began to watch him constantly even during cookies and juice break. One day his lip was covered with tomato juice which seemed strange because everyone else had pineapple juice. Just a nosebleed, she later learned.

It seemed to Melly that Alexa always sparked Stanley's attention. She'd drawn a red fire engine for him and he'd made a paper fan for her. She could get him to chase her in and out of the jungle gym at recess. Once into the bushes she would push him down onto the moist ground and plant sticky kisses on his face.

Melly's competitive spirit caused her to entice Stanley to race but she usually beat him. As he caught up with Melly afterward, he panted and puffed and his eyes seemed like cracked bird's eggs. When he beamed at Alexa, though, his eyes simply glistened a robin's egg blue.

In the spring, the class studied the post office and built one of cardboard for the back of the room. Each student's name personalized the cubbyholes. Alexa sent notes to all the boys, of course. She kept it simple, "I Love You! Lovingly, Alexa." When Stanley read his note, his face went as red as it had during the tomato juice incident.

For some reason that flipped another switch that sent new animals tripping through Melly's confused body. With pencil poised over her oatmeal paper with blue lines, she scrawled undying affection to top Alexa's message. "Dearest Stanley —I like you, I love you, I would do anything for you. I would kiss you. Would you? Forever lovingly, Melly." She beamed confidently and placed the note in Stanley's slot at the post office.

"This is not good!" proclaimed the teacher when she confiscated Melly's heart-grabber. She directed Melly to stand in the cloak room and pay her penance. Melly had spent lots of time in that dark interior for obvious crimes such as talking in class or causing distractions. Now she little understood the punishment and stood facing the coat pegs, still as a statue.

Mrs. Carter seemed likable enough especially because she smelled like apple pie with cinnamon. Every day she read from a book designed to enrich developing minds. Each selection lasted a week. Melly loved to watch as the lady cocked her head from side-to-side during the dialogue of a story. Often she stared at the children and recited lines as though she had memorized them for a performance. Story time took most of Melly's attention from Stanley and the surge of feeling that she felt for him.

Mrs. Carter fetched Melly just in time for the story and the wrongdoer slinked back to her seat amidst the titters of her classmates.

Mrs. Carter removed the day's reading book from her top drawer and opened it to page one. Lodged in between the pages for all to view, sat Melly's note of true and undying love. She could barely see "Stanley" scrawled across the back of the paper. A flush of panic seized her. Would her teacher read it in class and add to the punishment?

Now the gremlins within her raced.

Melly's eyes became glued to the note. Black and red blobs turned to polka dots and flashed in front of her failing vision. Could she creep out of class unnoticed, slither on the floor to the door, melt like an ice cube or become invisible? Trapped within an unresponsive body, she just wriggled in her seat.

She never heard a word as Mrs. Carter began reading *Charlotte's Web*. The sounds echoed as though hitting the sides of a deep well. As the teacher casually flicked each page, Melly flinched. Now and then Mrs. Carter shifted the note and Melly's heart nearly exploded through her chest. Would she read it . . . now?

After the day's reading, Mrs. Carter took the note from the front of the gray book. Melly's clammy hands gripped the seat . . . Now . . . ?

The teacher positioned the note as a bookmark, closed the book with a clop and returned it to the top drawer which she locked with a tiny key. Melly slumped in her seat with momentary relief.

For a week, until the finish of the story, the note moved farther and farther toward the back cover. Mrs. Carter fiddled with it, tapped it on her desk or waved it in the air to make a point in the story. Melly's short life had passed in front of her.

As a result, by now she didn't even feel the rising currents of excitement each time Stanley walked by. She went to sleep with thoughts of the note and woke up each morning with renewed terror. She dreamed of all those words coming to life. They'd be running off the page and climbing all over her, tying her up, shooting her with tiny arrows. Should she give up and confront Mrs. Carter? Could she break into the drawer and steal the note?

Day after day Melly dreaded story time and remained frozen in her chair. She didn't dare miss class in case Mrs. Carter would read the note without her being there.

Today must be the day, Melly thought, because

not many pages remained. Mrs. Carter's drawl seemed endless.

Suddenly, with a simple motion, Mrs. Carter turned the last page and placed the note at the end of the book. She removed her glasses, smiled at the class and zipped the book in her book bag to return home.

Now it was over.

Melly stared at the zippered bag. She'd surely served her sentence.

Love for Things Unknown

by

Phoebe Newman

The Rainbow is a big old bar out near the south end of nothing on the coast of Alabama. There is still a bubble-light-jukebox in The Rainbow, and a smooth wood dance floor. Blue and green Christmas tree lights line the edges of the roof and hang from the lower limbs of the tall pine trees ringing the parking lot. The bar is smoky inside and outside. Roy Owens has set up an oil-drum grill on the front porch and is selling sweet, crusty ribs. Roy has turned his Pontiac's searchlight toward the grill, and his big hands move like a magician's, into and out of the hard light.

Early in the night, most people are joking and easy. They play George Jones records over and over, and become quieter and more sentimental until closing time. Only a few started drinking sooner, right after work. They are laying their heads on the bar now, and look belligerent and pitiful. Some nights they strike out into brief, pointless tussles, like tired children.

At one round table three ladies sit together, wearing shiny, skimpy dresses and beads and bracelets that click and rattle like little snakes. The ladies dance with the single men—young and old, handsome and homely—and disappear from time to time for a half hour or so.

This particular August night a stranger has come in the screened door. No one has ever seen him before. They would remember. This man is over seven feet tall, with a huge jutting jaw and mammoth hands. He is wearing high-heeled cowboy boots and a towering ten-gallon hat with turkey feathers encircling the crown. A beat-up traveling circus is parked out at the fairgrounds, featuring some heat-struck lions, listless clowns, a Fat Lady and The Giant. And here *he* is, in their own bar!

"Now we got everything!" Virgil Loomis hoots. "We got The Giant and we got plenty of fat ladies we can look at for free!" His wife, no longer plump, pokes him hard in the side.

There is a hush in The Rainbow as The Giant walks directly over to the table where the three ladies sit with bowed heads. The Giant bends over and speaks softly to Darlene, the tiniest girl of all. Darlene is barely five foot, even with her hair all teased up! Virgil's jaw drops and many beer bottles are held still, halfway to open mouths. Only the jukebox continues its bubbling and colorful noise.

The Giant's hand covers Darlene's naked back from shoulder to shoulder as they walk out the door. She is not smiling and her purple eyeshadow gleams above her downcast eyes.

All the dancers and all the drinkers and all the tusslers listen for the sound of The Giant's car leaving the parking lot. The men try to look tough and the ladies pretend to be unconcerned, but a part of everyone's mind is tucked into a corner of Darlene's little beaded pocketbook.

Just before midnight Virgil's wife Leona is the first to hear the car pulling into the gravel lot. Everyone hears Darlene's high heels dotting across the porch. The screened door slams and she walks so beautifully, so calmly, across the room to her table. Her girlfriends welcome her back, offering sips from their pastel drinks.

Darlene sits down, leans way back, takes a wad of Dentyne out of her mouth, grins her biggest grin, and says to one and all, "He's my uncle! The Giant is my Uncle Wayne. I ain't seen him for six years. We been eatin' catfish." She turns then to Sue Ann and Tiffany and their sweet smiles.

The men think, "Ha. I doubt that!"

The ladies think, "Well . . . that makes sense . . . But some of them find themselves wondering what it was they fell in love with so many years ago. Seeing their puzzlement and sorrow, the men feel suddenly helpless, and pat their wives' bunchy behinds and give them quarters for the jukebox.

There has been a definite kind of click, a gap in the texture of the evening. Their own Darlene has been out with The Giant, has laughed with him and maybe wiped grease off his chin. Yet Darlene is still the same small and sparkling and sweet beneath her storm-cloud hairdo.

Is it really possible that nothing has changed? That danger, glamour and wonder have slid past them like summer rain? That the most magical person any of them has ever seen up close is just Darlene's old uncle?

Drinks are poured and shoes kicked off and it all starts over. But talk of fishing trips and new dress patterns grows hushed as they hear The Giant's car leaving the soft circle of light falling from The Rainbow.

Some part of their bewildered dreams has slipped out the screened door, past Roy's cooling grill, down the dirt road. Like quiet billows of dust rising behind his car, their confusion floats softly off into the hazy summer night. Their hands rest lightly on their partners' shoulders as the dancing begins again, and again.

Training Wheels

by

Lynne Conroy

Here I am. Waiting to begin. Ready to teach her to drive. As soon as she gets off the phone, that is. She's failed the test for her license twice, but I wouldn't call her a terrible driver. She just needs experience. That's where I come in. I'm her mother.

The first time she failed, she blew through three stop signs. She told the Registry officer that she didn't know they were for her. The last time, the Examiner got in the car and closed the door, She turned on the ignition, looked over her shoulder and backed into a utility pole. The electricity blacked out a fire station, two hospitals, and Lower Manhattan. I thought the guy who failed her was really nice about it. He said she needed a little practice. She said he didn't like her. I kept my mouth shut.

After that, I signed her up for a few more driving lessons, so all we have to do now is practice. But these practice sessions drive me crazy. I can't reach the brake fast enough with this cast on. It's useful, though. I just have everyone she runs into write their names and insurance info right here on the cast.

Anyways, it's been a week since the accident, and I've gotten philosophical. It could have been a bigger truck. Or she could be twins. Still and all, I fasten my seat belt. Check the buckle. And make sure there's no slack. Here she comes. Ready to drive.

Okay, Honey, let's back out of the garage. Great so far. Only one thing you forgot. Open the garage door.

Now, before you back up any more, look. Careful of that hydrant. Turn your wheel in the direction you want to go. No, the other direction. Watch out for the hydrant. The *other* direction! *Stop!*

Are you okay?

Honey, you stepped on the gas when you turned the wheel in the wrong direction. Water's *pouring* out of the hydrant. I think we might have broken it off at the stem. Pull ahead. Let me see how much damage we did. I need a moment to hoist myself out of the car with this cast on.

I'm out. The car is lurching. Stop. I said, *Stop the car!*

Oh, I see. I forgot to tell you to put it in 'Park'. I want you to shift into 'Park' every time the car has to stay still. Right now, though, I want you to listen carefully. The car is on my foot. Now, don't start crying. There's a lot of plaster between me and the tire. Roll about six inches down the driveway, please.

All right, it's off my foot now. Put on the parking brake while I get in. That's the lever thing between the seats. I'll call the Water Department when I get back. If I get back.

I'm sorry. You're right; I made a crack. Don't be upset. I'm not really mad or anything because I drove worse than you do. I remember when I'd make a right turn and have trouble straightening the wheel. So I'd run over someone. While they were in their living room watching TV. One guy was taking a whiz when I came through his bathtub.

Ignore the honking, Honey. And don't stop when you want to change lanes. Make sure that you do the turn signals, too. Good. You did good. You took your chance and missed the grey Jaguar by a few inches anyway.

Now don't take both hands off the wheel to wave. Or to comb your hair. All right, if I'm making you nervous, I'll change the subject.

What a great car this is! A 1971 Saab 99. They built them like bulldozers. Starts good, too, with the new battery in it. Maybe, when you get your license, we'll sand off some of the rust. Then, we'll paint it a snazzy color. When you get to be a real smooth driver, we can take off the 4 x 4's I bolted onto the bumper and those tires I strapped on the front. Oh, it's not so bad. Sure, not many cars have them, but plenty of boats and piers have tires all over them. They protect us, Honey.

You know what I did the first week I had my license? I was driving down the expressway in

Grandpa's '57 Studebaker during rush hour when the Studie conked out. Someone pushed me over into a turnout. I thumbed a ride to a pay phone and called my mother to come get the car because I had to get to class. You know what? She came and had the car towed for me. Because she loved me the way I love you.

Before you get your license, you and I should check out one more thing. Skidding. Nothing is worse than being in a skid and not knowing what to do. You're completely out of control. You have to stop thinking and just steer towards the skid. And don't brake. Or else you lose control again. But don't worry about it. We'll find a nice patch of ice to practice on.

Truth Like Enormous Flakes of Snow

by

Barbara

She is three days from dying, and knows it.
Twice the Fair Havens Nursing Home has
rousèd me from my nightgown.
But Grandma clings to that last crevice
with the strength of a rock climber.
She's disgruntled with death;
expected it to answer to all those questions
stored under her bed year after year. She
hoped
that truth would fall onto her upturned
face
like enormous flakes of snow.

Yet Grandma still isn't sure
who clipped off her pigtail one Halloween
night;
if the baby she lost was a girl or boy;
and whether Daniel Morgan remembers
that indelible green day
tucked between the corn rows.

The Man Who Owned a Mountain

by

Maureen Williams

"To my only son Ned," the lawyer intoned, "I leave my worldly wealth . . ."

"What's the use of a lousy mountain?" Ned complained of his inheritance. That the old man had loved the place counted for little. Ned knew that geological surveys had revealed nothing of value, no gold, nor diamonds, not even a seam of coal.

Ned's father had been left the mountain by his father, who inherited it from his father, and so on, way back to the seventeen hundreds. Who owned it originally, or how it came into the Thomas family, is not clear. The Indians called it Kittatinny, meaning the endless mountain, which was strange since it's quite small, a mere thousand feet in height.

Yet it is splendid: gently curving slopes covered in pine and maple, rising to a magnificent head crowned with hawthorn, white-blossomed in the spring, red-berried in the fall. So it is "endless" in this sense maybe: ever-changing, illusive, unknowable, endless in moods and colors and magical wavering airs.

Ten years ago, when this story begins, Ned Thomas, whose given name means the prosperous one, was youngish and very ambitious. A builder by trade, Ned helped folk move in on the wilderness, taming it with strong and practical A-frame houses constructed of the trees he cleared from their land. Ned's customers liked to civilize their purchases with patios and swimming pools and vast windows through which to gaze up at the wilder untouchable parts of the district. Ned thought of his own small mountain as another piece of real estate, to be tamed and somehow turned into gold. He took time to ponder the problem of Kittatinny, sketching in his mind scheme after scheme.

Ned had a son, Emlyn, twelve years old at the time, named for his grandfather. While Ned schemed, Emlyn was exploring the mountain as only a boy can. He learned many wondrous things about Kittatinny. A bear, black and about the size of a large dog, lived in a cave on the south side. Stealthily Emlyn had watched the bear feast on fruit and berries and the succulent lower branches of trees. There was an elk too; most rare, as the boy knew from his teacher who said that elk no longer lived in the area. Only once had Emlyn seen the elk. He had known at a glance that it wasn't a large deer by its wide flat horns and its beard. He had remembered elk from his teacher's picture book. Emlyn reckoned zillions of creatures lived on Kittatinny. He'd seen groundhogs, chipmunks, turkeys, snakes, lizards. His list went on and on. Flowers of brilliant blues, yellows, and reds that smelled glorious. And the leaves in autumn, so bright it seemed the trees were lit up from inside, much brighter than any Christmas tree.

Sometimes Emlyn wrote stories about what he'd seen. His teacher said: "Very good Emlyn! You have a most vivid imagination." Emlyn liked it that way; he wanted people to think that Kittatinny was an imaginary place. He never took his friends on exploratory rambles of his secret territory. Neither did Emlyn tell his father what he knew about the mountain, but this for a different reason: Ned rarely conversed with his son.

Ned was so busy building and scheming. Once he'd made his fortune, Ned told himself, there'd be time to relax and enjoy the boy's company. Emlyn's mother, May, had died giving birth to him. Emlyn often talked to her in dreams; with her he shared all secrets.

Ned came up with a most impressive scheme to turn Kittatinny to gold. As soon as it was clear in his mind, he announced grandly to his banker: "A ski resort! I've got the equipment to clear the slopes, and build lodges and such. But I'll need the bucks for lifts, winches, lighting, plows, groomers . . ." He had a long and costly shopping list. This banker, bored by paltry loans to farmers for tractors, harvesters, or the occasional silo, was impressed and excited by Ned's courageous scheme. Imagining his best customer on the brink of great riches, he wanted to be a part of such glory. They shook hands, Ned and the banker, to clinch a business deal and a new friendship.

Ned's bulldozers went into action, uprooting trees to make alleyways down the face of Kittatinny, some steep for expert skiers, some curving more gently, some trailing off into the remaining forest to snake around interestingly for long distance enjoyment. There was, too, a wide short area near the base for the bunny slopes, where skiing could be taught. Then the heavy machinery moved up, to drill and pound pylons into the rock-hard surface, with massive cranes standing at precarious angles to haul the huge steel structure into place. The men who dared to work on this project were paid the wages of danger.

Meanwhile, the wildlife of Kittatinny fled from the fearful cacophony of churning and pounding. Young Emlyn, walking in the pastures below the mountain, watched his father's treachery and wept for his animal friends. He could hear the bear crying out for help: a terrible wounded wailing that caused him to tremble. Nor was Emlyn alone in hearing this eerie sound.

The workmen began to exchange horror stories of disturbing Indian burial grounds, of hauntings at night around the cabins where they lived. But Ned increased their wages and the work continued.

By October, Ned's ski resort was ready. Silver cables glinted in the sun; rows of bucket seats jangled in the breeze; gigantic piers stood guard at top and bottom, with pylons at attention between. Log cabins at all stages sported bright signs: "Ski rentals," "Lift Tickets," "Picnic Lodge," "Fondue and Hot Wine!"

The hotel at the base, with a dining room looking up at the slopes, boasted a chef of international renown. Also promised was aprs ski entertainment of the most exciting kind. Vast billboards along the freeway yelled: "Come Ski the Big One!"

Even the farming families were agog; Ned's project would provide a bonus for them, a chance to turn their traditional period of rest into pin money. The entire community could benefit from the extra tourist trade. Some locals, worrying about an avalanche of Coke bottles and beer cans, nailed up signs saying: "We love our countryside! Please do not litter!"

In six months Ned had transformed Kittatinny. "At last that mountain's worth owning," he proclaimed. The banker agreed heartily: "This area could do with more men of vision and courage like you!" They shook hands again, pumping one another's arms gleefully. So great was Ned's self-congratulation that he failed to notice his young son hadn't spoken to him in months.

And oddly for so foresighted a man, Ned failed to give thought to the simple fact that a ski resort needs snow. To his utter astonishment, one month, then two months of his first season as a resort owner passed without a flake of snow falling on his prepared slopes. He had some customers, folk who came to look at the newness, and impressed, hung around for drinks and a meal cooked to perfection by the famous chef. They told their friends who came to see for themselves, bringing their friends. But no one could actually ski in this ski resort.

Ned travelled north to see other resorts where snow was falling, though not enough to make a good covering for the slopes. There he found cunning contraptions that blew out frozen water of the right consistency. They were expensive machines, but a must for the successful resort owner. Such machines were immediately installed upon Kittatinny, adding to Ned's power over his mountain.

To Emlyn, who still spent days wandering dejectedly in the fields below, they looked like tanks, lethal weaponry crawling over his beloved scarred Kittatinny. These huge blowers kept the locals awake with their din and could cover the slopes with Ned's "snow" in one night. Nature watched the performance in bright-eyed amazement. The electricity these powerful machines used per night could light an entire town, but Ned was well-satisfied by the results.

Each morning Nature smiled upon Ned's cunning—a cynical smile, and a little too warm. Under her warmth, Ned's snow didn't stand a chance. His eager customers managed only a few hours of skiing before the precious powder vanished. Yet Ned persevered. Night after night he laid powder. By dawn his slopes were groomed and ready for those few hours of skiing at least.

Through February, Ned had some financial relief in the form of ten, fourteen, then eighteen inches of real snow. His resort became a teeming success. By the end of that season, Ned did his sums and thankfully, he'd only suffered a modest loss.

"Next winter," he told the banker, "we'll really strike it rich!" His banker agreed, for long range weather predictions were saying that the season had been a freak and would certainly be followed by a long hard winter.

Actually, those next four years are still being talked about by the farmers who live in the vicinity of Kittatinny: "Remember when that weird southern climate crept up here?" they say, "and we had no winters at all?" In their heart, they believe themselves victims of a southern curse.

Emlyn Thomas, he knows better. When he returned to Kittatinny after some years away at college, and after his father had moved to Florida, Emlyn came back to shout joyfully to the tangle of ruby-leaved vines that now covered Ned's constructions:

"No man can own a mountain!" he shouted. He called it out over the wild slopes: "A mountain belongs to all creatures for all of time." Then for a few weeks the young man camped out on Kittatinny's gentle face.

Emlyn hoped to make his way in the world as a writer, a seeker of clues left behind by his ancestors. He wanted to tell of the way things were once, and could be again, he was sure. Some things are meant to continue, not be spoiled by "progress."

He had read of the tribe Lenni Lenape, the original people of these forested mountains, who made companions of the flora and fauna, taking only what they needed to survive in a simple manner, existing in harmony with the earth.

And then he'd read of his own people, the early settlers who arrived in winged canoes, as the Indians called the tall sailing ships that came to their shores across the Great Sea from the Land of the Rising Sun. The immigrants, too, treated their wondrous discovery with respect, agreeing with the Indians to share the bounty. Though later, as Emlyn was sadly aware, promises were broken, and bitter wars fought. Eventually the Lenni Lenape were driven out or destroyed. Yet in the beginning, there had been trust and harmony between settlers and settled, between Earth, her meeker creatures, and the human race.

"With Ned gone," some complained, "that mountain's dying." What they actually meant was that it had escaped the clutches of "progress." In truth, Kittatinny was coming to life again, while her surrounding fields were still farmed by simple folk who got along very well without Ned's enterprise.

On his mountain Emlyn again dreamed of his mother, May. Lovingly, she explained how to banish the shame he felt at being Ned's son, and maybe earn a pardon for the Thomas family. So Mother May spoke to Emlyn that starry night on Kittatinny: "Go set it down beautifully, my son. Tell of flowers and trees, their colors and virtues, and of all creatures living in peace. Dare to dream that your words will be read, and understood by some, and that a few may be inspired to return to our aboriginal ways."

"Maybe," Emlyn cried out with a sudden gush of hope in his strong young heart, "maybe Dad will read what I write, and begin to understand too!"

Then Emlyn crept off on moccasined feet in search of signs that the bear and the elk had returned to Kittatinny.

The Black Sheep of the Family

by

Thomas H. Davis III

I grew up in a small southern town. In so far as religion went, you were either First Baptist or First Methodist, and I was well into High School before I realized that you could be something else. If you know those Methodists, then you know that they change preachers about as often as they change their underwear. We Baptists, on the other hand, latch on to one and, good, bad, or ugly, we keep him forever.

Dr. Cutts had retired after twenty-something years with us and a new preacher took his place. Mama was fulfilling her obligation to the church when she invited him and his wife for Sunday dinner.

I remember it like yesterday. Mama went all out. For dinner, we had her and Daddy, me, my sister Marrlee, Aunt Josie, Uncle Bud ("no-a-count Bud" as Daddy called him) and, of course, the new preacher and his missus. We put two extra leaves in the dining room table, and Mama covered it with that real nice white, lace table cloth Aunt Polly had sent her from Germany.

It was in the early spring. We were supposed to eat at two o'clock, but of course, we didn't sit down until after two-thirty. I was particularly antsy. My two best friends, Bobby Newby and Bobby Carr, were waiting for me in the front yard with their fishing poles and a big tomato can filled with peat moss, cow manure, and red wigglers.

Instead of asking daddy to give the standard family blessing, Mama felt compelled to ask the preacher to say Grace. You know, preachers don't say the blessing; they say Grace.

Well into the prayer—indeed at the four minute mark—I peeked out the corner of my eye at Uncle Bud to see how he was handling this. Sure enough, he was nibbling on flakes of fried chicken!

The preacher finally finished, and before the chorus of "Amens" died down, I commenced eating. In no time, I cleaned my plate and asked Mama if I could be excused. Well, you'd have thought I'd asked permission to strip naked and dance around the table. "No, you can't be excused!" she said. "Our guests haven't finished."

I was through early mainly because I hadn't felt compelled to tell Mama how "golden flaky" her fried chicken was, or how "wonderful" her creamy mashed potatoes were, or how "delightful" her congealed salad was. And I already knew how she made such "magnificent" iced tea. Anyway, that's when she plopped two spoonfuls of smelly, slimy, boiled okra onto my plate and said, "You haven't had enough greens. Eat this okra. It's good for you."

I stared in horror at that okra, watching the slime ooze over my plate. The smell got up my nose, and turned my stomach, "Mama," I protested. "'You know I hate okra. I can't eat it. It makes me sick!"

"That was a long time ago," she said. "You haven't had any lately. You aren't being excused until you've tried a bite."

It wouldn't do but the new preacher had to get involved. From his seat directly across from me he leaned over and said, "I love boiled okra, son, and this is the best okra I've ever put in my mouth."

Why wasn't I surprised? Everything he had put into his mouth today was the best ever. I couldn't help but wonder what that said about his wife's cooking. My guess was that he would hear about it when she got him home.

Anyway, to prove his point he cut the end off a smelly, slimy piece of okra, gigged it with his fork, shoved it into his mouth, and commenced to chew. When he swallowed it, he said, "Ummmmmmm." Then he grinned like a fat possum stuffed with ripe persimmons.

I knew if I was going to leave the table early, I'd have to try that okra. It had been a long time since I'd tasted any. I figured if I didn't chew it and thought a happy thought as I swallowed, then it would go down okay. So that was what I did.

I threw that piece of okra into my mouth, thought about the catfish I was going to catch that day, and swallowed hard. It slid down fine. But halfway between my mouth and stomach it decided to turn around and come right back up. Trailing close behind, unfortunately, was fried chicken, Mama's famous mashed potatoes, some creamed corn, scrambled eggs from breakfast, and probably some pork chops from the night before.

Now this wasn't the namby-pamby kinda throw-up. You know the kind where you can cup your hands and catch it while you make it to the toilet or somewhere. No sir, I looked like a fire hydrant turned on full force. What was worse, I was facing directly at the new preacher. My load hit him square in the chest and splattered all over his red and black striped tie, clean white shirt, and pin striped suit. I figured he'd change his opinion about okra after this.

The new preacher jumped back as anyone would who'd been hit in the chest with the remains of someone else's dinner. When his shoulders slammed the back of the ladder-back chair, he started falling over. In an attempt to catch himself, he reached for the table but only succeeded in grabbing Mama's tablecloth.

Over he went, taking with him his plate of food and that whole bowl of smelly, slimy, boiled okra. His wife and Aunt Josie were sitting on either side when it happened. From their faces, you'd have thought his nose and ears had just fallen off.

Things got pretty quiet. After all, what do you say when the new preacher is laying toes up on the floor all covered with smelly slimy okra and your son's throw-up?

Everybody's plate was either on the other side of the table or in their laps. Uncle Bud, who had been gnawing on a drumstick at the time, broke the silence saying to Mama through a mouth full of chicken, "The boy done told you that he couldn't eat that okra." And pointing his chicken leg at the new preacher, continued, "Besides, the preacher there did say he loved boiled okra, didn't he?"

You know, I wasn't the only family embarrassment. No matter what I did, old Uncle Bud could always top it. I guess that's why I liked him so much. I sure do miss him and to this day remember that last time I saw him.

Not only was it the first time I'd ever seen a dead person, it was the first time I'd ever seen anybody actually die. And when I tell you about it, you'll see why I remember it so well. Kinda like when you heard the news that President Kennedy had been shot.

But first, I gotta tell you more about my Uncle Bud. He was first of all a Yankee and a traveling salesman who sold ladies lace and other unmentionables. He always had a cigarette or a big cigar in his mouth. Quite often, even in the morning, his eyes would be all glassed over from too much "Juice of the barley" as Uncle Bud would say or "rot-gut corn liquor" as my Daddy would describe it. Since he'd married Aunt Josie, his stomach had grown so big that he couldn't see the tips of his toes without bending forward until he was all red-faced. He didn't always treat Aunt Josie right either. Paw Paw had to talk to him about that more than once. Finally, it was known, but not spoken, that when he went on the road he was a womanizer. And this was the fellow who married into a family of staunch Southern Baptists. Need I say more?

All my aunts and uncles were polite to Uncle Bud, but Daddy, being an open and honest man, couldn't hide his feelings. As a matter of fact, whenever he referred to Uncle Bud he called him that "no-a-count Bud." I was nearly eight before I learned that "no-count" was Daddy's opinion and not a part of Uncle Bud's name. What I think Daddy liked least about Uncle Bud was that he borrowed things and didn't return them. Most often what he borrowed was money. Paw Paw wasn't too thrilled about this either.

Anyway, back to my story. It was a family tradition to get together for Thanksgiving, Christmas, and the Fourth of July, with the most important of the three being Thanksgiving. And so it was during a Thanksgiving that it happened.

Aunt Polly came in from an army post somewhere. Aunt Ann came down from Wilmington, North Carolina; Aunt Lasa from Atlanta; and Aunt Linda from Nashville. They brought their families with them. Including my sister Marrlee and me, Paw Paw's house bulged with thirteen eager and excited grandchildren. The only ones without children to add to the confusion were

Uncle Bud and Aunt Josie. I knew this made Daddy happy and thought Paw Paw felt the same.

For our Thanksgiving Day feast, Mama had whipped up a bowl of her famous creamy mashed potatoes. It was so big that I could hardly get my arms around it. However, Maw Maw and her cook, Annie Mae, were the ones who did most of the fixing. The big table was covered with bowls of turnip greens with pot liquor, creamed corn, fried okra, scalloped oysters, and sweet potato pie, two platters of crispy fried chicken, a ham from the smokehouse, baskets of homemade biscuits and golden brown cracklin' bread, the biggest turkey I'd ever seen, and, of course, mama's aforesaid mashed potatoes.

The adults sat around the dining room table. The children were relegated to card tables scattered between the dining room and the living room. That Thanksgiving I managed to capture a seat at a card table in the entrance way. This offered a full view of the adult's table and a way back to the kitchen for seconds without anybody counting.

Paw Paw stood and tapped a water glass with his spoon. When things quieted down he said, "Let's all bow our heads for this family blessing." And he prayed: "May the Lord be praised and the ladies pleased, which is but now and then. Let us eat our diet in peace and quiet, in the name of the Lord . . . Amen."

Amidst echoing "Amens," Uncle Bud staggers up, grabs his chest, lets out a holler, and falls flat across the table, landing face down in Mama's bowl of mashed potatoes. As he lay there, he jerked several times and then went limp as wet toilet paper. Well, I haven't got to tell you how flabbergasted everybody was. After all, it wasn't every day that a grown man, or anybody else for that matter, up and flings himself across the dinner table and buries his face up to the back of his ears in a bowl of mashed potatoes.

Well, Aunt Josie fainted and everybody else either screamed or gasped for breath. Daddy ran to the telephone and called for the ambulance, but it was too late. Uncle Bud was dead, dead as dead could be.

The funeral was set for Sunday afternoon. Everybody was in town anyway so they decided to stay. Friday the word came down that Uncle Bud had had a heart attack, but that it wasn't the main cause of death. It seems that while he was jerking around with his face buried in the potatoes he had inhaled several helpings. I haven't felt the same about Mama's famous mashed potatoes since.

After the funeral, we were riding back to the house in Paw Paw's white Cadillac. Daddy was driving, with Paw Paw sitting on his right. Marrlee and I were sandwiched between Mama and Maw Maw in the back. Mama sat holding a knotted-up Kleenex tissue. Marrlee was crying because that's what she thought she was supposed to do. I sat there all stoney-faced because that's what I thought I was supposed to do. Maw Maw wasn't doing much of anything but humming “Rock of Ages” as she stared out the window.

It was then Daddy cleared his throat like he always did when he was about to start a conversation. “It was real bad the way old Bud died,” he started. That got everyone’s attention. It was the first time we’d ever heard Daddy refer to Uncle Bud without calling him “no-a-count.” And it seemed like he was feeling kind of sorry that Uncle Bud had died. Then he looked over at Paw Paw and continued, “‘You know . . . he dearly hated mashed potatoes without gravy.

Paw Paw nodded, smiled knowingly, and grunted, “Uh huh.”

Golfers in the Fog

by

Richard Ploetz

The wipers wumped softly, squeegeeing mist on the windshield. The red light turned to green, and I let in the clutch. The '56 Plymouth jerked ahead.

"Gas," growled my grandfather, balancing his coffee mug.

As the car accelerated, the wipers slowed, then beat a flurry as I went up into second. At sixteen I reveled in the feel of clutch, gas, shift.

"Take it easy," said Poppy as I snapped down into third and we swished up Delaware Avenue. "I'd like to get some of this mocha on the inside."

A block beyond the Dutch Reformed Church, my buddy Leo Thompson loomed beside the curb, his plaid Bermudas, white basketball sneaks, and white tee shirt contrasting with the dripping gloom of the elm-hung street. Leo climbed into the back seat, clapping my grandfather on the shoulder. "Hi Pops!"

Poppy half-turned, "I'm not deaf yet."

Leo leaned forward, arms on the back of the front seat. "Watch out, guys, this is gonna be my day!" With the windows up, his Aqua Velva was pretty overpowering.

A car approached with its lights on and I switched ours on. "Real pea soup," I said.

"Think we'll be able to play?" asked Leo.

"It'll burn off," I said. "The only way to play is to get out early."

"Yeah, beat the crowds," Leo added.

Poppy was staring at the fog-shrouded landscape as it rolled by. An Elm Dairy milk truck loomed in the fog and passed.

Leo settled back. "Hey, remember that piece of shale I got on the field trip last Spring? Split it open and there's a fern inside, a fossil. Like it was pressed in the pages of a book. I wonder if it's worth anything? You know about fossils?" he asked Poppy.

"No," Poppy said stiffly. "They were before my time, believe it or not."

We were the second car in the Albany Public Golf Course parking lot, the first being Winny Crennel's black bullnosed '49 Merc. He was the clubhouse attendant.

"Only three loonies would be here at this ungodly hour in this stuff," said Poppy, lifting his folding golf cart out of the trunk.

I paid our green fees in the clubhouse—Poppy's treat—and Leo rented clubs. Through the window we could see my grandfather taking practice swings.

Looking off the first tee, you couldn't see twenty feet. It was like TV with the station gone off the air. You couldn't tell you were high over a long fairway hemmed in by pine woods and a swampy stream.

"Well, here goes nothing," my grandfather said, nesting the ebony head of his driver behind the white ball.

"It probably won't even land," said Leo. "I mean, the fog's so thick, it'll probably hold the ball up!"

Poppy settled his weight, then slowly swung the club back and then forward, cleaving the air with a "click." The ball vanished and he followed through. Even at the age of seventy-four, he had beautiful form. He plucked up his red tee. "You next, Leo," he said.

Leo stood, the seat of his Bermudas striped from the three fog-soaked slats of the bench. He teed a ball, wiggled his hips, and swung like Mickey Mantle.

"Watch the back of your head," said Poppy. "That one's coming right around."

Leo was studying the ground.

"Don't bother," laughed my grandfather. "The tee went further than the ball."

I got off a fair drive. We plunged downhill into the fog, Leo and I carrying our golf bags slung on our shoulders, Poppy being led by his cart. Leo left us, disappearing to the right.

It was still. Bushes dripped. Trunks of trees went up and disappeared in the fog. My sneakers were soaked already and squished with every step. The golf course was like those dried-up star fungi that swell in the wet.

"We should have brought a compass," I said to Poppy. We were walking together in the fog, just the swish of shoes through the wet grass, the easy jangle of clubs. But then he came right up on his ball. I asked if he had x-ray eyes or something.

"You hit a ball straight," he said, "two hundred yards and a blind man can find it. What do I want here, spoon or mid-iron?"

I answered, "Better use the iron. You don't want to overshoot this one."

He drew the long blond-shafted spoon out of his bag instead.

"Yooooooo!" Leo's voice floated on the fog.

"Find it?" Poppy shouted.

"Nooooo . . ." Leo called again.

Poppy trod a few times in place like a cat in your lap, and then hit the ball. "Long. Had to get that out of my system." He gestured to the right, "You sliced over there."

I'd out-driven him by twenty yards, but lay in the rough.

"Fore!" came from behind us. Poppy cupped his hands and called, "Who's that for, the woodchucks?"

"Up my snout!" Leo's call came back, surprisingly close.

I hit, and, as we moved ahead, Poppy and I separated. He grew fainter, merging with the mist, until I was alone.

I learned golf by caddying two summers for Poppy. When I played my first game, he didn't say anything for eighteen holes. Afterward, he went over the game stroke by stroke—a hundred and twenty-one of them. He then considered my apprenticeship over. We could play golf.

My ball sat in the green's dew, on the end of the curve it had rolled. I could hear Leo coming up whistling. Poppy stood under some wild grape vines above the green.

"You should have used that iron," I said.

"Yes, yes. Come up here," Poppy told me.

I held the vines back, and he exploded the ball to the accompaniment of dead leaves and soil. It sailed high and landed, bouncing up two feet from the flag.

By the long dog-leg Fifth, the sun was burning off the fog. It would be a scorcher. Leo had put on a sailor hat, brim turned-down, and looked like a guy from a backyard cookout.

"Whoa!" called Poppy, as Leo began a swing. "This isn't a butcher shop. Slice, slice, slice! Keep the left arm straight, snap the wrists and follow through."

Leo hooked the ball.

Poppy put his hand on Leo's shoulder as they advanced: "Golfing is like eating. You have to forget about it to do it. However, to forget about it, you have to know how to do it." They arrived at Poppy's ball; he continued offering commentary, "Downhill lie, two hundred yards to the flag; green trapped, sides and back. Strategy for the par?"

Coming up the long slope to the ninth green

in front of the clubhouse, I could see Poppy's swing had eased up and he was taking more time with his shots. The usual ram-rod posture, learned from his Prussian father, had melted a little in the heat. He leaned into the golf cart, pushing it up the hill. Poppy was timeless in his baggy beige pants, white shirt with the crossed drivers under the pocket, white Ben Hogan cap. He wore real spiked golf shoes: white saddles over brown, with fringed tongues that hung down to cover the laces. They reminded me of Fred Astaire.

We sat at the clubhouse bar drinking lemonades. The bartender had moved away after serving us, as if we gave off too much heat. Leo looked at me and raised his eyebrows.

"Ready to call it quits?" I asked Poppy.

"'You talking to Leo or me?" he replied.

"It's going to be a wicked back nine," I cautioned.

"We'd better get started then," he said.

"We should have played the back first . . ." Leo murmured.

We were taking a break under the big maple at the thirteenth tee, spread out on the bench, not touching. Leo had filled his hat at the last drinking fountain and emptied it over his head.

I knew better than to suggest shortcutting to the seventeenth to play out just the last two.

The part of the course we called the "Alps" lay ahead. I don't know if they were so bad, but you came to them tired. There were two strategies: power-drive clear across the valley and land on the opposite plateau, within chipping range of the green; or, like Poppy, play it smart and stroke easily into the valley, then take another easy shot up and over the rim.

I got up next and blasted.

"Jesus . . ." Poppy shook his head staring down at the acre of brush that had swallowed my golf ball. I think he would like to have done something to save me the trouble of being young.

An hour later, I was helping Poppy up the steep gullied hillside to the fifteenth hole, pulling him by his seven-iron. Leo, laden with his own golf bag and dragging Poppy's cart, pushed upward against the old man's behind. Poppy was grabbing grass tufts with his free hand. We must have looked like Moe, Larry, and Curly.

"Let go of that club," grunted Leo, "and I'm a dead man."

We went a few more feet like that, then started to laugh. Then Poppy dropped to his knees. Leo lurched forward spilling clubs and letting go of the cart. "Oh no!" Poppy said. Then he fell over sideways.

There was another of those big maples at the top. Leo and I each got hold of an arm and dragged Poppy up pretty fast. We laid him on his back in the shade, and I got his head propped up. Leo ran toward the green and disappeared behind a sand trap. I fanned Poppy with his cap. His chest was going up and down. Leo came back, hurrying, spilling most of the water in his hat. We splashed some in Poppy's face. His eyes opened and closed. The golf course right then was like the moon. Poppy's hand lifted off his chest and dropped back. He mumbled something.

"He's off his head," said Leo. "We'll rig his golf cart so we can drag him to the clubhouse!"

"That's a dumb idea," I said. "It wouldn't hold him."

An electric golf cart was floating like a mirage over an adjacent fairway. Leo ran toward it yelling.

I continued fanning my grandfather with his cap. Wisps of his silver hair moved back and forth. I was surprised that we had the same soft fine hair.

It was so still. No birds sang and there was a scorched dry smell. Leo was gone. The electric cart had vanished. Poppy's chest rose and fell more easily. He seemed to be sleeping. This air breathing was like taking a bite and chewing and swallowing it.

Thunderclouds were piling up in the West over near where we got the fossils. This had all once been a swamp of trilobites and ferns. A dog day like this a million days ago. It felt as though Poppy and I had died and were sinking into the mud, getting to be fossils. In a million years they'd find Poppy laying there with his wisps blowing, and me next to him, waving this cap. I wonder if they'd connect us? Same DNA in the bones?

A locust began a long summer wind-down in the gully.

There's a picture of Poppy as a kid. His hair

is thick and he's skinny, but his nose and eyes are the same. He is standing with his father, and Poppy isn't even 'Poppy,' but 'Emil Junior.' I am not born. He isn't even thinking about what's to come. This minute.

I wondered what I'd be like when I was old.

Another locust started up as the first wound down.

Poppy's eyes opened.

"Stop waving that cap," he groused. He propped himself up so he was sitting against the tree. "That me?" he asked, and pointed. A ball lay twenty feet left of the green.

I was shaken. "Are you okay? You keeled over and . . ."

"I know, I know." He took the cap from my hand. "You pick up the clubs?"

"Clubs?" I asked.

He said, "It's gonna look like Custer's Last Stand to the next party coming along."

"I was worried about you," I began.

"Get the clubs!" he insisted.

I crisscrossed the hill gathering golf clubs, balls. Poppy's cart was clear at the bottom on its side. One of the struts had bent, jamming the wheel.

Poppy was standing on the edge in the tall weeds, shielding his eyes and pointing. "Over there! Wood!" he yelled.

"Get back!" I bawled. "Get in the shade!"

He wobbled, or maybe it was the heat, and was gone. I dragged the cart over to the club, slammed it in, and scrambled up the hill expecting to find him in the weeds right there, saddle shoes pointed at the sky. But he was back under the tree.

"Hey, Poppy," I said. "take it easy! I don't want you dying out here!" He didn't look at me and I was sorry I'd said that.

We just sat under that tree in the complete heat and silence. If there was a clock you would have heard it tick.

Poppy drew in air so suddenly that it sounded like a sob. He gave a little wave at the golf course. "Hard to imagine, but I guess this ain't gonna go on."

"Hey," I reassured him, "you gotta teach Leo to hit a straight one."

He just stared out.

"We'll just play the front nine," I said. "We'll get out early and play nine. That's plenty."

"Next it'll be miniature golf," he snorted. "Then checkers on my bed!" He rose up steadying himself on the tree. "Leo must have gotten a flat tire," he complained. "Fetch my ball. Let's not play it out," he said. The wheel of the cart dragged as he started off, and with a kick he freed it.

Sightseeing

by

Thomas Claire

We'd traipsed all through
Rome's city streets
seeing the tourist sites,
Michelin in hand,
and had arrived atop
the Spanish steps,
my traveling companion
and I.

We'd gotten on
each others' nerves
and he'd gone off
to sulk in the shade
of a gnarled
chestnut tree on
the grassy sloping
hill above.

I gazed below
at the maze
of winding stairs
that seemed so derelict

with their drunken bums
and blaring radios
and wondered where
the fabled charm
I'd fantasized
the place to have
had gone.

I noticed a middle-aged
foreign couple
standing nearby,
dressed simply in
modest and sturdy,
not trendy,
travelling clothes.

The wife was blind
and I thought it odd
she would have climbed
all those stairs
to survey these sights.

After a bit, I realized
they were speaking French,
a language I understand,
but in the sweetest tone
I'd ever heard,
and I began to listen
as the husband delicately
depicted for his wife
what lay below:

"In the center of the square
there is a clear-flowing fountain
whose waters sparkle like a rainbow
in the high afternoon sun.

"Nearby there stands
a silver-streaked,
care-creased widow
in an antique ebony,
fringe laced shawl.

"She's sharing her
lunch with the
grateful white doves
that are floating
so gracefully about
her open hand.

"On the other side
a young couple
is embracing
at the ice cream
vendor's cart.

"You can see the love
his eyes are pressing
into every brightly
colored scoop
of perfumed ice
he is offering her,"

and he tenderly pressed

the soft folds
of his wife's arm
as he whispered the scene
into her ear.

"They all look so beautiful,"
she sighed,

and then inquired gently:
"Are there any flowers?"

"No, my love," he replied,
"but perhaps we'll see some
when we descend below
into the city."

Their kindness and care
had cast a glow of amber charm
above the city skylight
and I mused
to myself
I would gladly
give up
my sight
to see
with their eyes.

Alysa's Father

by

Amy Schildhouse

That winter after my father died I was thirteen years old, and I pretended that Alysa Schulman's father was my father, too. I caught a ride to Eastmoor Junior High School each frozen weekday morning with Mr. Schulman and Alysa. Their family lived in the house across the street from ours on Harding Road. Mr. Schulman dropped us at the junior high on the way to his law office in downtown Columbus.

I got to know him because his daughter Alysa and I were the same age. We used to play together in elementary school, and our families became friends. Once we began junior high, Alysa started playing with her girlfriends, and I hung around with the other guys. By that time it didn't matter, because I already knew Mr. Schulman. He was the one who offered me the lifts, anyway.

I began my friendship with him in the weeks after the funeral. He used to come around a lot, and talk to me about fishing or baseball. Once he surprised me in my retreat behind our woodshed. He told me it was all right for a guy to cry.

He'd cried when his own father died, he said, and he was even older than I at the time. No one could replace my father, but I told myself that Mr. Schulman was the next best thing.

Every morning I scraped the snow and ice from the front and rear windshields of Mr. Shulman's black Buick, parked in the driveway overnight. My lungs ached in the arctic morning air, and my fingers burned inside my green wool gloves, as I hacked and scraped at the ice. No one asked me to clear the windows. I wanted to do it for Mr. Schulman.

"David, just the driver's side is fine," Mr. Schulman commented one freezing morning. "It's too damn cold to stand out in this weather for so long."

He stood close to me by the side of the car. I breathed in his mixture of cigarette smoke and cologne. I admired Mr. Schulman's soft, black overcoat (which Alysa had told me was cashmere and very expensive) and then looked down and saw how his polished black leather boots gleamed against the trampled snow on the drive.

"Don't worry, Mr. Schulman, I don't mind," I assured him. "In fact, it rather gets the blood running, you know?"

He shrugged, and got into the car.

'*Rather* gets the blood running.' What a stupid thing to say! I kicked the front tire with my beat-up work boot, but Mr. Schulman seemed not to notice. He'd opened his *Columbus Citizen-Journnal.* He always read the morning paper while we waited for the engine to warm up, and for Alysa to come out to the car. I finished my scraping and took my place in the back seat of the Buick. Mr. Schulman's wristwatch beeped at 8 a.m. He glanced at it and frowned.

"What can be taking that daughter of mine so long?" He shook his head affectionately. Thirteen years old and already she spends more time in front of the bathroom mirror than Rochelle."

Rochelle was Mrs. Schulman.

"Alysa!" he rolled down his window and yelled. "Get out here!"

Alysa sailed out of the house and glared at her father as she opened the car door. I thought she was beautiful. Her skin was clear and white, and she had dimples, sometimes even when she wasn't smiling. She had her father's wide, red mouth and his same dark, bushy eyebrows. When Alysa slid into the front seat of the Buick Royale, I glimpsed her narrow hips beneath her short blue ski parka and felt the breath catch in my throat. She didn't turn around to say Good Morning to me, and I knew that meant all I'd see of her was that fluffy ponytail, bobbing above her long, pretty neck.

Throughout the rides, I kept my eyes on Mr. Schulman. He drove impatiently, his forefingers tapping against the steering wheel. He repeatedly glanced into the rear view mirror. Was he looking at me? He chain-smoked, pulling cigarettes from a pack of Marlboros he kept on top of the dashboard. Grey smoke billowed above his head. What was he thinking? Was he thinking of me?

Our trips always seemed magically eternal. The heater's fan kicked in with dependable frequency. Mr. Schulman kept his radio tuned to WNCI-FM, so the same hit songs or local commercials or Paul Harvey's hypnotic drone came over the radio. Once in a while Mr. Schulman and Alysa spoke, but only to say which parent would take the carpool, which sister's turn it was to set the table, who had flute or ballet lessons after school —that sort of thing. Mr. Schulman would ask questions and Alysa would respond grudgingly or belatedly, or not at all. The smoke from Mr. Schulman's cigarettes hung in the air like motes of dust in sunlight. I never wanted to reach the schoolyard. I was a willing prisoner in Mr. Schulman's warm Buick cocoon.

That morning, I hardly even noticed it when Mr. Schulman cleared his throat, lowered the volume of the radio, and said to Alysa: "I'd like to know the cause of your tantrum at breakfast this morning." Alysa stared out her side window. "Hon'?" he said. As usual, she ignored him. "Alysa Jane, I'm speaking to you."

Alysa turned languorously to face her father.

"Flute," she said.

"Alysa, what is that supposed to mean?" he asked.

"Watch my lips. I-have-a-flute-lesson-after-school," she enunciated. "Mom's going to pick me up after." She rolled her eyes. "It's Thursday, Dad, remember? On Thursdays I have flute and Beth has Hebrew School. But the Friedbergs drive this week, so you won't have to pick her up. Mom told you all this last night at dinner, *remember?*"

I leaned forward to watch Mr. Schulman pluck the coil lighter from the dashboard and light a cigarette. He returned the lighter to its socket on the dash. A few minutes passed as he smoked silently.

Then Alysa said: "You and Mom are really going to screw us over."

Mr. Schulman turned sharply to face her. "What are you talking about?"

"I know what's going on," Alysa said. "I heard you guys fighting again last night."

Mr. Schulman braked for a red light at the corner of Elbern and James roads. I glanced anxiously at the rear view mirror, trying to catch his eye.

"We weren't fighting," he said. "We were having a discussion."

"Yeah," Alysa sneered. "Some discussion."

Mr. Schulman glanced at me in the back seat and said, "Honey, let's talk about it later."

"I don't want to talk to you ever," she said coldly.

"Look, sweetheart," he continued, "there are a few things we do need to discuss."

"Forget it," she replied.

"Actually, Alysa, your mother and I have been meaning to speak to you girls. There are some things . . ." He glanced back at me again, ". . . but we'll talk about them at home."

"Dad, can I have five dollars?" Alysa asked

abruptly. "I have to pay my French Club dues today and they're five bucks."

"Okay, honey—" he began.

"Also, I forgot to tell you, Dad," she said, "some man from the Temple Board called for you last night while you were out walking Jeepers. I told him to call back in ten minutes, but I don't know if he ever did." She seemed to enjoy telling him this. "I think it might have been Mr. Sonnenstein, because he sounded familiar—"

"Alysa!" Mr. Schulman broke in, his voice suddenly loud and frightening.

Alysa bit the back of her hand and bent her head down to her chest. I watched her bring the other hand up to shield her eyes.

"Baby doll . . ." Mr. Schulman reached awkwardly across the space between them to touch his daughter's cheek.

Alysa jerked her head away from his fingers. She scrunched herself as close as she could to her car door. The traffic light turned green. Mr. Schulman drove through the intersection.

"Alysa, sweetheart," he began.

Alysa hunched over. "Don't talk to me," she said.

Then she was silent and still.

Mr. Schulman was steering his big, wide car along the route we took each morning. I rubbed a clear spot of my steamy window and looked out at the familiar snowy lawns of our neighborhood. We were entering the parking lot of the junior high school. Pairs and groups of kids weaved between the cars and across the asphalt to the courtyard. Mr. Schulman waited with unaccustomed patience for them to move out of the way. He pulled up alongside the curb and put the car in park.

"Here we are," he sighed.

Alysa jerked open her door and leapt out of the Buick. Then she bent over and stuck her head back into the car. Her dark eyes were wet and glittering.

"I hate you!" she whispered fiercely. "You're ruining my life, and *I just hate you!*"

Alysa slammed the car door and ran.

Mr. Schulman, who had been staring at the space vacated by his daughter, looked up slowly into the rear view mirror. He squinted his eyes and regarded me as though he had never seen me before. "She doesn't really mean that," he said, at once frightened, lonely, apologetic, strange.

I stared back at him, at his thinning brown hair and at the dark, puffy circles under the eyes. I saw his slackening jowls, and then I noticed how his overcoat bunched up in a fat, stiff, sad way above his seat belt.

Blackberry Island

by

Joanne Seltzer

The Sault Ste. Marie, which we called the Soo, was a fairyland that I heard about from my mother until a special summer when she and I were invited up north for a two-week visit with our relatives. We boarded the overnight boat that sailed from the port of Detroit up rivers and lakes, to the northern peninsula. Those lakes were like my dreams of an ocean, with waves that rolled to the end of the world.

I awoke early the next morning in the top bunk of a windowless cabin, retching from my first attack of greatlakesickness. I was still heaving when we changed to the Mackinac ferry which crossed us over the Straits to the town of St. Ignace. My stomach settled down while we waited for the train.

The train tracks north bisected a wilderness covered with second growth timber. I was frightened by the scenery that rippled past my window. I might see a bear in the lonely forest, or perhaps a tomahawking Indian. Besides, my stomach was churning again from the chugging of the train.

My aunt and uncle were waiting for us at the railroad station in the Soo. We rode in their shiny Packard sedan, arriving in style at the house on Spruce Street. My cousins were both away on vacation, so I was taken to Beverly's bedroom. I put my brand-new suitcase beneath the daytime moon and wondered if the star-shine would keep me up at night.

Soon it was time for lunch, and Aunt Sylvie introduced me to her Indian servant, Victoria. She looked just like I had imagined, except that she wore a housedress instead of buckskin clothing. And her face didn't smile when she said, "Hello, Louise."

I wish I could remember every detail of that three-story house. It seemed like a sultan's palace to a child brought up in a city apartment. Spruce Street was where the rich people lived. Aunt Sylvie's furniture had been ordered from Chicago. A grandfather clock presided over the stately foyer, chiming at every quarter-hour. Oriental carpets nearly covered the polished floors and a winding staircase led to the bedrooms. A grand piano was the feature of the formal parlor and a big shiny table filled the dining room. A servant's bell was wired into the dining room floor, right by Aunt Sylvie's seat, so she never had to raise her voice to call for Victoria. A secret gesture of the foot, and Victoria would appear, just like the-jinni in *Arabian Nights*. How I wanted to steal that bell!

There was a special staircase leading to the

third-floor attic where I was allowed to spend one rainy morning. I sat at a dusty old wooden table among trunks and boxes and all kinds of treasures: a domino game, children's books and grown-ups' books, baby dolls and doll clothes, baby clothes and baby bottles, a set of doll dishes from Belgium. Some of my cousin's twenty-six sweaters (now spoiled by tiny moth holes) were up in that magic attic.

I opened Beverly's private trunk: it was filled with Indian clothing in all different sizes. I found a leather dress that fit me, a feathered headband, a string of colored beads and Beverly's outgrown moccasins, which were almost too small for my feet. I pretended that I was an Indian princess, puffing on a broken peace pipe, having just escaped from an enemy tribe. Then I was told to put everything away, just like I had found it, or Beverly would be very, very angry.

The oriental rugs were perfectly designed for playing hop-scotch, especially the rug in the dining room. I would hop from square to square, even under the dining room table, careful not to step on the secret bell ihat would call Victoria. When I tired of my game, I played tag against the wallpaper above the spiral stairs. Touch a flower, skip a flower, touch a flower, skip a flower. A voice from behind—Aunt Sylvie's—made me jump:

"Please don't touch the walls, Louise," she said. "I had them repapered just last year, and it cost Uncle Max over four hundred dollars. That's a great deal of money, you know. The old wallpaper lasted for almost seven years, and it may be another seven years before I'll be able to decorate again, so I'd like this paper to stay fresh and pretty. In seven years, Louise, I'll be an old lady."

I turned and saw the furrows in my aunt's round face. "But Aunt Sylvie, you're old already!"

Aunt Sylvie thought it an amusing story to tell my mother. My mother laughed politely but her face turned red.

The main social event of our vacation was the Saturday night dinner party when friends from the Club came to the Zuckermans' house to meet my mother. It took my mother almost an hour to get me dressed and to comb my hair into Shirley Temple spirals. Meanwhile I received instructions:

"Remember, these men are soldiers from the Fort. Don't say mister. Always call them captain or colonel. And remember that none of these people are Jewish. I want to be sure you make a good impression. Don't shout when you talk and don't reach across the table and don't wiggle in your seat and don't eat more than four black olives. Black olives are very expensive. It would look nice if you would help Victoria serve the nuts and olives before dinner. Try not to seem shy."

Our guests that night were a group of professional soldiers and their wives. The regular army regarded the Soo as little Siberia. The soldiers were assigned to guard the border against a Canadian invasion that would never come.

The real enemy was a northern winter which set in early and lasted for most of the year. I was awed by the deep-chested laughter of those military officers, dressed for the night in civilian formal jackets. Their sourpuss wives wore long gowns and kept refilling their whiskey glasses while they talked about traveling south for the winter. I was so scared that I might say something wrong that I decided not to say anything at all, even when I was spoken to. I was glad when, after dinner, I was told to say goodnight. Kept awake by indoor starlight, I heard a lady repeat in falsetto, "But Aunt Sylvie, you're old already!" High-pitched laughter, mixed with booming laughter, lulled me to sleep.

One day Uncle Max decided to take the family for an all-day boat ride out on the lake. He lined the trunk of his Packard with an old Indian blanket. Then he carefully filled the trunk. A picnic hamper stored the silverware, dishes, tablecloth and napkins. There were boxes of sandwiches, boxes of cookies, a gallon jug of lemonade, another jug of iced tea, heavy jackets in case the wind was cold, kerchiefs to cover the ladies' hair, and containers for the blackberries that we planned to pick. One pail was kept inside the Packard in case I got carsick on the way to the dock.

The boathouse was ragged with splinters, but the boards were proudly lacquered. Our gear was lowered into a bobbing boat named "The Trading Post." I refused to go near the water for fear I'd slip and drown. So Uncle Max lifted me up and handed me down to my aunt and mother. I curled up in the hull of the rolling boat like an unhappy house cat. I wondered when I would learn to swim and if Uncle Max would save me if the boat turned over, or if he would rescue my aunt instead. Unlike the Detroit River, the great-lake water was very clean.

Off we went past the piers onto the open lake. We picked up speed as the motor roared, but I was only a little boat-sick while the sun beat down on my nose. It seemed as if we rode forever across the waves and through a freshwater spray. It took a while to find our island because that part of the lake had never been properly charted. At first we thought we had gone too far, but at last the inland pulled over to meet us, swimming out in the water away from the mainland. The anchor went down, and we waded ashore to taste the sweetest berries that grew in the world. We were allowed to nibble only a few because Aunt Sylvie was planning to put up jam the next morning. Stolen berry seeds caught in my teeth, but the seeds would be strained from tomorrow's preserves, leaving a sweet jam which would be sealed inside of tiny glasses. A slender cover of paraffin would protect our treasure from the germs of the world.

We didn't unpack the picnic boxes until the middle of the afternoon. It was fun to squat on the ground for lunch, pretending that we were Indians off hunting deer. We picked more berries after we ate, and soon the blackberry bushes were bare. Then, my mother had me walk behind a clump of trees, and she told me to make peepee before we started back. My city bladder wouldn't function without indoor plumbing, and I said I couldn't. My mother started yelling, "You gotta go. It's a long trip home and no one wants to hear you complaining." I began to cry that I couldn't, when my bladder started working. I was proud of my big round puddle which we covered with sand to keep the island clean.

Then we packed up our basket, berries and trash, leaving the island immaculately stripped of fruit. We rode back on the lake to the Soo, taking our supper from the leavings of lunch. My head began to nod from the motion of the boat and the blur of grown-up conversation. I heard talk about the locks that would soon be built on the St. Mary's River, joining Lake Superior to the other Great Lakes. The canal would open the northland to commerce and would surely be good for Uncle Max's business. I wondered if my sunburn would peel and if I'd get carsick riding home in the Packard. But I was sound asleep when we reached the dock and had to be carried, like a portaged canoe, between the boat and the car and the bed. I woke up next morning, beneath the wallpaper moon, tightly wrapped in an Indian blanket.

When it was time to go back home to Detroit, my aunt handed my mother a basket packed with six small jelly glasses. We put our supply of homemade preserves in the front-hall coat closet, safe away from kitchen ants. Six times during the next rawcold winter, we returned to the warmth of Blackberry Island. We finished the last sweet scrapings before the Passover season.

Elly

by

Stanley Field

Matt sat in the living room contemplating the flames roaring warmly in the fireplace. He was dressed in his best suit, tie and all. Tonight Elly and he were celebrating their twenty-third wedding anniversary. Elly had decided they were not going out. She would prepare the dinner and they would be by themselves, a quiet, happy celebration.

Their two children were off at college. Josh was in his junior year, taking pre-law courses. Meg was a freshman—or was it freshwoman?—looking forward to a teaching career.

All in all, it had been a happy life for Matt and Elly, although the beginning of their marriage was hardly propitious.

Matt leaned forward in the chair, staring into the fire, remembering:

. . . Ah, Elly! Maybe you wouldn't want to remember. I drove the pickup as slow as I could, careful about the bumps in the road. You'd knitted yourself a new sweater and you insisted on wearing it. Having a baby was a real occasion and you were going to wear the sweater even if you did bulge. It was blue because you were so sure of having a boy.

I remember how you looked at me and laughed. "Matt," you said, "don't act so scared. And drive a little faster or he'll be popping out right here in the pickup."

I was *really* scared then. I stepped down on the gas pedal once we were on the main highway. That ten miles to the hospital was like a a thousand. I remember when we stopped, you just sat there and I saw the pain in your face, and you gripped the seat till your knuckles went white. Then you smiled again and I helped you down.

Everybody was calm in the hospital. I kind of felt funny. I expected to see the nurse rushing you off to bed. But she told you to sit down while she asked you a lot of questions. And where was old Doc Nolan? I phoned him when you first got your pains, Elly, you remember that. I gave him plenty of time. Then the nurse took you to your room and left me sitting there, waiting, worrying. Where *was* Doc? He'd delivered me and he'd delivered you and now I was waiting for him to deliver our baby.

I remember him walking in with his little black bag, a big smile on his face and a cheery greeting: "Buck up, Matt. Old Doc Nolan's here and everything's going to be all right. What's your choice, boy or girl?"

I answered, "It doesn't matter, Doc. But don't you think you'd better hurry?"

"First born," Doc Nolan said. "No hurry. Only, Matt, I think you'd enjoy that cigarette more if you put a light to it."

I put a light to it, but I don't remember enjoying it. And I don't remember how long it was before Doc Nolan came out to see me again. There was a smile on his face, but it wasn't a cheery one. Like the smile my Dad used to have when he'd tell me there was something I couldn't get that my heart was set on. I felt sick to my stomach.

"It's a boy," Doc Nolan said.

I grabbed his hand. "A boy! A boy!" I must've misread that smile. "How's Elly?"

"She's fine," he told me. Then he put his arm around my shoulder. "Listen to me, Matt. We've got the baby under oxygen."

I panicked. "Huh? Oxygen? What's wrong, Doc? What's wrong?"

"His lungs," the doctor said. "He may pull through all right. Other babies have. We'll know in twenty-four hours. If his lungs don't collapse in that time, he'll be all right."

"But how'd it happen?" I questioned. "Elly's fine. I'm fine."

"Well," he answered, "it's . . . oh, Matt, it's no use my going into a lot of medical terminology now."

"Can I see Elly?" I asked. "*Should* I see her? Does she know?"

Doc sounded tired. "She's asleep, Matt. I put her to sleep. She doesn't know. You'd better go home and get some rest. I'll be here all the time. You come in the morning."

"I'll stay here," I insisted.

"No, Matt," he said. "You go home." He walked me out to the pickup.

It must've been about midnight. I don't remember that drive home, Elly. I don't remember going into the house and falling asleep. But I do remember that phone ringing. Three sharp rings. Somewhere far away somebody was ringing a tiny bell. Three sharp rings. Now the bell was coming closer and closer. It was right there in the house. I jumped out of bed. I picked up the phone.

It was Doc Nolan. "Matt, I'm sorry. We did everything we could."

I remember the sun breaking through the mist on the horizon and I remember thinking it should be raining. I didn't eat anything. I couldn't. I parked the pickup in the hospital parking lot, Elly, but I didn't go right in. I walked around the block twice. I wondered whether you knew. Lord, we'd wanted that child so much.

I remember how you smiled up at me and said, "Morning, Matt. Hope you got a good rest."

"How're you feeling, Elly?" I asked you. I could see your eyes cloud up and I knew you knew. I turned away to the window because all of a sudden my eyes were smarting. Then I turned back to you. "It's a nice day out, Elly." I tried to smile.

"Don't try so hard," you said. "I knew this morning when they brought the other babies in. Did you get to see him, Matt?"

"No," I said.

"Just as well," you sighed. "Just as well we didn't have time to get attached to him . . ."

Matt turned away from the crackling fire. The remembrance was vivid and still poignant. Thank God for Josh and Meg, both healthy, vibrant, wonderful children. He shut his eyes, this time thinking of his mother and her dire predictions about his relationship with Elly:

. . . You remember how Ma used to feel about you, Elly. She put on a happy face at the wedding, but you knew that she wasn't too pleased.

"Trouble with Elly Matson," Ma kept telling me, "is she's too pretty. She's had too many beaus. She'll have you doing everything around the house. She won't be happy tending chores. But it's your life, son. You'd been mooning around her long enough. Now you got her or maybe she's got you. Only don't think of moving in with me. I can take care of this land with the help I got. I've been taking care of it long since your dad died and I don't want any pretty thing around that probably doesn't know which end of the skillet is which."

Lots of folks in the county wondered why we didn't stay with Ma in that big house. Eight rooms and a pantry wide as a barn. Forty acres and twenty-four cows. A dozen pigs and a hen house. Soon as I finished high school, my life was the farm, but I figured Ma was right. We'd do better starting off on our own. There wasn't anything else we could do with Ma feeling the way she did. One thing about Ma. When she made up her mind, it took a small miracle to change it. You were a small miracle, Elly.

Those first few weeks Ma found plenty of excuses for not coming over. Said it was the best thing for young folks to be left to themselves at the beginning, and not have any mother-in-law come snooping around the house. I wanted her to come. I wanted to show her how wrong she was. I wanted to show off the curtains you made and how you kept our little place neat as a pin. I remember when you put the new kitchen curtains up and painted the shelves yourself. I said, "I'd sure like to have Ma see what you've done, Elly. She'd be as proud as I am."

You just up and flared at me. "Matt, you've asked your Ma here a dozen times now. I know she thinks I'm not much good around a house. But the least she could do is pay us a visit. Her saying that it's best to leave us alone at the beginning is just an excuse. I'll tell you what the trouble is. You're her only son. You've been a great help to her. She feels I've kind of stolen you from her."

I tried to soothe her. "Now, look here, Elly, maybe you've got Ma all wrong."

I remember how those hazel eyes of yours just blazed. You turned to the sink and scrubbed those pots like you were going to tear them apart. You didn't say a word to me all the rest of that night.

I never told you, Elly, that I went to see Ma the next day. I said I was going into Elkins to pick up some supplies. Ma was at the barn watching Hank fix the door that had blown loose in the night. I parked the pickup in the roadway and walked over to the barn. "Hello, Ma," I said. "I want to talk to you."

"Hello, son," she answered. "What about?"

"It's private," I told her.

We walked away from the barn toward the house. I remember she was wearing an old shawl around her shoulders and how there wasn't even a sign of grey in her black hair, cut short around the back.

She gave me a kind of stern look. "Well, son?"

"Ma, I think you've let us alone long enough," I said. I had decided I wasn't going to beat around the bush. "I want you to come over for dinner.

"Who's cooking the dinner," Ma asked, "you or Elly?"

"I don't find that funny at all, Ma," I said.

We stopped walking. She stared at me, pretty surprised.

"Ma," I said, "I want you to get on that phone as soon as I leave here and tell Elly you want to take her up on that invitation for dinner she gave you a couple of weeks ago."

"Did she put you up to this?" my mother asked.

I remember that made me madder than hell. "You're not being fair to her, Ma. Elly doesn't even know I'm here. Maybe you better phone her while I'm here so I can be sure you'll do it."

Ma laughed. "I see she hasn't broken your spirit, son. No need to stand guard over me. I'll phone her and tell her I'm coming tonight. She won't like that but neither will I. You better go back tending your chores. I'll see you both later on."

I remember you were waiting for me on the porch, Elly. I carried the package of hardware I'd bought, so you'd know I'd been into town. You studied me but I looked right back at you. Then we went in for lunch.

"Your Ma called," you said pretty casually.

I tried to be just as easy as you. "Did she? What did she want?"

"She's coming over for dinner tonight," you replied.

"Tonight? Wonder what made her break down?" I asked with practised innocence.

You kind of looked me over again. "I wonder," was all you said.

I finished my sandwich. "What're you going to cook?" I asked.

"Chicken," you said. "And better than she ever cooked it!"

You just shook your head the way you did when you were mighty determined about something. I just loved you for it, Elly, and I tried very hard to keep from smiling and giving myself away.

Towards the evening when I came into the kitchen to see how you were doing, you shooed me right out. I remember I started to ask, "How's the chicken . . ."

"You're in my way, Matt," was all you said. "Now just leave me alone!"

I got cleaned up and waited nervously. When you were through in the kitchen and had set the dining room table, you hurried upstairs and in a little while you came down. You were wearing that blue silk dress with the white collar and you looked as if you'd never set hand to a skillet. You smiled at me, but I could see you were as nervous as I was, and I kept thinking *What is this?* It's only Ma and you'd think it was the Queen of England we were expecting.

Ma came on time like she usually does. And if it was an occasion for us, it was for her too. She had on her taffeta dress with the gold brocade and her hair was all done up fine. I could see the two of you sizing each other up and I was wishing I could read minds.

We didn't say very much to each other except "Good evening" and "The weather's fine" and "Looks like a good crop—"

Then I remember you getting up, Elly, and excusing yourself. Ma was eyeing the living room.

"Elly made the curtains herself," I said.

Ma just nodded.

"Made the kitchen curtains, too," I told her "and painted all the shelves. Makes the place real pretty."

Ma nodded again.

You came back just then, Elly, and said dinner was ready, and we went in and sat down. I was watching Ma and she couldn't hide her look of pleasure at the grand way the table was set up. Still, she didn't say a word. When she finished the vegetable soup, though, Ma said: "They do a pretty good job of canning soup. Makes it easy on young housewives."

I could see you struggling to control yourself, Elly. But your voice was soft and gentle when you told her: "It ain't canned soup. It's homemade."

"Oh," Ma said, not the least taken back. "Mighty good."

I remember carving the chicken neat as I could. I gave Ma the leg and part of the breast. She took a small bite then she really set to. I was breathing easier. One thing, Ma was a good cook and she recognized good cooking. She looked up at you, Elly, and nodded her head and you smiled back, although I was sure you were going to break out crying.

What did it finally was the deep dish apple pie. Ma's favorite. She came over and kissed you and you both had tears in your eyes. You started jabbering at each other about cooking and sewing and taking care of a house. I walked into the living room and picked up the newspaper. No use my being there. Neither of you knew I was around . . .

"Matt!" It was Elly calling him. He shook his head as if to dispel the reverie, and walked to the dining room.

The table was spread with Elly's finest linen. Two candles gave a soft, romantic glow to the room. Elly was dressed in a blue spangled evening gown. She looked radiant.

Matt took her in his arms, held her close and kissed her fervently. "You're beautiful," he said. "I love you very, very much."

Dear Mary Lou

by

Dorothy Rose

You wouldn't believe
The things they have in Little Rock
We visited Aunt Stella there
Last week

They have a toilet in the house
Before we knew what it was
Pretty Boy sailed his boat in it
Ruby Nell washed her doll clothes in it
and I gave the cat a drink from it

When Aunt Stella explained
What it was for
Pretty Boy was afraid to sit on it
So we just let him
Pull the chain
When we used it

Aunt Stella made ice tea
We ran for bowls and spoons
But found that ice tea
Is very different

From ice cream
You drink it from a glass
It tastes like medicine

We ran to the railroad
To watch the train go by
Ruby Nell counted 87 hobos
I counted 105 boxcars
Pretty Boy threw rocks at it

We heard an airplane in the sky
Everyone ran outside to watch
Uncle Zeke said
If God meant us to fly
He'd of give us wings
Daddy said
Zeke that's dumb
If he'd meant us to wear clothes
He'd of give us fur or feathers

Mamma got real embarrassed
You know
The thought of anybody
Being naked

So then grandpa changed the subject
To that awful
President Hoover

The thing we liked best
Was the electric lights
One beautiful bulb

Hangs from the ceiling
Suspended in midair
Like your own special star

Well I've gotta close now Mary Lou
I want to go play with Zelda Prichett
She told me all about
That Santa Claus stuff yesterday
She promised to tell me
About that God stuff today

And
She says there's something
Fishy about
That stork bringing baby stuff too

With love
Your cousin
Jessie Mae

Better Man

by

Tricia Lande

Herschel Bybee got killed in a manhood contest—there is no other way to say it—and that's a sad way to die. It happened in 1925, when three of us were running whiskey up from the coast of Mexico. We had this old fishing boat, the *Annie B.*, that belonged to Herschel's daddy who bought it right after he came to California from Oklahoma. The old man had intended to use the boat for fishing, but he was a farmer, not a fisherman, and things hadn't worked out well. So in the end, to feed his family, he turned to running whiskey. He usually came with us, but not that trip. Then it was just me, twenty-three years old and still with a head of brown hair, and hollow-eyed Herschel, a skinny mouthy seventeen year old who never wore shoes. Wade Comstock was there too. He was two years older than me, with a tangled grass-brown beard, and big hands. I once saw him put a man's eye out in a fight over the right way to gaff a tuna. There was also a deck hand named Paco who kept pretty much to himself and I don't have any real strong memory of him.

We had waited around several days for our whiskey dealer and if we had connected with him right away, things would have gone better, no doubt about that. Wade never took to sea travel and had belly problems hard that trip because we had hit rough weather. Sailing up the Gulf of California was especially bad. The wind blew hot, carrying the stink of tropical decay, and the swells were high. Even anchored in a protected cove at the mouth of the Jardin Rosales, a river that flowed past Culiacan some miles beyond, we all felt poorly, though I think Wade took it worse than Herschel and me. Herschel was on him about it the whole time.

Herschel took more than a respectable amount of pleasure in Wade being sick, and I think size had a lot to do with that, Wade being a big man and Herschel built small. His body was all angles, his plow-sharp bones ended round where they came together, with shoulders so knobby they looked like gear handles. Even if Herschel had finished out his life, I don't think he would have gotten any bigger, and he knew that too. But Herschel was a good kid—though mouthy, as the very young will somctimes be—who wore his daddy's old canvas pants and looked smaller for it.

The sight of a man like Wade down on his knees in the head, hanging onto the bowl, while Herschel held himself back, must have made the kid feel more than equal, and when he said, "Orin,"—that's me, Orin Neck—"Orin, size don't make the man," loud enough for Wade to hear, I knew we were headed for trouble.

We were below deck, really the worst place to be if you are seasick, and Herschel and me were sitting around the little galley table. Herschel leaned his chair back so that it touched the wall and held his chin in the air as if he had just been made captain, then he said, "Size don't make the man," a second time.

Wade came out of the head, his shoulders hunched and his arms just out from his side. He didn't say anything, just looked at Herschel and I think that made me feel poorer about things, because I'd seen Wade in action, and I knew how mean he could get.

There was this thing about Wade's eyes. His white-blond lashes made him look as if he didn't have lids, and his eyes were so dark you couldn't tell their color, like they went way back inside his head sucking in light, but none shined back out because his soul was so black.

I watched him the way you'd watch a rattlesnake that somebody had picked at. You just know it's going to strike, and when it doesn't right off, you feel that hardness in your gut and you don't want to move. So I kept my silence, and with my little finger, traced the names carved deep in the oak table top by men who once served aboard the *Annie B.*

Wade stood there looking at Herschel, but Herschel seemed not to take notice because he said, "It ain't how big you are that shows your manhood. It's how you maintain yourself." He went on like that for a time. Then he was quiet and put his feet up on the oak table and looked off out the porthole like he could see all the way to tomorrow.

Finally, Wade said, "Maybe we ought to go ashore. Maybe we ought to just find out if our connection went north on us."

Looking back, I should have known better because, on land, Wade would be himself again, take the lead, but I'd had all I could stand of that boat myself. I was tired of looking at their faces and feeling that thick dark distance that had grown between us. So I agreed to the idea, and the next day, in that still hour of the morning just before sunup, the three of us rowed up the Jardin Rosales toward the village of La Salida, leaving Paco in charge of the *Annie B.*

The weather had quieted and it was an easy row. Along the banks, long oval-shaped banana tree leaves, still covered with droplets of water from the rain the night before, were shining in the first light, and rubbing together in the slight breeze. They made a shushing noise as if they were trying to hush the parrots that screamed overhead as we passed. It sounded like the way parents quiet their fighting kids so no outsiders would overhear any bad family business. There were lime orchards along the way, their blossoms sweet. In the time it took to get to the village, no one said a word, because it seemed that everything had already been said and things were wrong on account of that.

The sun was up by the time we reached La Salida. A dirt road ran down the middle of the place, but the road was mostly mud, and the water along the sides smelled like cow plops. Pigs stood knee deep in the mess, next to bare-bottomed little kids who watched us like we were something from another world. I had never been ashore before and everywhere I looked there was something to see.

The thing I couldn't take my eyes off was a man who sat on a stool with a wooden cage full of live chickens in front of him, and a pile of dead ones to his right stacked up like a cord of wood. He reached through the little opening, pulled one out by the neck and swung it up over his head, the chicken's wings flapping wildly, throwing feathers all around, trying to fly, trying to do something it couldn't have done even if nobody had ahold of it. The man swung it around until its neck cracked. Just a tiny noise and it was dead and was laid on top of its kin.

A child stood near the old man holding the biggest lizard I had ever seen. A mass of tough skin hung under the lizard's chin, and it had such dead eyes. Some people think lizards look like rocks, like a thing that was never alive, but to me they look dead. Even when the kid swung the thing around by the tail, it didn't try to get away. It just went along for the ride, swinging around and around.

I watched all this with Herschel. We were sitting on the stone steps by the village fountain, him with his head in his hands. The fountain was probably new when the conquistadors ran through the place. The tile around the circle of stone was hand painted in blues and yellows by somebody whose bones had long ago turned to dust. Women, more Indian than Spanish, with skin the color of rusted metal, knew us to be the smugglers that we were. They ignored us as they dipped oval clay pots into the fountain's water that was green with algae.

Wade was off talking to this one and that, trying to find out what happened to our dealer. Pretty soon he came back and said, "We got to wait in the cantina. I put the word out. If he's around, he'll show up there."

That one-horse town cantina, *La Casa de Maximilian,* wasn't much to see. The roof was thatched with straw and palm fronds laid across beams. The floor was dirt, and the back and side walls were wood. The front of the building was open to the street. A black metal fan, its blades thick as a man's wrist, moved hearse slow. It hung down on a long pole that was attached to a cross beam. A red tassel dangled on the end of each blade. There were a few wooden chairs and tables scattered around in a way that made it seem like they were only temporary. The bar, constructed from fruit packing crates, with words like *meln* and *frutas* stenciled on their sides, ran the length of the place.

A short walrus-faced man in a dirty apron stood behind the crates and there was a row of whiskey and tequila bottles on a shelf behind his head. A

Victrola was there, with a brass handle crank, and out of the black S-shaped horn came music. The words to the song were in a language I knew to be German, because I had a grandfather who was both German and crazy, and sang that song most nights. It was an *Abendlied,* a German supper song, and the words meant *Child, be careful! Best of luck to you for the future.* The singer's voice was harsh and grating.

The barkeep said, in good English, but with a German accent, "We got no food, just booze."

"Well, that's fine. We're all men here." Wade slapped the top of a crate then looked at Herschel. "Men don't need food. What a man needs is a drink! Right, Herschel?"

Herschel, with his hollowed-eyed face, answered, "That's right."

I had that bad feeling again and was trying to think of some way out of this, and I said, "Maybe me and Herschel oughta look around town some more. Ask us some questions about Chewy." Chewy was our connection.

"I already done that. What we need now is man-sized drinks. Barkeep, give us a bottle of tequila and the fixin's for it."

Which is what the barkeep did, setting out a flat dish full of salt, a couple of quartered lemons so full of juice that it ran into the crevices in the top of the weathered crates, leaving marks like long shiny vines. Then came the bottle with the worm laying near the bottom, floating upward when the liquid sloshed around. Finally, the German put down the shot glasses, three of them, one sitting inside the next.

The Victrola began to grind to a stop, the guttural words stretching, *zuuuuuu diiiirrr, zuuuuuu rrrrrrrr.* When the barkeep finished setting our things out, he went to the Victrola, holding its wooden side with his left hand, gently as if it were a friend, and cranking the brass handle with his right until the music came to life once more.

Wade took up the lemons in one big dirty hand and the bottle in the other. "Bring the other stuff, men."

The place was empty that time of day, so we had our pick of the tables and Wade took one near the open front of the building. Water had run up inside there and somebody had brought pebbles from the beach and spread them around on the floor, but Wade's heavy work boots ground them into the mud, leaving full imprints, because he laid his feet straight down, sort of like he was marching. Herschel was looking down as if he was tracking Wade by those prints.

We sat at a table and spread everything out.

"You done this before?" Wade asked.

Herschel and me both shook our heads no. So Wade gave us a lesson. He spit on his wrist and smeared it around a little with his tongue, then laid the wet place in the salt dish so that the large grains stuck. He licked his wrist, then took a shooter of tequila, sucked on a lemon quarter quick-like and so hard that juice ran down the sides of his mouth and dropped on the front of his cotton shirt, leaving round stains.

I watched, then followed the lesson exactly, but not before trying one more time to leave. For I really was worried now. I had seen Wade drunk and a drunk Wade was about as mean as mean got.

"I think maybe me and Herschel oughta go out for a while," I said. "I told his daddy I'd keep an eye on him. His old man ain't gonna like it if I get his kid drunk, Wade."

Well, Herschel got right up in my face and said, "I ain't no kid, Orin. And to hell with my daddy. I do a man's job of work and I can drink with the best. I sure can drink you under the table, Orin."

"What kid you talking about, Orin?" Wade said. He looked around like he was trying to see something. "Ain't no kids around here. Just us men here. Right, Herschel? Unless of course you're a kid, Orin. You a kid?" Wade said this with his teeth tight together. Then he pushed the shot glass over to me. "I don't hang around with no kids."

So I said no more and drank, and Herschel drank, and Wade drank and drank. After a while there was only about a shooter full left in the bottle, plus the worm laying at the bottom. Wade said, "Well now. That worm goes to the best man. Only the better man gets to drink that worm."

By this time I was feeling more than sick and I said, "That's okay, Wade. We knew all along you are the better man. Don't we know that, Herschel?"

Herschel allowed as how that was the total truth. "You the best, Wade. That there worm is yours, for sure."

"Nope. Nope," Wade said. "We got to find us a way to prove who's the best." Wade leaned back so that his chair stood on two legs that sunk into the soft sludge floor, then gave completely out dropping the big man on his back and landing him on those muddy pebbles. He just laid there for a minute, not saying anything, just staring up.

Now I was drunk, no doubt about that, but I hadn't had as much as Wade and neither had Herschel. I figure Wade ran about three drinks ahead of us, and I was still sober enough to hope Wade had passed out. But that wasn't to be. Turns out Wade was just laying there figuring out a way to prove who was the best.

"These pebbles is going to do it," he said. Then he raised up, took a bunch, and staggered his way back over to the table. "Best man is the one can hold his liquor. But how we going to prove who can hold his liquor?"

Herschel said, "You already done drunk more than us, Wade. And you're still standing. That's what proves it."

"Nope. Nope," Wade insisted. "Man who holds his liquor is the man that can maintain his skills."

"What kind of skills are we going to maintain?" I asked.

"Rock throwing," Wade said. "See, that makes it fair. Give you and Herschel a handicap. Me being older, I got more practice at drinking. You being younger, you got more recent rock throwing experience. You men understand?"

Both Herschel and I said we did, though that was a lie on my part. I was too drunk to really follow his line of thought.

Wade explained how things were going to be done. "See that fan?" The black metal fan turned slowly, red tassels trailing after each heavy curved blade, trying to move stale air around the room. It was about noon and the sun was full and high and the humid stink of that day made me feel as if I was trying to breathe with a pillow pressed over my face. My clothes stuck to my body and all I wanted now was to find a place to sleep.

The black fan purred overhead and Herschel watched it for a second, then whispered to me, "I feel sick." And I could hear the barkeep cranking his machine again, gears clicking against cog heels.

Wade said, "Remember, now. I don't hang around with no kids. I ain't rowing back to the boat with kids."

So Herschel and me each took the pebbles Wade set in front of us and did what he said. The idea was to see who could throw a pebble between the fan blades without hitting one. According to Wade that would prove who was able to maintain his skills.

Two things happened. First, nobody could

throw a rock between the fan blades without hitting one. Those rocks hit the fan blades the way a baseball hits a bat, flying off in all directions, bouncing off the wall, pinging against the bottles on the shelf behind the bar, rocketing off the palm frond roof, which led to the second thing that happened.

The German barman, who up to that point, minded his own business reading a newspaper and cranking his music, was pelleted with rocks and came up screaming. "You crazy! You crazy!" he yelled. "You kill me. You wreck my place!"

Wade moved quicker than you would have thought a drunk could. He was at the crates, reaching across and grabbing the German faster-than-Jack. "We're proving our manhood. You understand that? You comprende manhood?"

The German didn't say anything, just shook his head up and down best he could.

"Well," Wade went on, "if you want to keep yours, you better get the hell out the way." Then Wade dropped him and the guy took off over in the corner and stayed there until what happened finally happened.

Wade looked at the rocks that littered the floor. "Damn, this ain't working. The fan needs to go faster. That's the problem. How you make this go faster?" he said to the German.

The guy pointed to a black round switch on the wall next to a poster of a skinny matador holding a cape in front of a bull. Wade clicked it and the fan roared and swayed from side to side like it was trying to pull free from the pole that held it to the ceiling beam.

"Okay, men. Try her again." Of course things only got worse. Everybody ducked this time. Rocks flew every which-way. Finally, Wade sat down on the floor and looked up at the fan like it had betrayed him.

He slapped his knee and said, "Wait. I got it! I know a better way to show how good we maintain our skills. See that cross beam the fan's swinging on?"

Wade explained the new game. There was a space between the beam and the palm roof. The plan was to jump off the bar crates and grab the beam, swing from it twice, then drop to the floor on your feet. The man that could do that was the best and got to eat the worm.

I figured I was safe from eating that worm because the shooters had caught up with me to the point where I didn't think I could walk to the bar, much less jump.

I was wrong. I did manage to make it to the bar. I just couldn't make it up on the crates and pitched backwards so that I was spread-eagled on the floor instead. I felt paralyzed from the hair down and so there seemed no point in trying to get up. Besides, I could pretty well see what was going on and the mucky floor was soft, so there really was no reason to move.

When Wade realized I wasn't going to get up, he said, "Orin, you coward. You failed to maintain your skills. Herschel, you get up there next.

Herschel made it to the crate bar, knocking down chairs along the way. His hollow-eyed face, white now, looked down at me for an instant, then he moved on, mounting those crates while that hard voice with its military pulse kept on singing from the wind-up phonograph.

The bottoms of Herschel's feet showed as he climbed. Mud stuck to his little toes. And his canvas pants caught on a ragged corner. He pulled loose, tearing them. When he finally reached the top he stood very still for a second, like he was judging his distance, then raised his arms the way a diver does, sweat stains round under his shirt sleeves. Bent at the knees, he held the position for the time it takes to pull a breath and pushed off arching his body forward. The Victrola went . . . *zuuuu dirrrrr uuuuuuu rrrrrrrrrr.*

Herschel's hands were maybe sweaty. That must have been the problem, because he caught hold of the beam with both hands, but one slipped loose and that made him swing sideways to his right just as the fan pulled left against the pole. I heard the crack, just a tiny noise when that thick metal blade hit Herschel.

He came down backwards, like he was floating down, moving this way, then that, the way a feather does, and he didn't make much of a noise when he landed on the soft floor. A noise no louder than the crack of the bones in his neck, and I was glad for that. Glad he was dead when he hit the ground, at least I prayed he was. I didn't want the boy to feel what happened. For sure he was dead by the time I crawled over to where he lay.

His head was at an angle and his eyes stared upward as if he needed to check that beam again, figure out what had gone wrong. His canvas pants were pulled up on one leg so that the knob of a knee showed, and a long red tassel lay across his neck marking the spot where the fan blade had ended him.

Wade stood there looking at Herschel like he was trying to understand, and I could see that his eyes weren't black after all, but dark blue, and there was light in them now, something I hadn't seen before. Finally, it seemed clear to Wade what had happened, and he covered his face with his big hands for a moment, then he was gone.

I lay on the floor awhile longer. It was silent then because the record was over, the song had ended, and silent because Wade was gone and so was Herschel, who hadn't lived long enough to find out who was the better man.

Set Free

by

Helen Peppe

The dog sat on the grass near the house, his tongue out. There was a red collar around his neck. A long cable wound from his red collar to a hook on the house. It was strong. The boy knew it was strong. Everyone knew it was strong. They had seen the dog lunge and jerk at the end of the thick cord barking at the cars, the cats, the people, forcing against the cable and hook with its black chest. It hurt the boy to see the dog strain so frantically, so uselessly. He hoped that the cable would break so that the dog could be free. The boy felt the dog's frustration as if it were his own. He knew it was like the frustration he felt when his father held him tight in his arms and wouldn't let go. Even though it was a game, and his father laughed, he hated it. It was no game to him. At those times, the boy felt hate that he was incapable of expressing to anyone, but he knew the dog knew how he felt. It was not right for the dog to be tied just as it was not right for his father to hug him tight and laugh at him as he struggled to free himself.

The pain was too real to the boy; he had to do something.

The boy walked to the dog and gently rubbed his black pointed ears. The dog responded by licking the boy's hand and butting him with his smooth black head. The boy slid his small hand under the dog's collar. The fur was hot and rumpled. He knew it would be easy to unfasten the clip from the hook on the collar, but other things were not so easy. The question of where the dog would go ran through the boy's head. Would he just run so fast that no one could catch him, not even his father, who could do anything? And the question that the boy wondered the most, would the dog ever come back?

The boy loved the dog. The dog was the only one who shared his hate and anger. The dog was his closest friend.

The boy removed his fingers from the collar and instead wrapped his small arms around the dog's neck. The dog endured this new form of attention for a minute, then struggled free, although he still sat next to the boy.

The boy sat down on the grass. A new thought entered his mind. His father would be angry when he discovered that the dog was gone. The dog had cost a lot of money and they had had him for only six months. They had needed a watch dog, a Doberman, his father had insisted. No other dog scared people enough.

The boy had found this to be true. The kids next door had not taken his bike or played on his tire swing since the dog had come. Cats had certainly been scarce too. His father hated the mess that cats made and they all hated the yowling of the cats fighting under their windows at night. The boy didn't like cats. They were not like dogs, and no one could convince him that they were as fun to play with or that they did not make as much mess. He could smell the difference when he went to his friends' houses in the city. He moved toward the dog again, this time gratefully, and patted the dog's head. Maybe if he let the dog loose, the cats would come back. The boy instantly realized that it was a selfish thought. Enduring the cats would be a small price for the dog's freedom. He made a move to set the dog free, but just at that moment his mother came out of the house with the dog's supper. The boy wished that he had thought of this himself. It would have been terrible to let the dog loose without his supper.

His mother patted him on the head and told him that his own dinner would be ready soon. The boy nodded but stayed where he was. It would have been awful if the dog had had to eat out of garbage cans to get his supper like the dogs he saw on his way to school. The boy hated that. He wished that he could feed all the dogs in the neighborhood so that they wouldn't have to eat someone's old potato peels and beef gristle. But the boy knew that he did not have enough money. At eight, he barely had enough to weight his piggy bank down. On windy days he always had to remove his bank from the sill or he would find it on the floor, the black eyes of the pig staring up at the ceiling lamenting its inadequacy.

The dog sure was hungry. The boy knew his mother did not feed the dog enough. An eighty-five pound dog needed more than one bowl of food a day. It wasn't right. But his mother had gotten mad at him for bringing the dog his own mashed potatoes. The boy had always hated potatoes even though his mother always insisted that they didn't taste like potatoes when they were mashed. He still had stray lumps of potato in his jacket pocket. He was beginning to think that he would never be able to forget about trying to feed the dog his potatoes. And anyway, the dog hadn't liked them either. That was how his mother had found out. Mashed potatoes don't disappear very quickly from black pavement. The boy smiled. He was glad that the dog didn't like potatoes either, even mashed. The boy bet that the dog also wouldn't like liver. For that reason, he hadn't tried to sneak it to him. It was not right to feed liver to people who did not like it. The slimy liver residue lasted indefinitely on the dinner plate destroying the taste of the best elbow macaroni.

He wished his mother felt the way he and the dog did. But no one seemed to care how he or the dog felt. Anyone could see that the dog needed to run, but his father only walked him once a day. The boy knew that wasn't enough. The dog had so much energy. And the boy's mother wouldn't go near the dog unless it was to feed him or clean up his messes. She said that the dog was dangerous. She had wanted to get a poodle. She thought that Dobermans were too much like Pit Bulls. But his father had insisted on a Doberman. No other dog could do it, he said. As far as the boy knew, his father had been right.

The dog started toward his dog house, then turned and studied the boy. It was obvious that the dog was puzzled by the extra attention. The boy thought instead that the dog was looking to him for more food. The boy turned an angry look toward the house. His mother should know better. She was the one always talking about paying twenty-five dollars a month to adopt a foster child. But his father always made a disgusted face and said there were better things they could do with twenty-five dollars. His father disliked those dark kids with the large bellies. But the boy knew though, that his mother sent money secretly. He wished that he could do things secretly too, but his parents always found out.

He wondered what his father would do when he saw that the dog was gone. Maybe he wouldn't do much. His father had called the dog the boy's when there had been a mess in the driveway last week. Maybe the boy had the right to do with the dog what he wanted. This thought made the boy move again toward the dog's collar.

The dog's short black hair tickled the boy's fingers. The boy looked anxiously toward the house. He hoped his mother was busy, maybe on the telephone. She was on the telephone a lot. The hook felt cold on the boy's fingers in relation to the dog's fur. He slid his fingers around the metal clasp. For a minute, he hesitated. He hoped that the dog would not get lost. This misgiving was quickly suppressed with the thought of the dog's approaching happiness, and, before he could change his mind, he undid the metal clasp. With his hand still on the dog's collar, he kissed the dog, and hugged him tightly. A tear squeezed out between the boy's lids. He hoped that the dog would come back. He was his only real friend.

He released the dog's collar from his sweaty hands and stood back feeling miserable at the near separation. The dog yawned and stretched, glad to be free from the boy's restrictive arms. He looked at the boy then he licked his whiskered mouth for the last vestiges of his supper. The boy waved his hand slowly and whispered a bye. The dog stretched again and yawned with a high pitched sound. Then he moved toward the side of his dog house, lifted his leg, and urinated against the rough boards. He gave the boy another look as if to ask, "Are you through? Is there anything else?" then moved to the front of his dog house and kicked up his hind legs scratching up the grass.

Then the dog went inside, turned around, and laid down resting his pointed nose on his strong paws. The boy stared at him in confusion then walked to the dog house. The dog raised his eyes not bothering to lift his head. "You're loose," the boy whispered. “Don’t you realize that?” The dog closed his heavy lids with a grunt. There was a gurgle from the depths of his black rounded stomach.

The Donation

by

Marion Rosen

The wind whipped the heavy church door out of Dora's hand, slamming it with a hollow thud. She winced. It wasn't proper to slam doors in a church. She shook the rain from her umbrella and dropped it into the umbrella stand. The dampness had crept into her bones. Her bursitis would flare up tonight, she thought.

A door next to the choir loft opened. Minerva, president of the church's Ladies' Aid Society, stuck her head into the church from the adjoining sacristy and squinted at Dora through her bifocals.

"Lord a mercy, Dora, is that you making all that noise? Take off that wet coat before you catch your death," Minerva said. "Better leave it on the last pew so you don't drip everywhere."

No matter how hard she tried, Dora was never able to shrug off Minerva's constant disapproval.

Minerva motioned for Dora to hurry into the little room. "No heat in the church again, but it's warm enough in here."

Dora walked down the center aisle, her shoes

clicking loudly against the cold marble. When she entered the sacristy, Dora felt a warm stream of air coming from a small electric heater.

"Is anyone else coming?" Dora asked. Minerva shook her head and pulled her sweater tighter across her chest. "Looks like just the two of us. Sarah and Effie can't make it, and Margaret has the flu."

Minerva turned to Dora. "Did you call the new member about the bake sale?"

Dora strained a weak smile. She didn't feel comfortable asking newcomers to bake for the Ladies' Aid. People were too busy nowadays, and it was awkward listening to the excuses they made. Dora would gladly bake all the cakes for the bake sale herself if Minerva would just stop asking her to make embarrassing phone calls. "I thought I'd call tomorrow," she said.

"Gracious, Dora," Minerva rebuked, "how will we ever get a new altar cloth by Easter if you don't do your share? You have to get people involved, or they'll drift away."

Dora felt her face redden. It was true. Over the years, she had seen dozens of their members move from the downtown area to the cleaner, roomier suburbs. They would drive back into town once or twice for services, but then they would transfer to a newer church where the minister invariably played a guitar. She could remember a time when the Ladies' Aid boasted over a hundred members. Now they had about six they could count on, unless, of course, it was raining.

"Well, how many cakes do you have promised for Saturday?" Minerva asked, her eyes fixed on Dora.

"Six," Dora said, thinking about the five cakes she would have to bake herself.

"That's all?" Minerva pinched her eyebrows together. "Well, I have pledges for eleven cakes, and, of course, I'll bake one myself."

Minerva's words were drowned out by a thunderous banging of the church door. Startled, they hurried to the doorway and peered into the church, staring down the long, center aisle toward the entrance. Two men, one with a ski mask pulled down over his face, stood there dripping wet.

"Jeez, Archie, you said this place would be empty," Ski Mask said.

Archie looked to be about twenty, a big hulking lad with a dim look in his eyes. His features suggested he had seen plenty of fights, and he hadn't known when to duck.

"How was I to know?" Archie said. "Aren't churches supposed to be empty on Tuesdays?"

Minerva pulled herself up to her full five feet three inches. "May we help you, gentlemen?"

Ski Mask walked toward them and studied Minerva through the slits in his green and black mask. Dora thought he resembled a big lizard with those darting, black eyes.

"Any more old broads back there?" He shoved Minerva aside and looked into the sacristy. "What're you doing in here anyway?"

Minerva folded her hands across her waist and

said, "We were having a meeting of the Ladies' Aid. May we help you?" She sounded terribly official.

Ski Mask pointed to the first pew. "Sit down while I think."

Minerva began to protest, but just then a siren screamed outside as a police car sped by. Archie jumped and looked at Ski Mask. Surely now, Dora thought, Minerva must understand what they were facing, but still, Minerva didn't budge. Dora pushed against Minerva's elbow, steering her into the pew. They sat shoulder to shoulder.

"Check outside," Ski Mask ordered.

Archie raced to the door and opened it just a crack. Dora felt an icy draft rushing under the pews, encircling their legs.

"Are you boys in some kind of trouble?" Minerva asked.

"Shut up," Ski Mask said. "How can I think with you yapping?"

Archie ran back to the first pew. "I don't see no cops on the street."

"Still, we'd better hang out here for a while," Ski Mask said.

"Goodness, what have you done?" Minerva asked. "Why are the police after you?"

Dora rolled her eyes. Hadn't Minerva ever watched cops and robbers on TV?

Ski Mask set down the rumpled shopping bag he had clutched in his hand and flexed his fingers. "You sure are a nosey old dame. You sound just like my old lady."

Dora eyed the shopping bag. She could see something black inside and just a hint of something shiny.

"We knocked off Bryson's, that's what," Ski Mask shouted in Minerva's face. "Now are you happy?"

"Oh," Minerva breathed, a flush covering her face.

Bryson's was the oldest, most reputable jewelry store in town, and now Minerva, finally catching on, grabbed Dora's hand and held it tightly.

"Maybe we'd better not talk to them," Minerva whispered to Dora. "They're in serious trouble."

"Hey, no whispering," Ski Mask yelled at Minerva. "You got something to say, lady, you say it to me."

As cold as it was in the church, Minerva's hand felt clammy with sweat. Dora dabbed her handkerchief against her forehead with her other hand.

"Hey," Archie said, "you got anything to eat?"

Dora was indignant. "This is a church, not a restaurant."

Minerva finally regained her nerve and sat up straighter. "That's right," she agreed, her voice booming.

Ski Mask reached out and slapped Minerva hard across the face, sending her bifocals clattering to the floor. Minerva cried out, throwing her hands up to her eyes. Tears immediately began to trickle down her cheeks.

"You didn't have to hit her!" Dora cried. She knelt next to the shopping bag and groped for Minerva's glasses.

Ski Mask turned his back in disgust and walked toward the altar. He fingered the silver cross and tried to lift it. Its enormous weight probably saved it from being added to the loot in the shopping bag.

Carefully, Dora checked Minerva's lenses. Good, the glass was still intact, but now they had to worry about what Ski Mask might do next. Dora had no idea how to stop two brutal thieves from hurting them further, but she did have a feeling she might be able to solve one of their problems.

Ski Mask suddenly turned around and spotted Dora on the floor. "Hey, old lady. What're you doing? Get away from there."

He rushed back and grabbed Dora by the arm. Yanking her to her feet with a painful jerk, Ski Mask glared at her with his beady, lizard eyes. "Listen, lady, you're getting on my nerves. I got problems, here. We have to get across town, but this whole neighborhood is crawling with cops. Now shut up and let me think."

Dora sat down and handed the glasses to Minerva. Still weeping, Minerva leaned her head on Dora's shoulder.

"I'm hungry,"Archie bellowed. "Ain't you got nothing to eat?"

"I could make a pot of tea," Dora said.

"We don't need no tea," Ski Mask said, through

clenched teeth. "Jeez, Archie, will you shut up? You're worse than the old ladies."

Dora cleared her throat. "You could take my car," she said flatly.

Ski Mask snickered. "What do I look like? Some stupid jerk?"

Dora shook her head. "You could get where you're going faster with a car, couldn't you?"

"Yeah, and then you call the cops and report a stolen car," Ski Mask said. "They'd grab us in nothing flat."

"The church doesn't have a phone." Dora persisted, "Where do you have to go?"

Archie grinned and said, "We have to meet some guys over near the high scho . . . ,"

Ski Mask's growl overrode even Archie's voice. "Why, Lady? You want to come along?" His eyes bulged, ready to pop through the little slits in his mask.

Dora stood up and tucked her hanky into the cleft of her bosom. "If that's what it takes to get you out of here, yes. Otherwise, drive my car to meet your friends. Park it in the high school lot and leave the keys under the floor mat."

Dora heard Minerva suck in a deep breath, but Dora continued, even managing to muster a smile. "The police won't have time to grab you if you drive straight to the school. I can take the bus and pick up my car later."

Ski Mask scratched his head.

"You think it'll work?" Archie asked.

"It might," Ski Mask said, nodding. "Like she

said, we'd only be in the car ten minutes before we connect with the guys. Just put on your gloves so we don't leave prints in the car."

"What about them fingering us?" Archie asked.

"They ain't gonna finger me," Ski Mask retorted. "I told you to keep your mask on your face."

"Aw," Archie said, "I got hot."

Ski Mask turned to Dora. "Where are the keys, lady?"

"In my coat." Dora pointed, "It's back there, over the last pew."

Archie went to the last pew and grabbed Dora's coat. "Hey, these pockets are too little to get my hands in," he called.

Ski Mask hurried toward him. "You big ox. Can't you do anything right?" Ski Mask fumbled in the pocket, then pulled out Dora's keys. "Here they are. Where's your car?"

Dora told him, "Right outside. The blue Vega."

Ski Mask ran back to the first pew and grabbed the shopping bag. "I don't know why you're helping us, lady, but thanks." In another moment, they heard the door slam.

Dora sat down again and listened to the thudding of her own heart. She thought she was going to faint.

"What will Father Gallagher say?" Minerva demanded. She fanned her face with her hand. "At least the police will know where to look for them."

Dora scoffed, 'They won't go near the high

school, and the police probably won't find my car for days. It'll turn up in some alley behind a bar."

Minerva's eyes widened and her mouth fell open. "But then why did you let them take it?"

"Don't worry," Dora said slyly. "I'll get my car back sooner or later plus enough cash to donate to the church for the best altar cloth money can buy."

"But how?" Minerva asked.

Dora reached down the front of her dress and pulled out a black pouch. She opened it and spilled dozens of glittering diamonds into her lap. "I'm sure Mr. Bryson at the jewelry store will offer us a generous reward for the return of his property.

A gush of air escaped from Minerva's lips. "A reward! Why, Dora, you tricked everyone, even me. You played along with them knowing exactly what you were doing!"

Dora grinned, recalling how she'd lifted the jewels from the bag while she was on the floor. "That's right. Now the money we get from the bake sale will just be icing on the cake!"

Hot Chocolate for Two

by

Dorothy Winslow Wright

Andrew, wearing his favorite baggy blue sweater, tossed another log on the fire. He stood back and rubbed his hands in front of the flame as if trying to absorb the heat into his long slim fingers. Nineteen year old Allison, sprawled on the couch with a book in her lap, glanced up and laughed. "You look like someone out of a Norman Rockwell painting just in from the icy blasts," she said. "Are you that cold, Grampa?"

He answered, "No, not really, but there's something about a fire that stirs that in me. I remember when your grandmother and I would come in from bobsledding . . ."

Allison had heard this before. She interrupted, ". . . and you had hot chocolate and sat on the floor, side by side, watching the sparks fly up the chimney."

"Humph," he said. "You're making fun of me—but I guess I had it coming. I do tend to repeat myself."

"That's okay, Grampa, but I couldn't resist it. You're such a perfect storybook grandfather, even to retelling the old-timey tales." She paused, then smiled at him. "But I love to hear them—really. It's all so ancient."

The word hung in the air between them. It stayed with Andrew after he returned to his chair. It filtered through the words in the newspaper. He let the paper slip to the floor. No point in trying to read. He couldn't concentrate. Allison was right. The way of life he knew was gone, unknown to this beloved granddaughter.

Wearing the warm windproof jackets of today with their snug stitched-on hoods, how could the young ones be expected to know what cold was really like? In the old days the biting wind cut through the heaviest of coats. It crept up sleeves and sneaked down necks. Fingers turned blue in spite of thick woolen mittens. He thought of the outside chill, the contrasting warmth of the inside heat. The beauty of a welcoming fire, his Abby in his arms. It was a warmth that transcended the physical.

He scowled, his eyes going beyond the icicles fringing the big bay window to the snow glistening on the hill. His and Abby's hill.

He glanced at Allison, her head bent over her physics book. She looked so content. Comfortable. He should be happy, but he wasn't. He wanted her to experience—just once—the wonder of the winter world that he and Abby had known.

"Allison," he said, "how about taking a walk with me."

"Now?" she asked as she looked up. "It's freezing out there, Grampa."

"All the more reason," he said. "I want to try an experiment. Will you go along with me?"

She eyed him suspiciously, then shrugged. "Okay, Grampa, I guess I've had enough equations for one afternoon." She yawned and stretched. "So, what're we going to do?"

"You'll see. Now, grab your coat—the woolen one, not your goose-down jacket. And wear the mittens your Great Aunt Sarah knitted for you—not your ski mitts."

Allison paused, "You're sure tossing out the orders, aren't you?"

"For a reason," he said.

He pulled on his red plaid cap with the ear flaps, and plopped a similar one on Allison's head. "You'll need this." He led her out the back door and around to the right-of-way between his house and the woods behind it.

"That way," he said, nodding toward the field beyond. "I want to show you something." White frosty puffs accentuated every word he spoke.

Allison shivered as they walked into the wind. "This coat isn't warm enough," she said.

"Walk faster and you won't be so cold, girl." He put his arm around her and pulled her close. "Does that help?"

She nodded.

"That's what I used to do with your grandmother. You'd have liked Abby, Allison. She was a lot like you. Sassy. Said what she thought, that one." He gestured to a rise ahead. "That's where we're going."

She frowned. "That far? We should have taken the car."

"And miss all this fun?" he teased.

"Jimmy is n-n-never going to believe this," Allison said, shuddering with the cold. "He thought I was crazy to want to come to Vermont for the semester b-b-break when I could have gone with him to the sunny South."

"I'm glad you came," her grandfather answered. "I don't see near enough of you now that you're in college." He paused by a snowbank. "Now you can see where I took your grandmother bob sledding . . . and this is where she tumbled in the snow." He grinned and gave Allison a playful push.

"Grampa, that wasn't fair!" she sputtered, spitting out the snow as she landed in the drift. "Oh, well, since I'm already covered with this fluffy stuff, I might as well make snow angels. I haven't made 'em for years." She flopped on her back and swished her arms and legs back and forth like a five year old.

"Come on, Grampa, you make some, too." She tugged at the cuff of his flannel trousers.

Andrew lost his balance and fell beside her. When he sat up, a pain shot through his ankle. He winced.

"Oh, Grampa, are you hurt?" she asked.

"No," he said, "it's just my trick ankle. Always gives me trouble."

"Can you stand up?" Her voice trembled. She helped him up, then slipped her arm around his waist.

He was a darn fool to try to recreate the past. "I don't need any help," he snapped, more angry at himself than at her.

"I know you don't, Grampa, but I'm cold. Too darn cold—if you want to know—and I need to be next to you to keep warm. This was your idea, remember?"

She kept her arm in place all the way to the house. Neither talked. Their white breath made statements enough. Allison's teeth chattered. By the time they reached the house, Andrew's were chattering, too.

She helped him off with his coat and into the chair nearest the fire, then propped his foot up on a pillow. "Now stay put until I come back with some ice."

"I don't need any ice," he grumbled.

"Yes, you do, Grampa—and this time I'm calling the shots." He leaned back and closed his eyes, disgusted at the way things had turned out. He had wanted to give his beloved granddaughter something special, but instead he'd given her trouble. It showed in her worried frown, in the flush of her cheeks. This wasn't the afternoon he'd planned.

"There," she said, as she tucked the cold pack around his ankle, "this'll do the trick."

He watched her as she tossed another log on the glowing embers. She stood back and rubbed her hands in front of the flame as if trying to work the heat back into her long slim fingers.

Andrew chuckled. "You look like something out of a Norman Rockwell painting," he said.

"I expect I do," she said, "and now, how about some hot chocolate? We could drink it while we watch the sparks flutter up the chimney."

"That's just what I had in mind," he said.

Crazy Hat

by

Frederic Carpenter

I was about fifteen when the old man came to town. That was a long time ago, about two years. We were standing on the street in front of the drugstore when this old guy came walking along with a pack on his back and dust and dirt all over him. Like he'd been living out on the desert or prospecting up in the mountains. When he came up to us and we all saw him, we just quit joshing each other and watched the old guy as he passed.

He was really old. His face was practically hidden by his scraggly old beard and mop of dried out gray hair that was all frazzled and tangled and that stuck out all around. You could see the wrinkles and crevices in his face and that leathery big-pored skin that comes from a long time in the sun. You could tell he was at least seventy, maybe eighty. But he stood real straight and that pack didn't seem to bother him, so he must have been in pretty good shape for an old man.

And there was something about his eyes, too, that made him different from most old men I'd seen. They were wide awake and looked like they were looking for something and knew what it was. Most old men have sleepy-looking eyes like they're waiting for something to happen and don't even know what it is. They're just waiting.

The thing I noticed most about the old man, though, was his hat. It caught my eye when I was looking at his face, and the funny thing was that, after the old man had gone by, I asked the other kids about it and they hadn't even noticed it.

The hat had a funny shape. I mean it was kind of big in the crown, bigger than most men's hats and all pushed out of shape. Well, like it didn't have any real shape at all and just took whatever shape the winds or the weather gave it. It was streaked and faded, bleached by the rain and sun so you couldn't tell what color it had been. But it stood high above the old man's head like it had resisted the weather in its own way and had given up its shape and color as a compromise and had made itself more durable that way.

One time at the old man's camp I saw the hat lying down upside down and it looked all right. It still had a sweat band. The old man saw me looking at it when he came over to put it back on and said something about it didn't matter about the outside, the important thing was the insides and especially the top. That was the part that protected you, the top.

Anyway, that first day, we watched to see where he was going. He went into the post office and then came out and went to the general store. He stayed in there a pretty good while and came out with groceries and a bunch of tools and even a stepladder. Then he walked on out of town, carrying it all.

We thought that was the last we'd see of the old geezer and just forgot about him. We used to see old coots like him every now and then anyway. Most of them would hang around for a few days before the sheriff would hint to them to move along. And they would go.

The next day the old man came back. This time he went right to the general store. He came out with a bigger bag of groceries and an old Army surplus five-gallon can. He took the can down to the filling station at the West end of town and filled it with water and strapped it onto a pack frame he'd been wearing when he came into town. Then he went on out the way he'd come, again taking all that stuff with him.

We began to get curious about him then. It looked like he was staying around town but somewhere out on the desert. Nothing ever happens in this town except maybe once in a while you'll see a movie star on his way to Las Vegas or coming back. But most of the time it's just cars coming and going, passing through and sometimes stopping to fill up or for the people to eat. So you see why we were interested in the old man. Especially after he came into town the next week and went through the same routine.

About this same time, the people who stopped for gas at the station where I worked began to ask questions. They said there was an old guy working on a rock outside of town about six miles and they wanted to know what he was doing. They said he had a tent pitched out there, too, like he was living there. Well, that was the old man. I didn't know what he was doing any more than those people did. When I told the other kids, we decided to go out there and see.

One of the kids had an old Chevy and we piled into that, the six of us, and went on out to the old man's camp. He had a camp all right, but it wasn't much. Just an old pup tent, one of that kind you button together in the middle, and a fireplace made of some rocks with a place in the middle for a can of Sterno. It was pretty cruddy, but I guess it was all right for the old man.

When we drove up he just looked at us for a minute without saying anything and then went back to work. He was up on his ladder chipping away with a chisel and hammer at a tall rock and once in a while letting out a muffled chuckle like he was happy or having a joke on somebody. But he never said anything to us and after a while we just left.

But we couldn't stop wondering about the old man chipping on that rock. In fact, by then the whole town was talking and everybody was trying to figure what the old guy was up to. So we went out there again. Only this time we waited until after supper so we wouldn't have to come back so soon.

When we drove up the old man wasn't up on the ladder. He was down by the fireplace cooking his supper. But when we got out of the car, the old guy blew out the Sterno and went into his tent. We could see he didn't want to know us but we walked on over anyway and Bill, who was sort of our leader, stood at the tent opening and hollered, "Hey! Old Man!"

When he did this the old man just pulled the cover of his sleeping bag over his head and ignored us. Bill just stood there about a minute and scratched his head. Then he said, "Aw, come on. The old guy don't wanta know anybody." Then we all left.

That week we heard something about the old man. The county sheriff went out there to see what he was doing and found out the old man was a veteran of World War II and was getting a pension. Social Security, too. So the sheriff couldn't run him off for vagrancy. And besides, that was Federal land he'd camped on anyway. The sheriff said something about the old man building a monument. We were really curious then. The whole town was.

The next time the old man came into town, Mr. Jensen down at the station where the old man got his water tried to get the old man to talk. When the old man wouldn't talk, Mr. Jensen got kind of mad and the old man just walked off. He still needed water, though, and so he came down to where I worked. When I saw him coming, I fooled around with the water hose but he didn't come by me. He went over to Mr. Godfrey and asked him if he could fill up his water can for a quarter.

Mr. Godfrey said he didn't have to pay but the old man said he'd rather. He said it real straight-like and Mr. Godfrey took a good look at him and then said it was all right. I was standing there listening and when the old man came over, I gave him the hose and he filled up his can. I could see he didn't want to talk so I didn't say anything. When he was through he left.

A few people in town went out to see the old man a couple of times but after a while they just left him alone. They figured as long as the old man wasn't bothering anyone, they wouldn't bother him. They still wondered about that rock, though. We did, too. The other guys and me.

The next time the old man came into town he did something funny. He paid Mr. Godfrey the quarter and came over to fill the can. I was standing there like before without saying anything and when the old man was through, he looked at me and said, "In this station Pro-mee-thoose is unbound." Or something like that. Then he smiled and left.

Well, that week we went out there again. Me and the others. We went on a Saturday night. It was hot and we took some beer in an ice chest. We didn't go as early as last time, figuring maybe the old man would be more friendly after he'd had his supper.

The old man was playing a guitar when we drove up. He was leaning back on a rock chording away and crooning to himself. His eyes were half-closed and he must have been feeling pretty good, because when he heard us pull into his camp, he just looked our way for a minute and then went back to his playing. Only he quit chording and really began to play that guitar. He was good. Real good. We all piled out of the Chevy and just stood there while the old man played faster and faster making that guitar do everything but talk. He could pick those strings so fast it almost seemed like he was playing a piano instead of a guitar he got so many notes out of it.

After a while the old man stopped playing and opened his eyes to take a good look at us. At first he looked like he didn't want to have anything to do with us like before, but when he saw me, he seemed to relax a little and waited for one of us to say something. Bill walked up closer to the old man and said, "Say, old man, you want a beer?"

The old man said, "Nope, I don't suppose I do," in the same real proud way he'd talked to Mr. Godfrey.

I guess Bill didn't know what to say to that because he turned around and walked off slow like and then all of a sudden hollered, "Well, I'm gonna have me one, by God." Then he walked real fast toward the car.

I kind of liked the old man, but we were still curious about what he was doing with that rock, so I didn't want the old man to get mad at us right off. We'd never find out anything then. So I said real polite like, "Well . . . er . . . would you mind if we just sat around and talked?"

And the old man answered, "Nope, sonny, I

don't mind. But I'm just goin' to go ahead and play my guitar."

Well, we all went to the car and got a beer and then came back and sat around the old man. At first we just sat and listened while we drank our beer. We were all too bashful to come right out and ask the old man what was on our minds, and we didn't know what to talk about with such an old guy, so we just didn't say anything. After a while, though, I said, "Say, Mister, where're you from?"

"Son," the old man said, "I'm from the whole wide old U.S. and A."

"Yeah," I went on, "but I mean what part? Where you *from?*"

"Well, son," he said, "I don't rightly know where I was *born,* if that's what you mean, but I do know I'm from this good earth that you see all around you."

Then someone piped in and said, "Good? Ha! Nothin' but desert."

The old man came back with, "That's not what I mean, son. It's not this very earth I'm talking about, it's the concept of the earth."

"Whatta you mean by that?" I asked.

"It's not worth explaining, son," he answered. "It's just something some men feel. If you can't feel it, you can't understand it."

"Oh. Yeah. Well, lemme ask you something else," one of us braved, "What're you doing with that rock?"

Well, it was out then. What everyone was wondering about. And the old man was taken aback. You could tell by the way he didn't say anything, just sat there for a minute or so and then got up with his guitar and started walking off. He stopped, though, and turned around. He talked sort of grumpy then. You know, like old men talk. "I don't know what I'm doing with that rock. Just wait and see." He walked off then for good. He stood in front of his tent shaking his head and stomping his foot. He really looked funny with his hair bouncing around and his arms flopping loose-like when he'd kick his foot. After a bit he went on into the tent and ignored us like before.

There wasn't any more we could do then. We did stay around a little to look at that rock, but then we all got into the car and drove back to town.

Next week when the old man came to get his supplies, he seemed more solitary than ever. He just walked along wearing that old hat and staring straight ahead like he didn't even notice the people who'd stop and look at him as he walked by. Barber Wilkins even spoke to the old man, but he didn't even slow down or turn his head. He just kept on going. Mr. Wilkins just shrugged his shoulders and went back into his shop.

Anyway, when the old man came into the station to get water he gave a slight nod to me as if to say hello and then went on to give Mr. Godfrey his quarter. While the old guy got his water I said, "What do you say, Mister?" hoping to start a conversation.

He said, "Oh, hello, son." Then he ignored me. He sure didn't act like he wanted to make friends.

Another week rolled on by and people began to say they thought the old man was cracked. They told us kids not to go out there again and said bad things about him. Some of the folks even tried to get the sheriff to run the old guy off, but he said he didn't have any reason to as long as the old man minded his own business.

But you know how kids are. Tell us we can't do something and we'll do it. So we went on out there the very next weekend. It had been about two weeks since the old man had come in for water so I figured he was low and might be more friendly if we took him some. We rounded up four one-gallon jugs and took them on out there full of water. When we got there, we drove right up to the camp and hollered, "Hey! Old man! We got some water for you!"

The old man was in his tent and when he came out he rcally looked tired. He was thinner too. He hitched up his pants and looked at all of us, taking his time. He looked lonely. He finally smiled and said, "Thanks, boys. I am running low. Thanks." So we piled out of the car and took our jugs over and poured them into his five-gallon can. Then one of us offered the old man a beer and he said, "Yep. Thanks. It's been dry out here."

While someone was getting him a beer the old man reached into his tent and got his guitar. You could tell the old man was tired and must not have been eating much lately since he hadn't been to town for two weeks, but he was acting friendly for a change even though he didn't say much. He just sort of talked low while he played soft music. He didn't drink much either. Just nursed along a couple of beers for the two hours we stayed there. He was in a quiet mood so we didn't push him to talk to us, just listened to him talking along in time to his music. He wasn't singing, just sort of talking to himself. Half of it we couldn't even catch. It was like stories, most of them sad but some funny. He got sleepy after a while and would doze off and then shake himself awake. Everything was friendly and we figured the old man was a pretty good guy no matter what the folks in town said. We asked him if he'd mind if we came out again and he said okay. Then we left.

The very next day the old man came into town. He went through his usual routine and nobody watched him or tried to talk with him. People just ignored him. When he came out of the store he came across the highway and walked toward me. I acted like I wasn't watching but he just came right up to me and said, "Hello, boy." He even took off his hat. "You boys come on out to the camp soon. That rock's taking shape now. Next time you come, I'll be able to tell you all about it." Then he left.

The next Friday we went out there after supper. The old man was in a good mood and was glad to see us. "Hi, boys," he said. "Look at the rock." We all looked and the old man said, "Mean anything to you?"

"It looks like a man," one of us said.

"Yeah. It's me," the old man said.

"But what're you doing?" I asked.

"Nothing," the old guy said. "I'm just standing there."

"Yeah? Well, what's the point?" Bill hollered.

"Boys, the point is I'm building a monument to myself!" He said this like it was important. Then he explained. "Everyone wants to be remembered. This way I won't be forgotten when I'm gone. And people will see me as I was in my prime. At the most vital time of my life."

"Yeah?" Bill pressed him. "When was that?"

"During the big war," the old guy said. "That was the biggest event of my life, and I was a part of it."

"You're proud of that, are you?" said one of the guys.

"Yep," the old man went on, "and I'm going to immortalize it. I was old for that fight, but I wanted to make it. And I did."

"That's not a bad idea, old man," I said. "This statue, I mean. Maybe we all oughtta do that." And I and the others half-laughed at the old man.

He ignored the laughter and said, "Yep. I always say every man should be his own hero. Look to himself for life's solutions. Don't count on anyone else. Well, that's what the rock is all about. It's going to be my final statement. But you boys didn't come out here for a lecture. Let's have some music." So the old man broke out the guitar and started strumming. We opened the beer we'd brought and had a good time until the old man got sleepy and we left.

Now that we knew about the rock we weren't so curious about the old man, so we didn't go out there for about three weeks. I'd see him every week when he came for water and he'd say a few words. Other than that, we just left him alone.

When it was time, we decided we'd like to see what shape his rock was in and drove out there on a Friday night.

Bill was in a pretty good mood that night and was saying how the old man was an all right guy and could really play his guitar. "Let's get the old guy to tell us about himself," he said. "I'd like to know about the old sun of a gun. He's been around. He's probably got some good stories to tell. Let's get him to talk some tonight and have a ball."

"Yeah," another kid chimed in. "That bull about sitting around and not saying anything gets old."

When we got to the camp, the old man was in his tent lying down. Bill went over and said, "Hey, old man, we've got some beer. Come on out and sing for us."

"No," said the old man, "I'm not up to it tonight."

"Aw, come on, old man," Bill egged him on. "We wanta have a party."

"No," the geezer said. "I feel bad tonight. I'm thinking of my wife. I lost her not long ago."

"Aw, come on," Bill said, "a party will cheer you up."

"No," the old man insisted. "The way I feel, I may never make music again."

Bill got mad, then. He was like that. Hot tempered. "God damn," he said, "come on out here and give us some kicks! We came all the way out here and you won't even talk to us!"

"Please," said the old man, "just leave me alone. I feel really bad."

"Ah, hell, guys, let's go," shouted Bill. "This old coot is a creep!"

So we left and went somewhere else to drink our beer. Bill was in a bad mood and after a while said, "Let's fix that old man. I've got an idea. Let's go to my house!"

So we drove to Bill's house and Bill got a thick rope and said, "Okay, let's go out to the old man's."

I didn't like what I thought Bill had in mind for the old man. But what could I do? I was only one guy. And the youngest. Bill was wild, and when he got an idea there was no stopping him. So I just kept quiet.

When we got there the guys were all charged up and went right to work. And they didn't worry about being quiet, either. There was a full moon, so we could see pretty well. It didn't take long to tie that rope around the head of the old man's statue. When they started tying the other end to the rear end of the car, the old man came out of his tent yelling.

"What are you kids doing?" he shouted.

Bill hollered, "Aw, shut up, old man! We're gonna tear down your statue!"

The old man screeched, "No!" in this pained voice and moved toward the car. He was in his shorts, and I was startled at how white he was where the sun hadn't touched him. It made him look real vulnerable. Bill grabbed him and spun him around and held him back and yelled, "Go on, guys! Finish up!"

"No, please," the old man begged. "I haven't done anything to you boys. Stop!"

I was just standing around while this was going on and I felt real sorry for the old man. But I didn't say anything.

It didn't take long to finish tying the rope, and then one guy got in the car and started pulling at the statue. All this time the old man was pleading and struggling in Bill's arms. It was pathetic. He was a skinny old guy and he seemed so helpless against Bill and the others. It just wasn't fair. I stood it as long as I could and then blurted out, "Aw, come on, leave the old man alone!"

Just at that time the head of the statue broke off and the kids let out a big cheer. They were laughing and jumping when Bill let the old man go. He just went over and sat on a rock and sobbed without tears.

Like I said, the old man was really pathetic. After all of his struggling with Bill, his veins were standing out against his snow white skin so he looked like he had been skinned or something. It made me sad and I felt real sorry for him.

Well, we untied the rope and got out of there.

The next day I was working in the station when

the old man came into town. He did his same old thing—into the post office and then the store. He loaded up on groceries and then came over to the station for water. When he walked up he said, "Don't worry, son. We carry on," and while he filled his can he told me he was going to start another rock and build that monument somewhere else. I thought what a lot of guts the old man had, and when he left, I just stood there watching him go on out of town. He walked real straight. And he was still wearing that crazy hat.

Jelly Rolls

by

Jyl Lynn Felman

"Is this where the bus for Durham comes in?" a voice asked.

Edith Jeanne Drinkwater needed an answer to the exact same question, so she turned half a circle around. When she saw that she was facing a fat woman, Edith wanted to immediately complete the circle. But she couldn't do that because the fat woman had got hold of one of her eyes and wasn't letting go until Edith answered the question.

Edith had a thing about eye contact; it was just plain impolite to ignore someone else's eyes when they were giving them to you. So she looked, expecting to see a single big eye in the middle of a huge face. Much to her surprise the woman had two eyes just like she did. And the woman's eyes were the exact same color as her very own eyes.

Unbelievable, Edith said to herself. It wasn't because she thought she had the only pair of green hazel eyes in the world; it was just that, who would have thought that *fat* women have green eyes?

Before she knew what she was doing, thirty-five-year-old Edith found herself agreeing with the woman that Gate Three was their gate. Edith had never agreed with a fat woman in her life. She did not know what to do. She worried that the woman would assume friendship, maybe think that the two of them could share a seat on the bus. Edith knew what she was going to have to do and she didn't like it one bit. She was going to have to force herself to take up an entire row of seats. In order to accomplish that—because the size of her own body was so small—she now planned to spread her packages out over both seats instead of putting them on the rack above her as she usually did.

For the next fifteen minutes, to make her own position perfectly clear, Edith planned to ignore the fat woman. They had absolutely nothing in common; it was sheer coincidence that the two of them were riding the same bus to the same place this very Sunday night.

Quickly she stomped her sturdy Thom McAns on the floor of the Greyhound Station. She had to keep her body firmly in place. Edith wondered if this woman understood the difference between herself and the rest of the human race. Edith knew the difference; she had always known the difference, ever since she was a little girl, and her mother had pointed all the way down the street to a huge blue bonnet. "*That* is a fat woman," her mother said. "we don't mess with them. So don't let me catch you bringing one of them home for a glass of whole white milk and one of my home-made walnut-pecan butterscotch brownies. Friends like that you don't need. They're contagious." Edith had never forgotten her mother's wisdom. In fact, last week she'd decided to point out that same thing to her daughter next time they walked down the street together.

Meanwhile, Edith's ears filled up. She knew that fat people always sounded like they were addressing the entire world in a single breath. They did not have small voices. The woman was trying to appear as though she were not addressing anyone in particular. When a young boy finally said, "6:15," Edith leaned over to make sure she had heard right. After all, it was her bus too.

Edith felt green hazel eyes hanging onto her feet. She knew better than to think anyone would stare like that at a single pair of Thom McAns, no matter how small the feet were that wore them. Edith was scared. For the first time since she'd entered the bus station, she wasn't precisely clear about what was going on around her. That wasn't like her; she wasn't herself today. She wasn't sure about anything except that after a few more minutes of feeling fat green eyes moving up and down her entire body, Edith's fear turned into panic.

The fat woman was seeing something she shouldn't be seeing. Holding her packages close to her small breasts, Edith begged her feet to move her body forward. It had to be time to leave. Once she got on the bus, she knew she'd feel more like herself.

As she started for the gate, Edith felt an entire

army coming after her. There must be some mistake; everybody had begun to follow Edith. This had never happened to her. She was no leader. She knew her place and that had always been toward the end of every line. She was not one to push her way forward. Thin people never had to push and shove. Thin people were always sandwiched in between the larger people so that nothing would happen to them. That was the way Edith had always seen life work.

She found herself glancing around for the fat woman, who, much to her dismay, was bringing up the end of the army.

What Edith had most feared *might* happen, already *had* happened. That is, everyone going to Durham, New Hampshire, had assumed the two women were traveling together, and that they knew when to board the bus. Edith sincerely hoped the woman would take over the lead; then the confusion would clear up once and for all.

Somewhere in the background their bus was called and the fat woman took over the lead at the same time. Edith had stopped moving. When the announcement was over, the woman's ticket was in the driver's hand. Edith smiled at her feet, feeling almost like her old self again. The fat woman had taken over the responsibility for leading the people home. That was the way all life should be.

In case there was any danger, it would happen to the fat woman first. Besides, there was always a draft at the beginning of the line. Edith knew fat people didn't get cold like the rest of them. She had seen their kind dressed in thin coats with hardly any buttons. That was definitely the only lucky part about being a fat person: you didn't feel the cold. Edith was cold now, and although that meant she might be sick in bed tomorrow, it also meant she wasn't fat.

She had been standing in one place for so long that everyone had passed her up. She was the last passenger to board the bus. Edith gave the driver her ticket without looking him in the face. She was keeping her green hazel eyes to herself and she was putting one foot directly in front of the other. She wasn't going to look for a seat until she was smack at the top of the aisle. No single individual was going to get this very cold but thin woman to lift her eyes until she was ready. When her feet were in place, Edith was amazed. The confusion was still not over.

The problem was that the fat woman had seated herself directly behind the driver while all the real passengers had seated themselves behind the entire first row. How could they do this to her: leave her up front with that woman? What if her daughter had been traveling with her? How could she have explained to such a young child why they had to sit in the fat section? Edith lifted her eyes slowly; before she took her seat she was going to have her say.

She made her eyes go from seat to seat until they'd been up and down the whole aisle; she wanted the people to know that Edith Jeanne Drinkwater knew exactly what had happened: they had deserted her, one of their own. Only the fat woman met her gaze, waiting for Edith to take the row of seats across the aisle from her own row. Edith stared into the eyes of her people. *Thank you, each and every one of you for making my dream come true. All day I was praying for the first seat on this bus. That way, as soon as we turn down Main Street, my daughter will see, even before I get off the bus, that her mother has come home. You are all good people and I thank you.*

Edith had made her eyes carry all the way to the back of the bus. Satisfied that she had excluded the fat woman from her gaze and that she had redeemed herself, she sat down calmly waiting for the bus to begin its journey. Her own mother would have been proud of her. Edith had seen the heat of the fire coming straight for her but she'd turned it ice cold without ever getting burned. For the first time since this whole mess had started, she'd almost forgotten the fat woman existed. With a little more concentration, she was sure she could finish her off for good.

She'd just close her eyes and see if she could imagine the woman's seat giving way. Then the fat woman would be left out in the road. In order to keep moving, the back wheels of the bus would have to roll right over her.

Edith thought she could do this. She'd been in strong control of her imagination ever since she was a child. But when Edith closed her eyes, nothing happened. She blinked fast and closed them again tighter, in case there had been a mistake. This time she concentrated more. But behind her eyes there was no fat woman falling through the floor of the bus.

Edith knew from past experience that some things took more work than others. She would try harder. After all, these were *her* eyes; if she couldn't get them to see what she wanted to see, nobody else could. She closed her eyes again, but had to open them immediately. Clearly there had been some confusion because, what was going on behind Edith's eyes was food. Lots of food. It was the fat woman up to no good, and Edith wasn't going to stand for it. Just because they both had green hazel eyes did not mean they had to see the world the same. Never before had she lost her own clear sight and never before had she closed her eyes and seen only food.

The bus was not due in Durham for over an hour. That was long enough to regain her own sight. Edith remembered there had been a single occasion in her youth when her eyesight had been impaired. She had not listened to her mother, who had told her never to look straight into the yellow sun or she might go blind for life. Edith hadn't gone blind for life though, she'd only lost sight for a few seconds. For those few seconds, she had felt separated from the entire human race. That had been the most horrible feeling she had ever hoped to feel. Even as a child, she could not stand being separated from her people. Although that seemed to be happening again, only this time, right in *front* of her eyes.

Edith could feel her body resting. Her eyes closed. The food came back into view, but Edith didn't even try to make it go away. Her small body spread out across the entire seat. She was careful not to interfere with her packages. It felt good to be going to sleep. She was one of them after all; Edith had seen lots of her people sleeping on buses, slumped out in all directions. Everything was going to be fine.

In the middle of her dreams, Edith woke to find herself staring at the fat woman's stomach. The woman had slumped over and spread out just like Edith had done with her own body. The woman had no right to copy Edith's body position. The fat woman was even taking up both seats. Edith could see absolutely no reason why they had to sit in identical positions. She moved her body immediately, careful not to squish her husband's sweet rolls.

Edith tried to bring her legs together before the bus driver looked into his rear view mirror and noticed the unladylike position she'd gotten herself into. But nothing happened. She couldn't get her eyes to remove themselves from the fat woman's stomach. Never before had she lost so much control of her faculties. She was clearly not herself today. She would have to try again to move her legs, because, as long as Edith had known her husband, he had refused to eat his sweet rolls if they were the least bit flat. Any minute, her right thigh was going to flatten those jelly rolls out for good.

Just as she tried lifting her legs, Edith's eyes started talking inside her head. She wondered what exactly was inside the fat woman's stomach. Maybe, if she stared hard enough, she could see in through all that thick flesh. Her eyes imagined piles of white powdered sugar where she supposed the inside of the woman's stomach began. She stared harder. The white powder was turning into a giant jelly roll.

She got hold of herself fast. She did not like the idea of the fat woman and her husband eating the same food even if it was only for breakfast. That meant her husband's stomach could one day look like the fat woman's stomach. Edith knew she could never serve a fat man dinner at her table. She was going to have to act faster than she had ever acted in her entire life. Edith's hand reached to secure from under her thigh the bag which held her husband's jelly rolls.

That was when Edith noticed the fat woman's mouth opened and closed while she slept. It appeared the woman was eating the air. When her mouth closed, anyone could see she was chewing and swallowing. Edith knew eating when she saw it; and the fat woman was eating in her sleep. Edith felt her left hand open her husband's jelly roll bag. She knew what she had to do to keep her husband from turning into a fat woman. Her hand sank fast and deep into the white powdered sugar. She crumpled some powder between her fingers while she watched the fat woman eating the very air on the bus. The next time the fat woman's mouth opened, Edith's mouth opened right along with hers. It felt good; Edith got her jaw moving in the same round motion as the fat woman's jaw.

She hummed to herself softly so she wouldn't wake the woman. She was beginning to feel weightless, which was not hard for someone of Edith's small size. Her hand caught hold of one of the big jelly rolls. All she had to do to save her man was bring that roll up to her mouth when her lips were parted. If she got it up there when her lips were closed, Edith didn't know what would happen. She might push the roll back into the bag and stop all this rescue work immediately. She pictured her kitchen table which was only big enough for three small people. She saw her husband sitting down to his breakfast and getting up too big to ever sit down again. Quickly she stuffed the entire sweet roll into her mouth.

Powdered sugar was everywhere. Edith couldn't see clearly because some of the white stuff had gotten stuck right in front of her eyes. She waved her arms, hoping her vision would clear. When she could see again, she saw the fat woman staring straight at her husband's bag of red jelly rolls. Edith said, "No!" out loud. Faster than she had done before, she stuffed another jelly roll into her mouth. The woman just kept staring as if Edith hadn't said a word. Edith tried to chew faster. Eating on the bus wasn't so bad after all; it helped pass the time.

She knew there were exactly twelve rolls left. She'd bought fourteen, a week's supply. They had all been for her husband who ate two a day with black coffee. After a week, the jelly dried up and her husband said the white powder started cracking. He wouldn't have to worry about that this week. Edith ate two more sweet rolls in time with the turning bus wheels. The fat woman was still staring at Edith's bag as if she understood what Edith was doing. But she couldn't possibly understand. Edith assured herself that she was only eating to save her husband. She was certainly not eating because she was hungry.

She swallowed hard; she had almost choked on the sixth jelly roll. She had stopped paying full attention to what she was doing. She had begun to think hard about the fat woman. Edith was positive that she had nothing in common with that woman. Their kind ate to save themselves, but Edith was eating to save her family. There was a huge difference. She had only four rolls left; she was going to miss all that white powder floating down in front of her. She had almost forgotten where she was; she'd actually begun to feel like when the dentist filled her up with gas. Edith knew she was not quite in control of her faculties, but that didn't matter anymore. She felt good. She had no idea red sweet jelly rolls made you feel so light-headed.

Her whole body was jumping. Instead of feeling heavy and full, she had those female twitches between her legs. She felt her whole body puffing up like a fresh hot roll coming straight from the oven to the table. Just as Edith pictured the baker filling the roll with all that sweet red jelly, she gave out a bigger groan than she'd ever remembered giving out lying right next to her very own man. Her thighs were calming down. She almost hated to let go of all that sweetness, but she'd finished the last jelly roll; there was no more white powder blocking her vision. Quickly Edith commanded her legs to relax. She looked down at her feet just to make sure her Thom McAns were still there. Then she pulled her dress down as far over her knees as it would go.

Then Edith did it; she couldn't stop herself: she locked her own green hazel eyes straight into the fat woman's eyes. Then her vision cleared clearer than it had been all day. The fat woman had got what she wanted. She was nodding her head slowly, pushing something out of her head directly into Edith Jeanne Drinkwater.

Edith had no choice but to accept what the woman was giving her; she had locked their eyes together. Besides, she had been waiting her whole life for a single moment of truth. She'd always known she was capable of visions sent by the Lord, only Edith never expected to receive them from a fat woman riding on a moving bus. Here they were, taking up the whole front row including the aisle; it was unavoidable. That was the way her mother said the Lord always worked. He was unavoidable whenever you most wanted to be avoided. Edith decided to act with courage. If this was her moment, she was going to receive and be hallowed. Only it was too bad she had come to peace through the fat woman's eyes. Edith decided to prepare herself. She quit thinking altogether and opened her eyes as wide as she possibly could.

She shook her head, shaking out what the Lord was pushing in. She was seeing herself staring out at her from the fat woman's eyes. Only it wasn't exactly Edith. It was Edith a wee bit deformed. She was still five feet one-and-a-half inches tall and her arms were still short and slender, but her stomach had been pulled way out of shape. In the eyes of that woman, Edith was fat, so fat that her stomach took up both of the woman's eyes. Edith was horrified; she had never seen such a big stomach before. She was not at all clear that this was what the Lord Jesus had wanted her to see when she gave her eyes to the fat woman.

Her stomach grumbled; the picture was making her ill. She thought for a moment that if she could just open the moving bus window, she could throw up all fourteen jelly rolls into the street and let the bus roll right over them, killing the red jelly out flat. Then she could forget everything. But Edith knew that was impossible. She'd swallowed hard every single bite of those sweet red rolls; she'd taken them in as if in preparation for her single moment of truth.

Edith was still staring at herself in the fat woman's eyes when she noticed her neck had disappeared into her stomach. All of a sudden she saw one head after another rise up out of the stomach and take over. There must be some mistake. The heads had begun to look like her mother's and her mother's sister's heads. It was horrible; the fat woman was gulping down all the women Edith had ever known. Finally, Edith's own head came back. She smiled out at herself, only the smile seemed far away. She forced her eyes to focus. The smile was hiding under a thick veil and Edith was wearing a blue bonnet. She was becoming that woman. They all were becoming one giant fat woman. Edith began to think that inside every thin woman was a fat woman waiting to get out.

Edith made a decision to walk off the bus as if nothing had happened. As if nothing concerning the order of things had changed. She was going to hold her stomach in for the rest of her life, just to make sure no one guessed the truth. Oh, she'd come around once the others did. But not until then; she was going to keep it all to herself just as her mother had done with her. She would not point out that blue bonnet to her daughter after all. Edith was going to keep silent and keep her stomach in.

When Edith stepped off the bus and put both feet on the ground, the fat woman was right behind her, putting down her own two feet on the very same ground.

Boarding House Days

by

H. Ray Pardue

It was hard to be critical of my roommate, Pete Anderson, especially when I recalled how one day he had walked into the room with a couple of cold beers and said, "Here, Herb, old gyrene buddy. Have one." I had been trying to decipher some illegible notes taken in class that day when I gratefully accepted his offer.

But even so, eight hours in the bathroom. Eight hours! Our landlady, Mrs. Simms, had done the timekeeping. "Yesterday your roommate," she said, "was in the bathroom from ten in the morning until six in the evening." She spoke firmly and decisively. It was clear she knew what she was talking about.

"Mrs. Simms, I remonstrated, "thats not possible. Nobody spends eight hours in the bathroom."

"It's not possible," she said, "but it happened anyway." Mrs. Simms was a World War I war bride from London, having married Earl Simms, private, U.S. Army Infantry, early in 1919. Twenty-seven years later she still spoke with a trace of a cockney accent. She and old Earl Simms ran the boardinghouse where Pete and I shared a room. Pete had been in the Navy and I in the Marine Corps. We had unknowingly suffered through respective boot camps just across the bay from each other.

"Well, of course," I said, "Pete does have pretty hair. I mean, for a man, he has pretty hair."

Mrs. Simms agreed. "Yes, Herb, he does."

"But nobody," I went on, "can spend eight hours shampooing and drying and brushing a head of hair. Nobody."

"I agree," said Mrs. Simms.

The phone rang; it always has priority, so Mrs. Simms rose to answer the thing. I left, shaking my head in puzzlement.

But I had other things on my mind. For starters, I quickly surveyed the clothes situation. One suit just returned from the cleaners, one clean, starched white shirt, new tie to match, shoes shined and in good shape.

Down the hall from the room Pete and I occupied there resided a girl named Jessie Belle. She wasn't bad looking, not bad at all, except when she opened her mouth. An orthodontist could have helped a lot. Now, Jessie Belle was a student at the University studying philosophy. I mean real philosophy, not like one of these football coaches that gets a Doctor of Philosophy degree in physical education, but the kind of stuff that Socrates and Aristotle and all those other old boys went in for. She already had her master's and was now after her Ph.D., a degree that, to me, seemed unattainable.

I paused before her door which was wide open, adjusting my tie, and there sat Jessie Belle by the window. She looked over at me and I said, "Hi, Jessie Belle, how goes it?"

She looked at me strangely and said, "Mr. Partridge, I want to ask you a question."

"Okay with me, Jess, but I am in just a little bit of a hurry." And then I felt like a bastard for having said that, and tried to mollify the situation by grinning like an idiot. I said, "But I always have time for you, honey."

I sat down on the chair beside Jessie's bed, where at that moment she stretched out in rather a sensuous posture. She extended her little lily white to me and, not knowing what else to do, I took it and shook it.

"Mr. Partridge," she said, "do you think I'm sexually attractive?" Just like that. I stalled. I looked around for an ashtray. She languidly found one. Using exaggerated motions, I snuffed out my cigarette. *Think, boy, think,* I advised myself. After all, we Marines are noted for our fast thinking.

"Now, Jess," I said, "what in the world does your question have to do with philosophy? Are you conducting an experiment on me, something to help with your degree?"

"Mr. Partridge," she said, giving what sounded like a poor imitation of Katherine Hepburn, "I had entertained some hope for you. You seemed to be just a . . ." She appeared to be searching for just the right phrase. ". . . cut above the others here." As she said, "others," I felt like she was talking about pigs in the sty or jackasses in the stable or something. I debated whether I should feel complimented. I glanced surreptitiously at my watch. Damn, I thought, I needed to get a move on.

"Jessie, dear girl," I said, reverting to an old pre-WWII line of mine, "I love you dearly, but I've got to get going. Rain check, okay?" No answer. "Okay?" I repeated.

She straightened up and God only knows what she was thinking when she said flatly, "Okay."

No question about it, Jessie Belle was one heck of an interesting chick. But she couldn't compare with Pete's wife. Now, I had never met his wife, didn't even know her name, but it was clear that night when I came in that Pete wanted to talk about her. Not right away, though.

He was sitting near the window with a beer in his hand and I could tell he was in a low mood. "What's the word, mate?" I inquired cheerfully. A bit too cheerfully I gathered, because he glared at me. "Any more beer?" I asked.

Then he said, in almost human tones, "Sure, there's half a case in the refrigerator. Help yourself."

I did so, and as I removed the cap from the bottle, I asked, "How come so glum? War's over, you know."

In the worst way in the world I wanted to take a close look at Pete's hair. He wasn't in the best light of all, besides, how could I do it without arousing suspicion? It was pretty, all right. Those golden curls. Man, that was rare. Okay, I said to myself, I'll go ahead and assume two hours spent on the hair. But what about the other six?

"World War II is over chum," he said, "but not mine." Then he withdrew into his own world.

I shrugged. *I* felt great. I whistled through my teeth the tune of "Darktown Strutters Ball." Pete roused himself and glared at me. He asked me if I had ever been married. "Nope," I replied, "but it's a great institution, marriage." Pete looked like he had just bit into a lemon, so I added hastily, "So they tell me."

He was silent so long that I had time to speculate about the remaining six hours. A long soak in the tub . . . But how long? One hour at the most. Longer than one hour and the water would be cold. Well, cool, anyway. Okay, two soakings. That's three hours used up. But boy, I said to myself, you've got a long way to go. Five more hours.

Pete brought me back to the present. *"Women,"* he said, "are nuts."

I took off my jacket and stretched out on my sack. "Well, Pete, old sailor of the seas, tell me about it. You and the little woman are separated. That's easy to figure, else you wouldn't be living in a boardinghouse." I took a quick look at his shoes, there beside his sack. Gleaming. Shined to a mirror glaze. Does he shine his shoes in the bathroom? No, can't be. Just can't be. Keep thinking, Herb.

Finally Pete said, "My wife is a beautiful woman." He looked at me expectantly. He reverted to GI slang. "I mean, she's stacked, mate. Get me?"

I nodded. "Roger. Proceed."

He abruptly shot out of the chair and left the room. Dang, I thought, something really is eating him. He came back in half a minute with two beers, handing me one. I said, "Thanks," and offered him a cigarette, taking one myself, and waited as patiently as I could for him to continue.

"Partridge," Pete finally said, "my wife and I have sex troubles."

"Oh," I said politely.

Pete continued. "That's right. Oh, she isn't frigid or anything like that. Fact is, she's a bit on the warm side." It was then clear to me that Pete's marriage was truly on the rocks. Otherwise he would not have broken the taboo men have with respect to talking about their spouses. Especially about such intimate matters. Of course, it's mainly a matter of male ego. Having married the girl, there couldn't possibly be anything wrong with his judgment. Simple as that.

Pete puffed on his cigarette and sipped his beer. "It's just that she had damn peculiar ideas about *when.*" He paused and looked at me to see if he was getting across. I nodded to indicate we were in rapport. "Worse than that," he added, "was *why.*"

We were no longer in rapport. "Why? I'm not with you there, mate," I said. "What do you mean?"

"Well, first," he said, taking care of the when, "it always had to be after dark. With the lights out. It had to be under the sheets, or cover."

"Well," I said, trying to make some sort of intelligent contribution, "that's not so bad. Perhaps a little unusual, but . . ."

"Right, pal," he agreed. "It could be regarded as modesty, A man can adjust to that." He took a deep draft from the beer. "Note, Partridge," he said, "how we have only covered the subject of the when." He paused again.

I nodded. "Proceed. The why."

"Yes," he said, "precisely. The why." He got up and strode about the room nervously. "This," he said, almost too loud, "is something I say no man should put up with." I had to admit I was curious. I thought it wiser, though, not to appear so. Obviously it wasn't easy for Pete to talk about his estranged wife.

Besides, if at all possible, I wanted to find out about those eight hours in the bathroom. I looked closely at his face. A heavy beard? No, no, out of the question. He was blond and blond men seldom have heavy beards. Shaving couldn't have taken more than half an hour. Hell, man, back in the old Corps, I could shave in two minutes. Allow half an hour at the most.

Pete stared out the window so long that I was tempted to prod him along. I thought better of it. Just as I thought he would never get on with it, he said, with his voice almost croaking, "Why? Why? Because she *wanted* something." He stood up to his full height and scowled at me. If there had been a podium he would have pounded on it.

"She wanted something?" I asked, feeling benumbed.

"That's right, Mac, because she wanted something," he repeated.

I was nonplussed. I asked, "Wanted what?"

"Hell-fire, man," he almost shouted, "anything. Any damn thing. A new hat, a new dress, a new coat, a new bracelet, earrings. Anything."

I said, not very brightly, "You mean . . ." I looked at the door fearfully to see if it was tightly closed, for Pete was truly in a state, yelling his head off. I hoped fervently we weren't disturbing anyone.

He seemed quite distraught. "That's exactly what I mean. She wouldn't let me have any until I promised her something." I felt dazed. "You think it was easy to live with a woman like that? Partridge, a man can put up with a lot of damned things from his wife, but how can a man put up with the idea that his wife is nothing but a . . . a . . ."

I tossed all discretion to the winds and asked, "A what?" suspecting that I knew what he was going to say.

"A whore, that's what. A plain old whore, h-o-r-e." He was unaware he had misspelled the word. "Now you know what kind of wife I have."

I thought, poor old Pete. Eight hours in the bathroom was nothing compared to that.

Next day was Saturday; I slept later than usual,

Pete was gone off to that real estate job of his, which called for peculiar working hours. Mrs. Simms handed me a hot cup of coffee there in the kitchen. I sat down, broke out my pencil, took a piece of paper, sipped on the coffee, and said, "Mrs. Simms, I can account for three and a half hours." She understood right away what I was talking about.

"Go ahead," she smiled, "let me see what you've got there."

I said, "Two hours for hair— the shampoo, the drying, the brushing and combing. Any argument with that?"

"Okay so far," she agreed. "Go ahead."

"One hour for the bath," I said, "including toweling." Half an hour for shaving. Three and a half hours. Now, dear Landlady, where do we go from here?"

"Well," she said, trying to be helpful, "how about manicure and pedicure?"

As she put the bacon and eggs and toast in front of me on the table, I protested, "Does one need to be in the bathroom for that?"

She laughed and said, "Look, son, with four and a half hours to go, don't knock it."

But then she turned serious. "His domestic troubles . . ." she began. She knew about Pete's wife. "Could it be that he was weeping; you, know, crying? And didn't want anyone to know it?"

I thought about that, but not too long, "No, Mrs. Simms, I don't think so. You must remember that boys don't cry."

Mrs. Simms and I spent a great deal of time on the problem. We never did come to any conclusion. We even went into wild imaginings, such as allowing an hour for tooth brushing, and we still couldn't account for the time. We each had other things to do, so we parted company.

One evening I came home, whistling jauntily as I walked down the hall to my room, when I tripped. I dang near fell on my face and would have, if it hadn't been for a lot of judo training I had had in the Marines. Recovering I whirled to the door and saw Jessie Belle there, withdrawing her foot. She said, "Well, Mr. Partridge, home at last, I see."

She grabbed me by the hand and yanked me onto her bed, which was quite near the door. As I lay supine, I said, with what I thought was considerable aplomb, looking into those green eyes of hers, "Jess, old girl. How's it going?"

She ignored my inquiry and panted in my face. "Mr. Partridge, I may be no Cleopatra, I may be no Theda Bara, but . . ." and she shoved her right arm under my neck, raised it up and planted a kiss on my lips. A long, lingering kiss. As my feet rose in the air, I squirmed out from under and asked, "But Jess, dear girl, what about the patrol?" referring to the periodic trips up and down the hall by Mr. Simms to enforce their rigid rule that there was to be no hanky-panky in the Simms establishment.

"They're out shopping," she hissed. Well, I suppose really it was more like a whisper.

"Shopping?" I hate to say it, but I think I squeaked.

"Yes," she breathed, "shopping." She straightened up a bit and said, in direct and forthright tones. "As to that implication that I am not sexually attractive, let's see how you like this." My feet didn't go straight up in the air this time, but my hair stood on end. It was similar to that time on Saipan two years earlier when I hadn't seen a white woman in a long time, and then there was Betty Hutton up on a stage, entertaining the troops. Even though she was a couple of hundred yards distant, my hair stood on end that time too.

Jessie Belle regarded me with triumph. "Ha!" she said. "So much for that little detail."

"Huh?" I admit that I sounded pretty dumb.

"And now, dear Mr. Partridge, one other little item."

She spoke so precisely, so determinedly, that I regret that I said again, "Huh?"

"I have wondered," Jesse Belle said, "whether or not you have a mind."

"A mind?" I asked. The Marines would have disowned me for that. But it was apparent we had dispensed with the subject of sex and were onto something else.

"For example," she said, "have you ever heard of Descartes? *Cogito, ergo sum.*" She looked at me, as if her half-formed doubts were becoming reality. She was waiting for my reply. I knew I was on the spot. But, heck, us Marines are used to that. I thought fast. It sounded like Spanish. In high school, once, many years before, I had studied Spanish.

She repeated, *"Cogito, ergo sum."*

Think, man, think. In desperation, I said, *"Si."*

"See?" she inquired.

"Si," I responded.

She persisted. "See what?"

Well, I knew I was licked. "See day car before de horse." I laughed, artificially.

She looked at me scornfully. "You have a body," she assessed, "but you certainly have no mind. None whatever."

A few weeks later, Pete told me his wife had filed for divorce, the papers having been recently served on him. This aroused my curiosity, since Pete was certainly the aggrieved party in that deal. He was being gallant, though, feeling that it wouldn't hurt him to take the blame. By this time I had decided that Mrs. Simms' speculation about what he did in the bathroom that used up eight hours, was correct.

Still, Mrs. Simms and I had made a sort of pact with each other that if either of us ever had any hard information on the subject, we would pass it on to the other, even after I had departed the city. I was about to do just that, having completed my engineering studies at the University.

I never heard from Mrs. Simms again, but she did hear from me once. I wrote to tell her that Jessie Belle and I had gotten married.

The Necessary Art of Salvage

by

Barbara Lau

In the dumbfounded middle of loss
we still manage to
open mail
feed the dog
answer the phone.

The letter came the same day
my doctor announced
that the minnow heart inside me
had stopped pulsing.
Back home I ate the lunch placed in front
of me.
And when the envelope fell through the slot
I opened it. The handwriting said
that a poem I wrote months ago
would be released on a polished
white sheet of daylight.

I will never think of it as a fair exchange.
But at least I know how to salvage,
how to search through the rubble
for that one unbroken teacup.

Missing Kin

by

Shelby Hearon

"Old people expect to be called early in the morning," my mother says on the phone.

My mother is talking about Joe Don's grandmother who has disappeared. It is her birthday, and we have sent her a dozen red roses and a Western Union Candygram, which we hope is a Whitman's Sampler. But she is not at home and, by long distance, we have to make the decision whether to spend our Saturday being worried that she has fallen and broken a hip, or whether to get back to our own life.

"She expected to be called in the morning," my mother says.

My mother is picturing someone frail, someone who lives a solitary life with no family or friends. Who woke up on her birthday and wanted the phone to ring. What my mother is not acknowledging is that Joe Don's grandmother is just her age, has dyed blonde hair wears long red fingernails and smokes four packs of cigarettes a day.

"Old people are like that, Flower," Mother says.

Is she thinking, I wonder of some elderly woman

in her past? It is doubtful. Her own mother died at 34; her grandmother at 29. The women in her family came and went in relation either to small pelvises and large babies, or to the high blood pressure that comes from handsome husbands and separate bedrooms. More likely she is imagining herself in some future time down the road at a stage called Old: waking before the sun, having her cup of coffee, watching the clock and waiting for her daughters to call. She is feeling future anger that it has become noon and later, and no one of us has got around to remembering her day.

The fact is that they—we, the daughter—would be doing what Joe Don and I were doing this morning while letting the long-stemmed roses and Candygram carry the message to his grandmother: making love, listening to old Sons of the Pioneers records, eating.

Eating. We make fun of couples who make a production out of it. Gourmet couples who spend Saturdays doing quiches and ceviche and their own special eggs (not Benedict or Sardou, but Eggs Charles or Eggs Betty). We think it an affectation peculiar to couples like ourselves, who cohabit late, after those early marriages and diapered babies; who get together as productive consenting adults, and, then, well, what do you do when there are not children clamoring for an excursion or common sessions over maintenance and upkeep? You cook, and we do it, too. Even as we acknowledge its origins.

This morning, because it was my turn, I made french pancakes with powdered sugar, sausages, and broiled fresh pears and bananas, and we ate in bed, on the love-rumpled dark blue sheets.

"You should have waked her," my mother continues, "with 'Happy Birthday.' You know there are services that call old people who live alone every day, check to make sure they are all right. I always thought that would be a nice thing, when the time came, a nice cheery voice saying, 'Good morning, Nan, and how are you?' "

"She's probably gone out for cigarettes," I tell her.

"Can she drive?" Amazement in my mother's voice.

"Mother, she's 74," I say.

"Oh," she hesitates, "I thought . . . his grandmother . . ."

We have been through this generational puzzle before. How is my mother the age of his grandmother? Is she, Mother, old enough to be a grown man's grandmother? I remind her that his grandmother was fourteen when she had his mother. Her mind jams at that. In some way it connects up to the women in her family who married late, had a child late, died from it or shut their doors. The fact of someone her generation beginning it all at 14 and living 60 more years in the bargain sets uneasily. She hasn't got over the guilt of her own survival of making three daughters and sleeping with my father to the end, and thus becoming the first woman in her family ever to bury a husband. To do such tricks as if it were nothing; well, it makes her nervous.

Joe Don thinks we borrow trouble. His grandmother he conveys, can take care of herself.

I am remembering the afternoon my mother in her distress at finding herself in a public place, husbandless, lost her keys in a department store, somewhere between Gloves and Better Dresses. Breaking into her house while waiting for a locksmith to arrive on a football Saturday afternoon, we crashed over her stand of African violets, deep purple from their daily feeding with cold coffee.

Those were the days of early marriages, when Saturdays were for helping the helpless; when there was $1.75 left to your name, and a young sullen cousin with red Janis Joplin hair appeared on your doorstep, and you got a can of tomato juice and some gelatin and everything in the refrigerator became an aspic.

"Mother says we should have called her earlier," I report.

"Your mother can't go to the store alone," Joe Don says.

"She keeps up with things; she's current," I argue.

"She's afraid of the dark," he insists.

We don't quite fight. We can't. We have made a choice for the present, people like us, and are careful not to tatter it with bits from the past.

Toward the end of the day, Joe Don gives in and deals with his missing kin. The time has been lost to fretting anyway, the pancake plates are still on the bed, the blue sheets half on the floor. Outside it is getting dark, the sort of early evening twilight in which the mockingbirds make their last pass at stalking cats, and the dry hot air carries the smell of drooping flowers.

"Could you call a neighbor to check on her?" I suggest.

"They're all Mexican," he answers. Which means, of course, that his grandmother does not acknowledge them. She lives in an old part of Houston, on the fringes of downtown in a neighborhood that is turning from rundown and triethnic to one that is fashionable to buy into and restore. It is hanging on the cusp of turning from one to the other, and so even walking around past the old elementary school and the small wood-framed hamburger stand feels unreal. It is no longer a place where people live; it is now a real estate value. An Episcopal church has bought a whole block in order to minister to the heart of the area—and for capital gains.

People like us, who take turns cooking for one another on weekends, who are well out of those early marriages and have been through upward mobility and come out the other side, are buying into his grandmother's neighborhood.

If something happened to her, we could live in the very house where Joe Don was born and raised, and it would be a good investment. The thought depresses him; there is no way now that moving back would be going home.

I have the address book out, making a list of

friends to ask, those who are sharing Eggs Helene with one another, when she calls.

She explains she went out shopping, and has bought herself a brand new pantsuit. "Red as a fire engine," she says. "I look like a million dollars. I thought, why not, it's my birthday. It was half price."

The roses and candy, which was Russell Stover, ended up next door. She thinks the Mexican woman who brought them over has sampled the candy. She tells me, "There's a piece missing from the bottom layer; she thinks I didn't notice."

My mother is relieved to hear that we've located the missing grandmother. It sits better for everyone to be where she should on a Saturday night. She has to get off the phone to watch the news—the Middle East has taken a lot of her best hours lately. Her mind is always engaged with what's going on; she's a young woman still, and active.

"You should have called her first thing this morning," she concludes. "Then you'd have known."

I hang up, looking down the road to some future time. I am unable to locate a red pantsuit; I lose my car keys somewhere in Better Dresses.

"I should call her once in a while," I conclude, feeling close to my mother. "Just to say 'Good morning.' "

Joe Don remembers it is his time to cook. "How about green enchiladas?" he says.

Notes on Contributors

CAROLYN BANKS earned an M.A in Creative Writing from the University of Maryland. She has had four suspense novels published and a number of her short stories and personal essays have appeared in a variety of national magazines and anthologies. She is presently working on a lighthearted mystery series entitled *She Rides, He Doesn't* a title based on her personal situation; she rides her horses almost daily and her husband, Bob, a travel writer doesn't ride at all. They live at Pinchpenny Farm in Elgin, Texas, and it is there that she co-edited *A Loving Voice*.

BARRY BAUSKA completed his doctorate at the University of Washington and, since 1971, has taught literature and creative writing at the University of Puget Sound in Tacoma, Washington. Barry has been published widely in such magazines as the *Cumberland Poetry Review, Cimarron Review,* and *Twigs*. He is married and the father of one son.

LUCILLE BELLUCCI was born in Shanghai, China and at 18, as a political exile, resettled in Rome, Italy. At 23 she immigrated to the United

States and ten years later went to Brazil with her husband, an engineer. They stayed in Brazil for fifteen years. Now living in Oakland, California, Lucille has been writing for about nine years and has written two novels which she is presently marketing.

JEAN LANGSTON BURGESS was born in 1942 on the edge of South Carolina's sandy-rich Lynches River swamp. Health forced her to retire early from the business world. Jean now writes short stories and poetry in her home at Lake City, South Carolina, where she and her husband, Bobby, live, not too far from that same swamp. Their two grown children, Beth and Ray, live nearby as do lots of other relatives.

FREDERIC CARPENTER went to sea at fifteen, during World War II. At 24 he went to Louisiana State University but was bored and left after one semester. Five years later Fred went back on a scholarship and took degrees in Sociology and Psychology. He presently lives in Clearwater, Florida, where he is a safety inspector.

THOMAS CLAIRE is a poet, writer, and translator living in New York City, A National Merit Scholar at Kenyon College, he later attended the Sorbonne as a Fulbright Scholar and also holds advanced degrees from Brown and Columbia. Listed in the 1990 *Who's Who in America,* Thomas has been published in a number of poetry and literary magazines. His first volume of poetry, *Songs of Surrender,* was published by Fithian Press.

NANCY CLIMER is a Texas homemaker married to a retired Army officer. This is her first national publication.

LYNNE CONROY wrote and directed in television until recently when she returned to teaching and writing in Milton, Massachusetts. In addition to short stories, she's working on a novel that will be a comic re-telling of *Moby Dick.* Lynne has a daughter, Melanie, who is a student at the Sorbonne.

J. MADISON DAVIS is senior professor in the Professional Writing program at the University of Oklahoma. His latest novel is *Bloody Marko.* His previous novel *White Rook* was called "spellbinding" by *Publisher's Weekly,* and his first novel, *The Murder of Frau Schutz,* was nominated for an Edgar Allan Poe "Best First Award." Jim's short stories have been published in a number of literary magazines. He lives with his wife, Simonne, and their sons in Norman, Oklahoma.

THOMAS H. DAVIS III is a career Army Special Forces officer living in Fayetteville, North Carolina. A graduate of the University of Georgia, Tom has a Master's degree from the University of Southern California. In addition to just completing an action/adventure novel, he is also the author of a series of short stories chronicling the antics of a boy growing up in the rural south.

LOUISE ERDRICH has received numerous national awards for her fiction. Her most recent work is the bestselling novel, *The Crown of Columbus,* which she co-authored with her husband, Michael Dorris. She is also the author of *Love Medicine* and *The Beet Queen.*

PAUL ESTAVER, of Gainsville, Virginia, has won the Virginia Prize for Fiction and a fellowship from the National Endowment for the Arts. His first novel, *His Third, Her Second;* was published by Soho Press in 1989 to enthusiastic reviews nationwide. Paul's latest book, *Fighting Me Every Step of the Way,* is expected out soon.

JYL LYNN FELMAN is an award-winning writer who lives in Wendell, Massachusetts. She completed her M.F.A. in Fiction on a writing fellowship at the University of Massachusetts. Her work has been published in a number of literary magazines as well as in other anthologies. Jyl's story, "Jelly Rolls" is from her first collection of short fiction, *Hot Chicken Wings,* to be published in the fall of 1992.

STANLEY FIELD of San Diego, California is the author of six books, numerous short stories and articles, plus radio, TV and film dramas and documentaries. Formerly Adjunct Professor at the

American University School of Communication in Washington, D.C., Stanley's work has won a number of awards including the Freedoms Foundation Radio Production Award. Born in 1911, Stanley is the oldest contributor to this collection.

LISA FISHER lives in Highland Park, Illinois where she is the mother of three. She has a degree in psychology and, before having a family of her own, worked with adolescents. Lisa has been writing for about three years and her poetry and short stories have been published in several literary magazines.

BETTY GRAY married an Air Force officer shortly after she graduated from Rice University in Houston in 1944. After World War II they moved to Austin, Texas where they raised three children: Ann, Bill, and Shelly. The children are all grown now and Betty is enjoying retirement, writing, sports, and an empty nest with her husband, Charles.

SHELBY HEARON is the prize-winning author of eleven novels including *Owning Jolene* and *Group Therapy*. In addition, her short stories have appeared in major magazines like *Cosmopolitan* and in several anthologies. She has won five PEN Syndicated Fiction Awards, including one for "Missing Kin." Shelby has also received awards and fellowships from the Guggenheim Foundation, the National Endowment for the Arts, the

Ingram Merrill Foundation, and the American Academy and Institute of Arts and Letters. The mother of a daughter and son, she lives in Westchester County, New York with her husband, philosopher Bill Lucas.

KATHLEEN HOFFMAN went to work for the federal government for what she calls a "brief and awful period" after she graduated from Mary Washington College in Fredericksburg, Virginia. Then she began writing for a newspaper in Culpeper, Virginia. She has written about politics and tragedies and community leaders and oddballs, and always animals. Despite her story, "Everybody Has a Snake Story", snakes are not her favorite; dogs and horses are. Kathleen has been married to her husband, Jack, since 1968 and has a daughter, Jennifer. Currently she is the news editor for the *Culpeper News.*

JOHN H. LAMBE was born in California just after World War II, but was reared in Oklahoma. A businessman for many years, John has gone back to family roots and an appreciation of the beauty of the American West in his writing of mainly Western tales and romantic poetry. He and his wife, Cherri, live in Valliant, Oklahoma with their three teenaged children.

TRICIA LANDE lives in Long Beach, California. It was there that, while working on a California State University demographic/ethnic research project, she found constant reminders of stories told her as a child by members of her family who had migrated to the area from Arkansas in the 1920s and 1930s. Tricia is using these stories as the basis for a novel she's writing called *The Unauthorized Biography of Juanita Sneed.* Her short story, "Better Man" is excerpted from that novel.

RUTH D. LANGSTON spent World War II at jobs ranging from working in a fish cannery, standing ankle deep in fish guts, to the Office of War Information in Calcutta, India. Later she worked for the United Nations and at various jobs in the Texas oil patch. Ruth also did church work for sixteen years. Now retired, she spends much of her time doing volunteer work in Bastrop, Texas.

BARBARA LAU has had a number of feature articles published in national magazines such as *Family Circle* and *Savvy.* She is also a widely published poet. Her poem "Old Women" appeared in the enormously popular anthology *When I Am an Old Woman I Shall Wear Purple.* Barbara lives in Austin, Texas with her husband, who is a musician, and their daughter.

C. S. KITTELMANN was born in Peru of German parents. English is her fourth language. She came to Massachusetts in 1977 and now lives in Brookline and works as an Occupational Therapist in the Boston area. Claudia recently completed a memoir of her Peruvian childhood and is now writing a collection of personal essays about working with emotionally disturbed children. Her story, "The Bear," is her first publication.

PHOEBE NEWMAN is a native Georgian who spent many years in New York and now—happily, she says—writes poetry and short fiction and teaches in the mountains of northern New Mexico around Los Alamos. Her work is frequently published in regional and national journals and anthologies.

LEON ANOGUES was married, had a son, Thomas, and lost her Air Force officer husband all within two years during World War II. Married again after the war, she had another son, Dan, in 1950 in Bowie, Texas. That marriage lasted until her husband died in 1987. Leona now lives with her present husband, Dewitt Nogues, in Cedar Creek, Texas.

CAROLYN OSBORN was originally from Nashville, Tennessee, but has lived in Texas since 1946. She has been a newspaper reporter, radio writer, and an English teacher at the University of Texas in Austin where she now lives. Carolyn's stories have been published in a number of literary journals and anthologies, including the *1990 O. Henry Awards.* Her story, "The Greats," first appeared in the *Antioch View* and was included in her latest collection of short stories, *Warriors and Maidens,* published in 1991. Carolyn has had two other collections published: *A Horse of Another Color* and *The Fields of Memory.*

H. RAY PARDUE lives in Cedar Creek, Texas. Retired now, he was a court reporter for 36 years, 27 of which he worked as reporter of administrative hearings for the Texas Railroad Commission's Oil and Gas Division. He has three daughters and six grandchildren.

HELEN PEPPE, a Maine native, graduated *summa cum laude* in English literature from the University of Southern Maine in May 1990. While there, she won first place in a University short story contest. Helen has had poems and short stories published nationally in magazines and anthologies. She's currently a free-lance writer living with her family in Gary, Maine. Born in 1967, Helen is the youngest contributor to this collection.

RICHARD PLOETZ earned an M.F.A. from Columbia University's Writing Division in 1989 and currently teaches Composition at Fairleigh Dickinson University. His stories have been published in a number of literary magazines. Richard lives in Manhattan's East Village with his wife and three year old daughter.

MARY CONNOR RALPH's work has appeared

in a number of magazines in the U.S. and Canada. She lives in Chicopee, Massachusetts, with her husband, Bill, their three teenagers, a guinea pig, and an iguana. Currently, Mary is working on a collction of women's oral histories entitled *Living Through the War: The Women Left Behind.*

JANIS RIZZO is a licensed pharmacist, a former captain in the Air Force, and free-lance writer whose work has appeared in a number of national magazines. Born in Calilornia, she was raised in Rhode Island and has also lived in New York, New Hampshire, and West Germany. After receiving an M.B.A. from Texas Tech University, she says she is now qualified to run her household in Cedar Creek, Texas, made up of four children under the age of five, six horses, three dogs, one cat, and Jon, her airline pilot husband. Janis is also the co-editor of *A Loving Voice.*

DOROTHY ROSE has had three of her collections of poems published and other poems and short stories published in more than 50 journals, magazines, and anthologies in the U.S. and Canada. She studied art at the University of California and now lives and writes in Westlake Village near Los Angeles. Her four poems in this anthology were all published previously in literary magazines.

MARION ROSEN decided to become a writer when she was ten. At that time Marion and a friend set up a detective agency in her grandfather's barn. Since clients were few, the two spent their time reading Nancy Drew mysteries, leading to her decision to become a mystery writer. But for the next thirty-some years she had to put it off while getting an education, teaching, writing textbooks, and raising a family. Marion says she has published mostly non-fiction, but her spirit soars when she writes a mystery. She now lives in Sherman Oaks, California.

PATRICIA LEWIS SACKREY was born and raised in Texas, but moved north twenty-five years ago and has since been a tree farmer, business owner, administrator, advocate for a number of causes ranging from the arts to equality for women, and recently served four years in an elected office. She now lives in Westhampton, Massachusetts, and says that it was only with the encouragement and support of the writers in the Amherst Writers and Artists that she found the guts to write for others to read.

AMY SCHILDHOUSE has been published in a wide variety of literary magazines in both the U.S. and Mexico. Her story, "Alysa's Father," is set in her native Columbus, Ohio, where she now lives with her son, Daniel, and her husband, painter Moises Zabludovsky. There, she is currently completing a collection of her own stories.

C. G. SEGRE has had essays, book reviews, and columns published in a number of national newspapers, including *The New York Times* and *The Washington Post,* and in magazines in the U.S. and Italy. His most recent book is *Italo Balbo: A Fascist Life,* a biography of the famed Italian aviator and Fascist politician. Claudio lives in Austin, Texas, where he is a professor of modern European history at the University of Texas.

JOANNE SELTZER was born in Detroit, but has lived in upstate New York, Schenectady at present, since 1960. Her poems have been published in literary magazines, anthologies, and newspapers, and in three collections of her own: *Adirondack Lake Poems* (1985), *Suburban Landscape* (1988) and *Inside Invisible Walls* (1989). She has also had published translations of French poetry, as well as her own short stories.

DOTTE SHAFFER says she has been writing as long as she can remember, but it wasn't until she sold a confession story that she got hooked on the idea that the whole world should read her work. She has written and has in circulation a novel and two children's books. Dotte lives in Klamath Falls, Oregon, where, in addition to writing, she's also an indulgent and loving grandmother.

STACY TUTHILL is a 1986 winner of the PEN Syndicated Fiction Award. Her stories and poems have appeared in a number of literary magazines.

Supported in part by a grant from the Maryland Arts Council, she spent the academic year of 1987-88 in Kenya where she completed a number of short stories set in East Africa. Her chapbook, *Postcards from Zambia,* was published in Zambia. Stacy is the founder of Scop Publications, Inc., and presently serves as president of the board of directors. She lives in Adelphi, Maryland.

ROSALIND WARREN has won several awards and prizes, including a 1990 Pennsylvania Council on the Arts Literature Fellowship. Her stories have appeared in magazines ranging from *Seventeen* to *Beatniks from Space,* as well as in a number of anthologies. She is the editor of *Women's Glib,* an anthology of humorous stories, essays, cartoons, photos, and poetry by women, and is now gathering material for the "sequel"—*Women's Glibber.*

BRUCE WICK was born in California and grew up in Pittsburgh, Pennsylvania and later in College Station, Texas. He has traveled the country working in construction, retail, as a musician, and an accountant. Bruce and his wife, Amy, now live in Austin, Texas, with their dogs, Lucy (the role model for Berto in his story "Dad's Wrench") and Blue. Currently completing his degree to become an elementary school teacher, Bruce is also working on a novel.

PENNY WILKES is a former editor and award-winning columnist. Her articles on travel, personalities, carousel art, creativity, humor, as well as her short stories, have appeared in a variety of publications. As a writer and lecturer with twenty years experience in creative communications, she presents "Creative Writeshops" to writers, educators, and health care professionals. Penny lives in La Jolla, California where she recently completed a children's book and is working on a book on creativity for writers.

MAUREEN WILLIAMS is, as she writes, "a Kelt from Cornwall, England transplanted to Pennsylvania" where she now lives and writes in Uniondale. Her stories have been published in the U.S. and Britain. Maureen's story, "The Man Who Owned a Mountain" was originally broadcast by BBC World Service and later published in short story form in *Read Me.* She's currently collecting her stories under the title *Time Belongs To the Moon.* She is also a contributing editor to the *Endless Mountains Review.*

CHRISTOPHER WOODS writes poetry, plays, fiction, and non-fiction. His works include a novel, *The Dream Path,* and a chapbook of poems, *Houses and Fugues.* He has received a fiction grant from the Mary Roberts Rinehart Foundation, and residencies from the Ucross Foundation and the Edward Albee Foundation. Although he lives in Houston, Texas, Christopher is currently resident playwright for the Stage Two Theatre Company in Illinois. Among his plays are *Interim, Moonbirds, Fire, Pillow Talk,* and *Women Alone.*

DOROTHY WINSLOW WRIGHT, a former Bostonian now living in Honolulu with her husband, is the mother of three grown children. Her fiction, articles, and poetry have appeared in a variety of publications in the U.S., Canada, and Britain. She recently completed a collection of poetry and is presently working on a volume of short stories. Dorothy (D. W.) also edits a church newsletter, raises tropical flowers, and is learning to play a keyboard.